Pleasure Tested for the Tropics
The Story of New Moon Theatre Company

Justin Macdonnell

Connor Court Publishing

Queensland

Published in 2022 by Connor Court Publishing Pty Ltd

Copyright © Justin Macdonnell

All rights reserved. No part of this book may be reproduced or transmitted in any form or by any means, electronic or mechanical, including photocopying, recording or by any information storage and retrieval system, without prior permission in writing from the publisher.

Connor Court Publishing Pty Ltd
PO Box 7257
Redland Bay QLD 4165
sales@connorcourt.com
www.connorcourtpublishing.com.au
Phone 0497-900-685

Printed in Australia

ISBN: 9781922815149

Front Cover Photo: New Moon on tour. Photo courtesy *The Townsville Bulletin*.

Photos in the book: Special Collections, Library and Information Services Eddie Koiki Mabo Library, James Cook University, Townsville.

Every effort has been made to trace the copyright holders and to obtain their permission for the use of copyright material, including photos. The publisher apologises for any errors or omissions or where we have been unable to find the copyright holder. If we are notified of any corrections or omissions, we will incorporate these in future reprints or editions of this book.

Do mo mhac breá Seán

Contents

Acknowledgments		vii
Foreword		1
1	A new arrival	5
2	Where did it come from?	17
3	What was the Context?	37
4	Who were the characters?	61
5	What was the Tale?	93
6	The Tale continued	119
7	What did it do ?	169
8	Why did it Fail?	229
9	What can we Learn?	259
Bibliography		277
Endnotes		279
Index		293

Acknowledgments

As always with a venture such as this, there are so many to whom thanks are due. First to the participants in and observers of the New Moon company who through interviews and the provision of notes and documents so generously gave of their time, consideration and memories to help build the story and its context: Anthony Babicci, Bob Baines, Helmut Bakaitis, Peter Barclay, Margaret Bornhorst, Malcolm Calder, Stephen Clark, Chris Cottrell, Brian Debnam, Ray Dickson, Gary Down, David Fenton, Michael FitzGerald, David Gration, Arthur Frame, Karen Jacobsen, Ian Jessup, Aku Kadago, Robert Love, David Malacari, James McCaughey, Jocelyn McKinnon, David Murray, Ric Nelson, Terrence O'Connell, Kevin Radbourne, Henry Reynolds, Hon Margaret Reynolds, Hon Mike Reynolds, Kerry Saul, Lucinda Shaw, Robert Spencer, Cheryl Stock, (the late) Bob Taylor, Kirsty Veron, Rod Wissler and Campbell Young.

Second, a very special acknowledgement is due to Bronwyn McBurnie, Manager of Special Collections at the Eddie Mabo Library, James Cook University and her wonderful, welcoming and patient staff whose outstanding custodianship of the New Moon archives made my research such a pleasure. Would that all Australian theatrical history had such guardian angels!

Third, to The Society for Theatre Research, London, Paul Iles Bequest which helped to make my research possible.

Above all, my deepest thanks and appreciation are due to Professor Ruth Bereson who set me loose on this fascinating trail; encouraged and prodded me along the way above all with recommendations for further and wider research; and whose invaluable first-hand knowledge, insights, rigorous scholarly critique and eagle eye helped shape whatever value this book now possesses.

Foreword

So often Queensland is remembered for a period of conservative leadership which ended over 35 years ago. The Joh years seem to have forever tainted the Sunshine State as a place to be mocked and forgot. There has been a wholesale wiping out of the public record of social innovation and progressive artistic movements that have come from Queensland and the denial of any ongoing contribution to the vibrancy of Australian cultural life. In recent times the north of the state has become politically synonymous with the redneck south of the United States, a place of extremes and problematic people. In contrast, the so-called progressive south of our continent has tried to woo the North with paternal, evangelical caravans of thought. The truth is there are all types, everywhere, all the time. Unlike the other states, Queensland has a huge decentralised population away from the capital and as such has always looked to the regions for political and social stability. This has contributed to building a state-wide identity that often contradicts the more nuanced experience of living in the diverse geographies and economies within the white-imposed borders of the federation. Whereas in many other places you may say you are a citizen of a city, in the North-East corner of the continent you are a Queenslander and to dismiss one is to attack all.

The building of Arts Centres and subsequent touring networks, railways, the decentralising of universities and other cultural infrastructure was in direct response to the demands of rural, regional and agrarian societies throughout the 20th Century to have access to arts and culture. Most of the time this need would be satisfied by touring shows from 'down south' even if that meant it came from overseas or mostly from a strong community and amateur practice which harvested local talents to play in "Gilbert and Sullivan and Noel Coward"-esque works. In Queensland, when the time came to want to see ourselves on our stages and screens, to hear our accents and witness stories about us there was a palpable tension between the communities that had always exercised extreme hospitality and pride in elevating the home grown star, with the trained outsider who came from 'down south' whose hands were too too soft.

Growing up in Queensland in the 1980s was a constant act of rebellion against almost everything – the politically stale and repressive government, the national climate of scorn and even the temptations of such consistently beautiful weather and landscapes that threatened to distract you from ever achieving your goals. I have a memory of visiting Townsville and witnessing the work of New Moon and La Luna Youth Theatre in the early 1990s and seeing the matrix of community expectations rubbing up against artistic adventure and innovation, the deep power and value of the amateur scene in a sweaty wrestle with professional practice, different cultural references and horizons that looked further afield.

New Moon was a culmination of hopes and aspirations to transition from being called the Far North (a place seen in relation to the distance from somewhere else) to the Tropical North (a statement of local identity and character). The inheritance of this sense of identity and character and the legacy and lessons learned from this company can be seen today in the vibrant arts organisations that grew up with and after New Moon in Townsville and Cairns – JUTE, Dance North, Northsite, Umbrella, TAIMA and Tjapukai to name a few.

New Moon helped shape the arguments for distinctive and homegrown talents to have roots in the fertile soils of the region yet always stay connected to the world around us. To find the balance between the export and the import, the extractive and the reproductive. This balance takes investment in people who live in a place, who have strong connections and loyalties to the place. This investment is not about economies based on FIFO sensibilities but on sustainable and vibrant communities who have long term vision for the intergenerational project of living in this country. Justin Macdonnell is the perfect teller of this story having grown up drenched in this complex environment. He doesn't pull punches and opens all the cupboard doors in search of the skeletons. He knows by documenting our history and understanding the fullest extent of what has gone before he is gifting us power to grow a future that does not wax and wane depending on the will of a far-distant capital. Justin Macdonnell reminds us of where we have come from and why we are here now.

Wesley Enoch

Ned Kelly . Photo: Yon Ivanovic
Clockwise from left- John Rush, David Sandford, Wayne Pigram, Stephen Clark
Joe Spano, Peter Barclay, Bob Baines

1

A new arrival

I've tried the new moon tilted in the air
Above a hazy tree-and-farmhouse cluster
As you might try a jewel in your hair.
I've tried it fine with little breadth of luster,
Alone, or in one ornament combining
With one first-water start almost shining.

Robert Frost – 'The Freedom Of The Moon'

What was it?

The ideal of a professional, touring theatre company in tropical Queensland flared briefly and died as soon. It was at its best and brightest an extraordinary, bold achievement involving some of Australia's most talented theatre artists and activists. At its lowest and most dismal, it was a succession of ill judgements, mistaken identity, *folies de grandeur* and sheer bloody-mindedness. To that extent, it seemed as if, while the actors and crew struggled to keep the wagons rolling from town to town across the immense area it had marked out and fending off raids from cultural marauders along the way, there was at least as much drama, if not melodrama, off stage as on it.

The facts of the matter are easily told. Which shows, who played in them and how they were received are all matters of public record and that record has been well-preserved. The chronicle behind the scenes, perhaps inevitably since some of the key personalities are gone, requires a little more detective work. The passage of time, too, has not been equally kind to everyone's memory. In addition, some participants came away bruised from the experience and have chosen largely to forget. All needed some prompting to recall.

In essence, the New Moon Theatre Company may be considered as a decade-long phenomenon. That is not so lengthy even in the fragile world of emerging theatre companies. But in its short career it achieved much and its visibility at the time far exceeded its lifespan. Even to say a decade is misleading. Effectively, it lasted just six years, at a stretch seven. The genuine span of the Company *qua* company extended from 1982 to 1986 and, to state it simply, in that time it had two Artistic Directors: Terrence O'Connell 1982/1983 and Helmut Bakaitis 1984/1986. From its inception until the end of 1985, Paul Iles was variously General Manager or Executive Producer, but always what today we would call CEO. It presented barely two dozen adult productions.

The full story is understandably more complex and the cast of critical characters much greater than the previous paragraph suggests. There was a later period (from 1987 to its demise in 1991, which makes it exactly a decade all told) during which New Moon stumbled on with scattered productions and the somewhat surprising emergence of a youth theatre branch, called appropriately enough, La Luna. That organisation survived until very recently[1] and may reasonably be regarded as having been New Moon's sole tangible legacy in North Queensland. Otherwise, it was an extended, slow decline punctuated by changes of leadership and direction and a series of rear-guard actions to retain or regain public funding and attendance, all valiantly fought. But above all it is, as was said of 'The Turn of the Screw', "a curious story" and one which bears retelling both for its own interest and as a cautionary tale.

The impulse

Nevertheless, we can claim with confidence that 1982 marked the beginning of this major cultural step for that hot and sweaty region: the founding of a full-time, professional, touring theatre company whose function was to provide a high-level, artistic service to the communities of the zone. It was a ground-breaking move and one that has had implications, both positive and negative, for so much regional arts development which has followed, or in some cases not followed. It was also based on a business model which has had few parallels and no real descendants. The Central and Northern Queensland Theatre, later and more famously to be known as New Moon, was developed initially to serve an urban population of approximately 250,000 living at that time in and around the major coastal cities of Cairns, Mackay, Rockhampton and Townsville and in their respective catchments. That ambition alone is remarkable. There had been many attempts in different parts of the country to create regional, professional theatre, which will be touched on later. So that move in itself was not especially distinctive. New Moon sits within a wider regional initiative but also oddly, and almost self-consciously, outside of it. However that may be judged, nothing before or since on this scale or with such idealistic (one might almost say hubristic) goals has been attempted. Such are the times and the shrunken aims of government arts agencies today, that it is highly unlikely such thing would be attempted.

From its first season in that part of the world New Moon quickly acquired a reputation for daring and derring-do, high energy, quality performances and colourful behaviour – a reputation which it maintained for some time after and for which, to a large extent, it is remembered today. That is true both among audiences and opinion-makers in the communities it served, as well as among the actors, technical crew and managements who worked with it in those critical and not infrequently harrowing years. Most seem to have come away with the feeling that they had witnessed or participated in something extraordinary. In many cases that has had an indelible impact on their lives; sometimes professionally sometimes personally; sometimes to the extent of shaping their future entertainment interests and needs; sometimes totally turning their later careers in unexpected directions. We will attempt to thread some of their stories through this account.

One impulse for the creation of this Company was the level of amateur theatre activity already happening in the region. That had already been growing at a greater pace during the 1970s from several active voluntary groups in each of the provincial cities. Another incentive was the recent creation of a theatre training program at the Townsville College of Advanced Education (TCAE) later to be folded into James Cook University (JCU). Then there was the ambition of local governments, in particular but not exclusively the Townsville City Council. Above all, there was a "summer stock" experiment that had occurred there. That had been an initiative of the Townsville Council whereby local actors were able to develop their skills through the opportunity of working with a professional directors and occasionally invited professional actors. All that was bound up with the idea that this was a part of the country that deserved to share in the better things of life. That was reflected most notably in New Moon's eventual charter from both federal and state government funding agencies that it service the whole of North Queensland not just one part of it. By that means it would potentially reach an audience similar to that contained in the south-east corner of the State then provided for by the Brisbane-based Queensland Theatre Company (QTC) which had been established in the late 1960s.

That principle was a cornerstone of the original mission and, as it transpired, was to impose a variety of difficulties on it over the years. Not the least of these would be the constant moving of its base so as to ensure that it would be "resident" in and thus "belong to" a different city each year or couple of years. Subsequent history was to show that for much of its life New Moon was, as a consequence, unable to become part of any one community in its vast region of responsibility. It grew or shrank accordingly as those stake-holding cities and their audiences waxed and waned in their enthusiasm and subvention, but it never really struck root in any of them.

The argument for providing professional theatre in those northern communities was much the same as advanced elsewhere in Australia. In some ways and certainly, to the founding fathers and mothers, it was regarded as a sort of self-evident truth. But in Queensland it went further. Those believers adopted a concept which was more radical and at the same time more risky, namely that of having a *permanent* touring ensemble company. It was a revolutionary step and taken because it was considered at the time that no one of these cities by itself had sufficient population or trained talent to support its own company nor that the supply from the capital through QTC or the Queensland Arts Council (QAC), not to say for-profit producers, was sufficiently regular or assured to satisfy local demand. Nevertheless, it was beyond doubt that an upsurge of "little" theatre activity had coincided with the opening of new civic theatres in Cairns (1974), Townsville (1978) and Rockhampton(1979). These facilities had been a remarkable catalyst in the provision of a greater quantity of performing arts product and commercial entertainment than had previously been available. However, the provision of quality professional theatre had proven to be a greater problem that not even the entrepreneurial activity of those arts venues had been able, at that point, to resolve. Accordingly, the new theatre company was conceived in answer to that need in those particular circumstances. For all these reasons, the prospective Company was intended to promote a substantial increase in the number of professional theatre seasons available in those centres and would, in effect, present runs of between three and six night stands in each city.

At the time, this was regarded very much as a pilot for the establishment further down the track of a year-round company to service the northern half of the State. For that reason, a program would be mounted initially as a six-month trial between January to June over the years originally intended to be 1980 to 1983. It would be designed to present four theatrical productions per year in the region, utilising the services of a contracted ensemble of actors and others. A subsidiary program to service smaller towns would be implemented after the Company was established on a full-time basis. It is clear that that concept originally provided for a phased development that would progressively test the waters and adjust in the light of experience, eventually becoming a 12 month operation. But somewhere along the path the colt from Old Regret had got away. As things turned out, the 4 productions x 4 cities x six months pattern became locked in and may be accounted, in large part, for New Moon's operational weakness in those critical foundation years.

Genesis

Although 1982 can be regarded fairly as the year of this project's fruition, its genesis lay further back, in 1979. Early in that year, the search for the necessary support and essentially the funds to underwrite it had begun. Detailed plans and proposals were submitted to City Councils in the Central and Northern Queensland area, explaining the objectives of the scheme. Those bodies were asked to contribute their own ideas and opinions on the concept and also whether they would be able to offer significant financial assistance as security for the embryonic venture. At the same time, lengthy discussion was held with and grant applications were made to the Theatre Board of Australia Council for the Arts (TB) and the Queensland Division of Cultural Activities (DCA).[2]

These proposals argued for six quite ambitious although not particularly exceptional goals: 1. to provide ongoing professional theatre services in North Queensland; 2. to maximise audiences and develop a theatre-going tradition within the various areas serviced; 3. to develop audience appreciation and expectation through presentation of a wide range of theatrical product; 4. to provide where practicable professional training and/or services to stimulate amateur and quasi-professional community theatre; 5. to provide a theatre-in-education service; and 6. to pursue the highest standards of excellence in the technical and creative areas.[3]

A Steering Committee comprising members appointed by five key local government authorities was set up and operated over 1979 and 1980 for the initial planning and development of the Company. It was composed of Alderman Sheila D Keeffe, Townsville City Council, Alderman Margaret Cossins, Cairns City Council, Alderman Carmel Daveson, Mackay City Council, John Lamb, Director of the Townsville Civic Theatre, Robert Randle, Manager of the Cairns Civic Centre, Ian Satchwell, Administrator of Rockhampton's Pilbeam Theatre, Alderman Tom Bencke, Rockhampton City Council and Councillor Walter Percival "Snow" Wright of the Pioneer Shire Council, which neighboured Mackay. Over that time, the Committee met variously in Townsville, Rockhampton, Cairns and Pioneer and consulted with local theatre and other interests as it went.[4] Its members were also responsible for liaising between their authorities and the developing organisation, with a view to its eventual registration as a company limited by guarantee. That, in the event, took place on December 3, 1980 at which point the Steering Committee was disbanded in favour of a legally incorporated Board. The new theatre, briefly called "Paradise Productions", but soon to become the much pithier and more saleable New Moon, was by then ready to spread its wings.[5]

The foundation Board set the stage for what was planned to be broadly representative of the main players in the scheme and thereby the key interests in that success. It was designed to be a balance between elected local government officials, local government employees (notably those managing the principal venues), leavened from time to time by a selection of worthy citizens and giving the Company's Artistic Director and General Manager a role, although as non-voting members. There were initially 14 directors: eight local government nominees with 3 year terms, four were elected by members of the community one in each principal performance city subject to approval by Council, together with the Artistic Director and General Manager. How that community plebiscite occurred was always far from clear and as with many such non-profit arts organisations somewhat fictional. Time would reveal the flaws in this entire arrangement, but for the moment it suggested strength and broad inclusion.

The first true Board retained some but not all of the Steering Committee members: Ald. Keeffe (President), Cr Wright (Vice-president), Ald. Bencke, Rockhampton City Council, Mr David Berker, elected Townsville, Ald. Cossins, Ald. Daveson, Mrs Val Hardman, elected Rockhampton, John Lamb, Robert Randle, elected Cairns, Ian Satchwell and businessman Bruce Shepherd, elected Mackay. To these were added Peter Barclay and Terrence O'Connell, then incoming as Artistic Directors, both non-voting.[6] Thus the main actors, bar one, were all in place but from the beginning it can be seen how diverse their locations, backgrounds and interests were likely to be and thereby how problematic it was that such a board would be able to form consistent plans and policies. One might speculate too how easy it might be for a shrewd manager to play them off against each other.

The team

The original intention had been to engage an Artistic Director and a General Manager to run a fairly classical theatre company structure such as had by then become the norm elsewhere in the country. The position of Artistic Director was advertised and after a couple of false starts the decision was taken to appoint not one but two Artistic Directors in tandem. They were O'Connell and Barclay, both of Sydney. With the wisdom of hindsight they were an unusual coupling. O'Connell was very showbiz and inclusive in his manner, Barclay somewhat cerebral and withdrawn, albeit volatile in personality. Both had co-incidentally worked at the Riverina (Trucking/Theatre) Company (RTC) in Wagga Wagga though not at the same time other than in one production. They were thus an oddly matched pair, notwithstanding they were seen jointly as an exciting team to head a brave new venture.

They were described as being "both extremely experienced and successful directors of a wide range of theatrical productions".[7] That was a slight exaggeration. While it might have been a fair description of O'Connell at that time, it was a rather ambitious claim for Barclay. Nevertheless, both were committed to the notion that the Central and Northern Queensland Theatre Company could be "one of the most exciting and innovative projects in Australian theatre"[8] acknowledging its importance not only to the northern communities of Queensland but to the future of Australian theatre generally and while the two were in total agreement with the original objectives of the Company, they had a few of their own to add. These would be critical in shaping the first two seasons and the excitement they generated.

Whether by co-incidence or design, both O'Connell and Barclay were occasional actors as well as directors and so they are able to share not only the directorial responsibility of the plays to be presented but could also appear in each other's productions. They had fulfilled both of those roles successively at RTC and elsewhere. They certainly aimed to provide a theatre experience to the North equal to what was being then imported from elsewhere or regularly enjoyed in any of the metropolitan centres to their South. Their other objective was to promote Australian work wherever possible. Indeed, a quarter of the productions in those first two years were Australian and in opening the Company with 'Ned Kelly' and following in the second year with the quintessentially Australian experience of 'Royal Show', they exhibited a marked attempt to find material that would, in theory at least, resonate with their provincial audiences. But above all, they were committed to the idea that the Company would become identified as an essential part of the cultural life of Queensland and reflect and encourage the quality of life in these towns as well as hoping to develop a rigorous coherent and individual character in its approach to production: "['Ned Kelly'] was bold, choreographed by the African-American choreographer Aku Kadogo, led musically by Queenslanders John Rush and David Sandford, designed by Queenslander David Bell and performed on white box with the company all masked."[9]

In an arts world that has today become weighed down with compliance and smothered in "sustainability" and when so called "mission" statements rarely rise above the platitudinous, there is something deeply moving in the vision of New Moon that these two young men presented to the Board on December 11, 1981.[10] It was nothing if not lyrical in both expression and aspiration: "This company, a new phase for the Australian theatre …[will be] a striking, colourful ensemble presenting new works and classics from the Australian and world repertoires. The company will have a strong bias towards music theatre. We aim to present theatre that will eventually attract audiences from all sections of the community. We aim to present theatre that does not patronise the audience, work that displays a respect and encouragement for the audience's intelligence and imagination… We *do* have high ideals, dreams and ambitions for this company and we need your help to achieve these." It continues in an even more poetic vein: "Let us be Diana's foresters, gentlemen of the shade, minions of the moon", William Shakespeare; and "Soon as the evening shades prevail,/The moon takes up the wondrous tale,/And nightly to the listening earth,/Repeats the story of her birth,/Whilst all the stars that round her burn,/And all the planets in their turn,/Confirm the tidings as they roll/And spread the truth from pole to pole", Joseph Addison; even: "The new moon hangs like an ivory bugle in the naked frosty blue", Dylan Thomas; and finally "Boys and girls come out to play, the Moon doth shine as bright as day, nursery rhyme".

The selection of Paul Iles soon after as General Manager of the new venture and thus the third of the founding triumvirate, was the most surprising choice of all. While O'Connell and Barclay were well regarded, both were in a way on the fringe of Australian theatrical life at that time. Iles by contrast was a highflyer at the centre of the scene. Recruited hot from Britain in his mid-20s he had been, in turn, the esteemed if idiosyncratic General Manager of Nimrod Theatre from 1976 to 1980 and then briefly General Manger of the State Theatre of South Australia (STCSA). Many at the time considered the latter move to have been an odd one. Nimrod was Sydney and freewheeling. STCSA was a statutory corporation and in rather stitched-up post-Dunstan Adelaide. Clearly, it would not be long before fresher fields beckoned, but no one could have dreamt it would be tropical Queensland! But then, Iles had always known when to leave the party for a better one.

The plan

Given such a leadership, it was not surprising that, unusually for the time and even more so today, the acting company would also be of a different mode. Planned as an ensemble of young performers, mainly in their 20s to early 30s, it would also be multi-skilled, so that a wide range of theatrical styles and genres could be presented and to a high level. For instance, virtually all those selected had some musical ability alongside their acting talents, whether this was singing or playing an instrument. Those who could not play, rapidly acquired a modest but serviceable competence. The ensemble was to be engaged for six months each year, at least initially, with the first contract period being from January to June 1982. While the precise reason for this was never articulated is reasonable to suppose that a variety of factors, not the least being financial in the initial stages, played a part. Climatic conditions in Northern Australia are also a major influence for any for who have endured the Wet there. But there was also the need to allow the civic venues dates for the all-important commercial hires that were central to their trading success. At all events, New Moon's plan was to repeat this pattern for a second year of the pilot project in 1983.

The aim was to offer four pieces of popular theatre ranging through comedy, musicals, classics and Australian plays. While various repertoire options had been canvassed during the period of advocacy which its prime movers had undertaken prior to the appointment of the Artistic Directors, the final selection of works to be produced obviously had to match the skills of the ensemble and the needs and interests of the existing theatregoers of the region, as well reach the potential but still uninitiated wider public. All that implied then that the productions would need to have broad general appeal without defaulting to the conservative.

Unique is a much over-used word these days. But it is fair to say that the concept upon which what was to become New Moon was based can genuinely be so described. First, it would be the only permanent touring theatre company in the country; and second, it was one of the very few strictly ensemble performing arts companies of any kind operating in Australia. Indeed, it was the only such theatre company of that time (there were of course ensemble dance companies and music groups). While the prime focus was always to be on the four main centres of Townsville, Cairns, Rockhampton and Mackay, both the "permanency" of the ensemble and its very existence would, it was hoped, enable it in the longer term to extend services beyond the existing circuit to other northern cities such as Mount Isa, Innisfail and even across the border to Alice Springs and Darwin, as both demand and opportunity arose.

So the Artistic Directors were appointed, the management was in place and rehearsals for a four-play season were due to begin in December 1981. The first tour of northern and central Queensland was scheduled to commence in January, 1982. The New Moon had begun to rise.

Life on Mars
Back row- David Sandford, Penny McCue, Gina Riley, Wayne Pigram
Kneeling- Nicholas Flanagan, Gillian Hyde
Front- Diedre Chambers

First Directorate. Photo: David Wilson
Left to right- Peter Barclay, Paul Iles, Terrence O'Connell

2

Where did it come from?

Pleasure tested for the Tropics
attributed to Paul Iles

Being entrepreneurial

The Civic Theatre in Townsville opened on March 31, 1978. Since that date, it had engaged in a number of entrepreneurial activities to present "a wide range of professional and amateur theatre events". They drew on a fund established by the City Council for the purpose of: a) presenting events that would not otherwise be seen in Townsville; b) keeping the Civic Theatre lit when it would otherwise be dark; and c) enhancing and developing professional standards in local theatre presentations.[11]

Mike Reynolds, Townsville's Labor Mayor from 1980 to 1989 and sometime New Moon board member, recalls: "we took building of the [Townsville Civic] theatre, which had been proposed but not enacted by the previous [conservative] administration to the electors. Later we campaigned on having an entrepreneurial fund. These were things that we believed in and which the people of Townsville voted for".[12] It is perhaps one of the few occasions in Australia when the general public has engaged in a plebiscite on an arts matter. He continued: "if you looked at the community there was a lot of support for sport and recreation and facilities for those [but] very lagging in the infrastructure and the necessary operational and innovative ventures like the New Moon Theatre Company ... And we also set up Sunspot Productions and Summer Stock".[13] These measures were indicative of the times generally, but were also a mark of how that city in particular was growing up and saw itself and its future socially and culturally.

The entrepreneurial fund, to which the former mayor referred, and the thinking behind it were crucial to the greater arts vision. Taking that action meant that the Civic Theatre (and many arts centres that came after it across the country) were able to prime their artistic pumps. They could intervene in the entertainment marketplace by buying-in shows and presenting them at their own risk, rather than remaining inert halls-for-hire that had to wait for a promoter, whether non-profit or commercial, to come along and rent their venue. It may sound all very obvious now, but in 1978 in regional Australia it was trailblazing and implied a level of awareness and foresight with which most cultural observers would not have credited Townsville or any part of Queensland at that time. Not even the Sydney Opera House engaged in entrepreneurial activities in those days. Perish the thought! But the idea of such a risk fund ran even deeper. It meant that, whether through buys-in or by creating its own activity, the Civic Theatre could take greater control of its own destiny. It could begin to 'curate', as we would say today, as against merely receiving whatever was on the road. In theory, it could start to respond more immediately to the tastes of its constituents even perhaps to shape them, and above all it could offer professional opportunities in the performing arts to local aspirants. It was a heady mix of possibilities!

Nonetheless, thus far it was still fairly standard operating procedure. While such an approach was then rare in Australia, it had long been in operation in the USA. Soon all the new civic-owned and operated centres across the country were doing much the same or endeavouring to. But the Townsville Civic Theatre's Director, John Lamb had a bigger and more expansive vision than most. As things turned out, he was also more persuasive in making it happen. The range of buys-in he managed was pretty well representative across the board, though a tad more adventurous than some would have chosen back then. If 'For Coloured Girls Who Have Considered Suicide When the Rainbow is Enuf' from the Adelaide Festival and 'Viva Indonesia' from Brisbane's political Popular Theatre Troupe were a little more radical than the regional norm, Twelfth Night Theatre's 'In Praise of Love', 'Clowneroonies' from QTC and 'Bedroom Farce' from the Australian Elizabethan Theatre Trust (AETT) were rather more mainstream. However, it was the presentation in Townsville of Nimrod Theatre's production of Ron Blair's play, 'The Christian Brothers' that was to prove the catalyst in bringing together two of the people who were to be critical to getting New Moon off the ground: Lamb and Paul Iles, then Nimrod's hyper-energetic and lateral thinking General Manger.

Lamb had come to Townsville from Cairns in 1978 to take up the role of Director of the newly completed Civic Theatre – the second cab off the rank of what was to be a succession of new, largely purpose-built, managed, municipal theatres along coastal Queensland. Eventually, they would extend from Cairns to Toowoomba and cover virtually all of the regional cities and towns of Australia's most decentralised State. Queensland was also the only State which has ever had a Country/National Party government – a fact not inconsequential in our tale but important in deciding to create these venues. Later, the theatres would link together into the Northern Australian Regional Performing Arts Centres Association (NARPACA) and extend into the Northern Territory making it then, as now, the most extensive such circuit in the nation. But back in 1978, Townsville's Civic Theatre was almost a lone wolf searching for content.

Kevin Radbourne, long-term official of the Queensland state government arts agency, noted that these cities: "had State Government subsidy to build the performing arts centres. [But] that it didn't come with operating funds. That was the responsibility of the local authority. So they got their capital subsidy which in those days was $33^{1/3}$% of the total cost of building [then] they had to take out loans and other subsidies. So they were keen to have product in them and, of course, they all had professional managements and they were the ones who were looking for product and driving a model of support to have something permanent."[14]

Consider the times. This was all untilled terrain. The various State-based Arts Council networks, reliant on their local branches, had for over 30 years achieved a virtual monopoly on the provision of performing arts product. If a professional theatre show was touring the bush, particularly in New South Wales, Victoria and above all Queensland it was almost certainly being done by an Arts Council and that had been so in varying degrees since the 1950s. Mostly, they were productions from Sydney and Melbourne such as from the Melbourne Theatre Company or The Old Tote and a seemingly endless succession of one person, 'While the Billy Boils' Australiana or their equivalents. There was the occasional, international show spun off from the AETT, Adelaide or Perth Festivals or foreign cultural missions such the British Council, Alliance Française or Goethe-Institut. Periodically, a commercial management might dip its toe into the field, but even there, as with something like the hugely successful 'Godspell', in did so in collaboration with the Arts Council networks which had, as they say, "boots on the ground" to market, provide front-of-house and entertain the troops CWA-like with tea and lamingtons.[15]

These shows played in town halls, church halls and Schools of Arts and sometimes elderly venues called the Theatre Royal or Prince of Wales Opera House and in the increasingly redundant cinemas as TV killed off regular movie attendance. There were few if any properly equipped, professionally managed venues in the bush. Many tales are told of an Arts Council bump-in to a country Town Hall when the caretaker/technician/jack-of-all trades had to be located and extracted from the nearby RSL club. There were, of course, exceptions. A scattering of larger cities like Launceston, Newcastle, Ballarat retained their old vaudeville road houses, but they were few and far between. Lamb himself remarked at the time that those new centres were different in others ways: "Unlike the old commercial theatres or subsidised theatres in the capital cities which usually play one type of attraction for a run of anything from six weeks to twelve months, the regional civic theatre is the venue for all branches of the performing arts, with seasons ranging from one-night stands up to a week."[16] This was all exacerbated by the extreme weather conditions in the tropical zone and in those days often extremely poor roads.

So, in that sense, though only just, John Lamb was a pioneer. He was noteworthy as being among the first to confront the needs of a brand new theatre in a world that had not seen such a phenomenon in ages, yet was about to see a rash of them. He was also somewhat ahead of his time in seeing the need to supply enough activity (or content, as we would say today) to balance the offerings of the local amateur societies, civic events, eisteddfods and occasional touring product with enough other activity to justify their existence not to mention the city's capital investment. This is not the place to enter in any detail into the various dilemmas that arise between community usage and professional operations. Suffice it to say, that those tensions have been with these centres worldwide since their beginnings and have seldom been adequately resolved. So, early in his tenure, Lamb looked around for ways in which to boost occupancy of his 900+ seat venue that were not reliant on the vagaries of touring either by the Arts Council or commercial providers.

In a way, music was easy. Those for-profit promoters who saw advantage in using a smart new auditorium with staff and client comforts switched in a flash from the ageing Town Halls, RSL or Workers Clubs that been their traditional stamping grounds for touring bands. The Queensland Symphony Orchestra's annual Northern tour and Music Viva concerts would or might transfer. The amateur musicals moved as well, if they could be persuaded to afford the rent and technical charges. But theatre remained a problem. What Lamb required was a regular, predictable source of product that could occupy recurrent dates in the calendar with a diet of quality, professional productions. There was also the not inconsiderable matter of productions that could reasonably be expected to fill his overlarge (for theatre) house.

Summer stock!

There was, however, a third element: not content with buying in, Lamb also wanted to raise local standards and create local opportunities. To that end, drawing again on Townsville Council's entrepreneurial support he created a summer stock program which essentially provided professional expertise for amateur productions. Neither idea was new. The concept and the choice of name itself came from the chance and timely return to Townsville of a man who had past experience of the City's arts scene. In 1974 Melbourne-born and trained, Ric Nelson had been a Lecturer in Creative Arts at the Townville Teachers College (TTC). He had a background in music and the visual arts as well as in theatre and had long dreamt of a professional theatre company in the North. After TTC he had headed to Adelaide to take a degree in drama at Flinders University and thence to the Bristol Old Vic Theatre school to read for a Master's. Returning to Australia and traversing the country, auditioning and looking for work as jobbing actor, he drifted back to Townsville arriving just as the new theatre opened and John Lamb was looking around for ways to realise his own theatre vision.[17]

Summer stock had been a fixture on the US entertainment scene since the 1920s. When city theatres closed for the summer actors, often working as co-operatives, moved to holiday resorts and ran seasons of lighter fare for the visitors. Despite occasional efforts in various places the idea had never taken off in Australia and by the 1980s even in America it was in its death throes. At the same time, the notion of injecting professional directors for short periods to work with amateur societies was scarcely new. The Arts Council of NSW had run the Country Producers' Scheme along similar lines for many years.[18] Lamb's innovation was to combine the two. He hired Nelson on a per-show basis to direct a series of productions to set the ball rolling. Nelson made an astonishing five productions between November 1978 to June 1979 and eight in all, up to early 1980. "Since I was paid on a per-production basis I had to do a lot just to make ends meet", he recounted later.[19] The actors were mostly local amateur with a sprinkling of what were described as "resting" professionals, like Sydney's Stuart Wagstaff, engaged on a "honorarium" basis. One may interpret that to mean accommodation, a modest fee, no living allowances but a lovely break near the Great Barrier Reef.

The choice of work was eclectic: five performances of 'The Summer of the Seventeenth Doll' were followed by fourteen of 'The Sound of Music', six of 'Beware the Ides of March' (billed as a fun entertainment based on Shakespeare!), eight performances of Williamson's 'Don's Party' and the same of the American thriller, 'Wait until Dark'.[20] As might be expected, some shows were more successful than others, but the point of it all was to take the temperature. Given the pace, one wonders whether sufficient evidence was garnered about the market and its prospects before Lamb rushed into the next, as it proved, fateful stage. However, one item stood out. Amortised across the spectrum of Summer Stock, total audience numbers amounted to the equivalent of 23% of Townsville's then population. That seemed an astonishing result and caught the attention of decision-makers well beyond the city. Lamb was quick to use it as a selling point in his advocacy to the Australia Council and the Queensland government. If we can achieve this on an ad hoc, pro-am basis, he argued, what could we not do with a professional company? In fact, the figures were not so exceptional. Arts Council tours over the previous decades had racked up any number of such statistics in country towns, though rarely it is true in places as large as Townsville.[21] What was genuinely impressive was that the figure had been achieved by consistently high levels of attendance over a large number of shows in a very concentrated period. In the light of this, Lamb went on to propose that: "It is intended to maintain the program in the second half of 1979 and depending on the timing of the establishment of a professional company in Townsville, to proceed in 1980 with a modified version of Summer stock".[22] Interestingly, there was also Summer Stock Education: a summer school in effect, as well as a youth theatre component. One might, with hindsight, regret that while the adult professional company was fast forwarded, in the interim the attention to outreach and youth fell by the wayside. When it was finally taken up it was, in the event, too late and too half-hearted to help sustain or justify the whole New Moon enterprise. Had it been otherwise, the history and ultimate fate of the Company might have been very different. Nelson today argues that for him it had also always been an integral part of the plan to incorporate the development of a training program at the Townsville College of Advanced Education (TCAE), which had succeeded TTC and ultimately merged with JCU, into a means of feeding the professional company. The course was established but the link was never forged in any coherent way. What's more, he'd always believed that an education arm would be fundamental to the Company's success with the various regional communities.[23]

When, in order to give more stability to this growing theatrical arrangement, a joint position was created, part-funded by Townville City Council and TCAE, at first Nelson did not put up his hand. Later he did. He recalls that his change of mind rather irritated Lamb who had meanwhile moved on to fresher fields. In the event, Rod Wissler got the job on the grounds, quite rightly, Nelson says today, that he had a PhD.[24]

Wissler was in Townsville in 1980 and 1981 and in this new capacity took over the running of Summer Stock. "The TCAE component [of the joint position] was lecturing in literature including drama to teaching students and the City Council component of it was directing the Summer Stock program which was four productions annually in the Civic Theatre, essentially community-based productions with unpaid local people supported by the professional staff of the theatre; but each year there was a big summer musical which involved very large casts, a local orchestra with a professional MD, a number of other professional staff both in the technical area and often one star."[25] Wissler had more of a commitment to Australian content than his predecessor producing works like 'A Toast to Melba' and Nick Enright's version of 'The Servant of two Masters' alongside musicals like 'The King and I' and 'South Pacific'. He did, however, include a workshop production of a local musical 'Beyond the Reef' about which he had a tussle with John Lamb who was more inclined to the Broadway works. "I had been employed from a professional career in theatre in Brisbane and in going to Townsville I was bringing a kind of professional work ethic if you like – a professional aesthetic to these productions which had to show well in the new 1000 seat Civic Theatre and to that extent I guess provide some kind of on-the-ground training for local people who aspired to more work at a semi-professional or professional level in theatre... There was always and still is a big itinerant population in Townsville of public servants, teachers and whatever, and those in Summer Stock productions included people from those ranks as well as long-time residents some of whom had worked professionally. So I certainly had the sense that I was making some kind of contribution [by] up-skilling local residents who aspired to professional work in theatre and, at the same time, I was seeking to lay the foundations for a professional training course at the CAE pretty soon after."[26]

Meanwhile, Nelson never saw himself as having the credentials to run the new theatre company which was to emerge out of all this. And it is a matter of record that he never applied to do so. But clearly he felt disappointment then and regret today that the incoming team of what was to be New Moon made little effort to pursue any of the outreach goals he considered so important. He was the first of many to be discarded by the Company when greater ambitions prevailed. It is not always an edifying tale.

Moreover, there was a tendency to behave as though New Moon came into entirely fallow territory. While Summer Stock had paved the way at the Civic Theatre, a thriving amateur scene was already operating in the city[27] and a successful pro-am theatre restaurant, the Stage Door which specialised in revues. The latter had been set up by a local couple, Mal Hodge and Lyle Hillway and significantly ran from 1980/81 to 1990 or almost exactly the decade of New Moon's existence.[28] Seemingly, none of that knowledge, talent or skill was drawn upon by the new venture. Reading the written record, whether in public statements such as media releases or privately in minutes of meetings and correspondence, one is left with the impression that it was as though none of that existed or if it did, it was of no interest to the new arrivals. Terra nullius, so to speak.

Wissler notes: "I don't remember actually having any formal input to the discussions around New Moon although it is very possible that I did through the City Council. I mean, my Summer Stock role reported to a City Council committee of which Sheila Keeffe was the chair."[29] At all events, the great plan was rapidly advancing. The theatrical Sunlander was off and running. By February 14, 1979, less than a year after the Civic Theatre had opened, an application was sent to the Regional Theatre Funding program of the Australia Council's Theatre Board with a copy to the Director of the Queensland DCA, proposing that North Queensland jump straight to the creation of a professional company. Amazingly, just one year after that the State/Federal funding deal was in place and a five-town local government package to underpin the venture was well on the way.

Recruiting

All that is a matter of fact. There are also scattered references that the Company resulted from a consultancy undertaken by Paul Iles, but no precise record of that survives. Certainly, Iles was appointed the Company's General Manager in mid-1981 (a title which morphs into Executive Director and Executive Producer at later stages). He is described in later documents as having been a "consultant" to the project from 1978 and then to the Steering Committee.[30] Whether this was an official arrangement is unclear. What is certain is that he was unpaid at that stage. It is also possible that Lamb subsequently related Iles's involvement to others and they in turn interpreted it as having been a more formal association than it was.[31] There are, however, curious twists along the way. The Minutes of the Board meeting on December 12, 1980 note that Iles was "invited to apply" for the position of General Manager and in a letter to him in Adelaide Lamb issues that invitation: "in view of your background interest in this project and your own expertise".[32] This was *after* it had been advertised and some 10 short-listed candidates from all over Australia were interviewed by a panel consisting of Peter Dent of the Queensland Arts Council and Twelfth Night Theatre's Joan Whalley.[33] However, to ensure that some degree of protocol was observed, the position was re-advertised in *The Australian* in mid-March 1981 in an advertisement which names Barclay and O'Connell already as joint Artistic Directors.

More certain it is that in 1978 Iles had "dropped in" on Townsville on his way back from a holiday in Papua-New Guinea. He was just 26. Almost a boy wonder. He gave an interview to the Townsville newspaper in which he floated the idea of a professional theatre company for the North. An ensemble of 6 actors plus Artistic Director, Manager and technical support was all that was needed, he observed.[34] To the local arts community and am-dram aficionados it must have seem like a declaration of the second coming. Here was the theatrical wunderkind from the South with his cheeky grin, Harry Potter glasses, déclassé English accent and persistent sniff, telling them that in this distant outpost of the Empire, by Jove they could do it, chaps. Whether the idea was his originally, came as a rush of blood to the head such as he was prone to experience when faced with a journalist's tape recorder or formed part of a carefully crafted scheme, we cannot now be sure. It seems likely he and Lamb had already by then spoken about it, though whether he planted the idea with Lamb or vice versa must remain speculation, since no correspondence between them on the matter has been uncovered and both are deceased. Whatever the case, the seed fell on fertile ground, struck root and flourished. The two men were to be instrumental in shaping both the concept and its implementation, albeit in markedly different ways and at differing speeds. It also seems probable that the newspaper interview was at least kite-flying on Lamb's part. In the event, for good or ill their destinies were to be bound together.

Given all this, one can with some assurance credit Lamb, the Summer Stock program and Iles with being the three driving forces in New Moon's creation. But there is another factor. One might dress it up as an acute sense of urgency or down as simple impatience. At various times, then and later, both Lamb and Iles displayed the latter trait to an extreme degree. However it is characterised, the project surged forward not entirely under control.

Since two of the three key persons involved in that foundation process are no longer available for comment, we may never know for sure. Yet there is no doubt Iles played a defining role. It seems most likely that the visit of 'The Christian Brothers' to Townsville brought him and Lamb together. Certainly, Lamb consulted Iles informally on funding tactics. Peter Barclay recalls that while still an Associate Director at Nimrod he was invited to sit in on meetings between the two in Sydney. It is likely that Iles himself had no thought of any future involvement and was simply helping a colleague. Certainly, Barclay had not the least thought then that he himself might ever form part of north Queensland theatre company.

"Paul believed it was not enough to learn to direct, one had to learn all the business so he generously invited me to things like that".[35] Barclay remembers Iles advising Lamb to get both the local governments and the State government onside before approaching the Australia Council considering that that way his case would be much stronger. Barclay believed that Iles probably acted as an advocate for the proposed company with, at least, members of the Theatre Board, such as Richard Wherrett and Elizabeth Butcher, but admits that is only supposition on his part.[36]

Finding backers

There is one further leading character in this genesis: Alderman Sheila D. Keeffe was the chair of the Townsville Council's Community and Cultural Committee and went on to preside over the Steering Committee of the embryonic company. For all his drive and determination Lamb was, in the end, an employee of just one Local Government Authority (LGA). It was a crucial LGA, with a brand new venue as a bargaining chip. But, when all is said and done, he was merely the hired help. Alderman Keeffe, by contrast, was an elected official and chair of a key Committee of the then Labor-dominated Townsville City Council and something of a force in the local land. Secretary to and later wife of Senator Jim Keeffe, himself a Labor stalwart from a State party that took no prisoners, the Keeffes were what later would have been called a "power couple". "She was a real dynamo", Margaret Bornhorst who at that time hosted an afternoon ABC radio talk program and was later an actor with New Moon recalls.[37] Keeffe had been one of the architects of the campaign to persuade the Council into building the Civic Theatre. But oddly for our story, the power couple that actually emerged to realise the dream of a functioning enterprise was Keeffe and Lamb and to them must go the credit not only of shaping a creative solution to the need to provide that recurrent professional performing arts content, but in the process "invent" a theatre company in Northern Australia whose business model was, it is not going too far to say, ground-breaking, even radical for the time.

The Keeffes were Labor in a state run as its fiefdom by the National Party (formerly Country Party) at the height of its ascendancy. They were also Labor in a National Party local government fortress that had been heavily guarded until only a few years prior to our story.[38] But Sheila was also a fierce North Queenslander which counted then and counts today for much and there is that camaraderie across local government which often transcends party political lines. Certainly, Keeffe was able to speak across those divides. She, Lamb and Nelson literally took their show on the road. They travelled down to Rockhampton where the redoubtable Alderman Rex Pilbeam had ruled for what seemed like generations, notionally as mayor but rather more like a South American caudillo. Nelson recalls the mayor slamming the written (theatre) proposal down on the table and storming out of the meeting.[39] Yet in time, they convinced even him of their case or somehow the more enlightened of his council colleagues did so. They duly named Rockhampton's new theatre after him so perhaps there was an element of Donald Trump's favourite quid pro quo.

The advocacy troupe went to Cairns where Lamb had been previously the theatre manger before moving to Townsville and persuaded the Council there. They were extremely well-received in Mackay and indeed achieved the amazing feat of reeling in both its City Council and that of the neighbouring Pioneer Shire as a joint venture in what must have been one of the great (and rare) acts of municipal collaboration in Australian arts history. Interestingly, while those two were early to buy in there, together with Townsville they were in the last to abandon ship. The team even trekked out to union-dominated Mt Isa where politically Keeffe was on friendlier ground than in some places on the coast, but was curiously unsuccessful there. And so the see-sawing went on for months. Margaret Reynolds, Alderman, sometime New Moon board member and later Senator and Federal Minister, remembers the three coming back sometimes full of optimism which reversed, sometimes downhearted only to be surprised by good tidings and sometimes both in rapid succession. It was important, too, for them to keep up the spirits at home in Townsville because while they had allies there not everyone was persuaded or equally persuadable.[40]

Another great champion of the Company was and remained the redoubtable Brian Sweeney, soft drink manufacturer who, in a curious move by the Fraser government, had been appointed to the chair of the Australia Council's Theatre Board and thence as a member of the Council itself. He became an outstanding advocate for New Moon and regional theatre in general, even travelling to Mt Isa to address a meeting of the recalcitrant City Council to urge them to change their minds about joining the growing band of LGA supporters of the scheme. In the event, Sweeney, too, would be rebuffed but he did at least persuade them to think again.[41] And he remained a staunch friend of the Company even after his term at the Theatre Board ended. He was later rewarded, if that is the word, by being invited by New Moon to become an "associate director". The significance of the appointment was never clarified but was another typically expansive and no doubt genuinely well-meant gesture by Iles, a man much given to gestures. Perhaps he believed that the wider and more prestigious the associations the better the advocacy. There is little evidence that his faith in this practice was justified.[42] Sweeney's appointment to the Australia Council had been widely criticised in the arts community. Later there were those who went on to claim that the Theatre Board was never better than under his chairmanship. "Interestingly, in 1985 a CAPPA (Confederation of Australian Professional Performing Arts) survey of Theatre Board clients found that 73% favoured an independent, non-artist chairperson for the Board."[43]

Bob Ellicott, then Minister for Home Affairs (which covered the Arts portfolio in the Fraser government), wrote to Sweeney as chair of Theatre Board that Keeffe and Lamb had paid him a visit about the new company concept. "The project seemed to be both interesting and worthwhile and I am conveying the representations made to me" with the request that they be taken into account when this subject was under consideration by the Board. Ellicott was an ink-in-the-veins silk, so this must pass for enthusiasm from such as him.[44]

Accordingly, it is than apparent that rather than popping fully grown like Athena from the head of Zeus (much as one suspects John Lamb would have approved of the analogy) the idea of the new company evolved more gradually and from a variety of sources. That said, it was still over a relatively short time that the notion emerged of a home-grown theatre enterprise which would occupy the Civic Theatre and, by extension, service the Townsville public with locally-made product and eventually create a circuit throughout the region.

Finding the money

Perhaps even more remarkable than all of this imagining and goodwill was the financial base on which the new company was launched. Few such ventures can have enjoyed so promising a foundation. While it may be a little difficult today to grasp fully the purchasing power of the dollar in 1981/82, nevertheless the sums are impressive as the starting point in any age for an untried organisation. The Theatre Board and the Queensland Division of Cultural Affairs were each committed to an annual contribution of $86,900. (In fact, because of the delayed start, it began with *two years* of Queensland subvention rolled into one). The five local government authorities provided box office guarantees between them amounting to $112,475 plus the municipally-operated theatres gave cost guarantees of a further $23,325. In addition, the Company had budgeted for corporate sponsors of $30,000 together with private donors' and foundations' contributions of $35,400 (in the first year the figure was $17,700, but by 1983 it had risen to $59,600). All this made an estimated grand total income of $375,000. To the two young men who had variously started at the RTC in Wagga Wagga and a fringe outfit in Sydney's Rocks and had worked in the small-to-medium scaled arts scene, the income figures must have seemed well-nigh incredible. Time would tell how everyone's credulity would be strained when the cost side also became apparent.

In a statement at the time, Ald. Keeffe somewhat grandly declared: "They will be unique in Australia. It is the first time local authorities, the State government and the Australian government have combined to provide a secure base for a regional arts organisation...It will be a model for other areas of Australia".[45] Sadly for New Moon itself and the rest of the country that part of her prophecy was not to be realised.

The scene

But beyond the politics, what can we say of the other dimensions to this cultural blooming? Take James Cook University, for example. It was a major employer as well as a significant cultural presence in the North. Since, in so many other ways, the University has been an important factor in the growth and change of Townsville over the past 60 years; and since, in that time, it has harboured many cultural activities within its bosom, one might have thought that it would have played some definitive role in the history of New Moon. After all, it had been a pioneer in teaching Australian literature at tertiary level. It had established one of the earliest university drama courses and distinguished figures passed through its teaching ranks such as Robert Love[46], Michael Lanchberry, Edward Cowie and even some associated with New Moon such as choreographer Aku Kadago.[47] That course's later incarnation with Jean-Pierre Voos and its harbouring of his company Tropic Line is another story, but it is indicative of the University's ongoing, enthusiastic support of the performing arts. Its music department incubated the Townville Chamber Music Festival which, through many a twist and turn, is still going. For decades its literary magazine *Linq* was among a small number in the country regularly publishing quality verse, prose and criticism.

One might have thought too, that the growing presence through the University of a body of scholars, scientists, administrators, technicians especially in Townsville and Cairns as well as those in other research institutions like the Marine Park Authority, might have been a factor in creating an educated audience for setting up a theatre company. Even if this were a factor lying below the radar in Townsville and later Cairns, clearly it was not in Rockhampton and Mackay where the emergence of tertiary education was somewhat slower. That absence may well have been why it did not rate any particular mention in those cities. Yet if that was in anyone's minds it seems not to have been stated at the time.

Meantime, Townsville City Council was also embarked on other cultural developments. More or less simultaneously it had created what was to become one of the leading regional galleries in the country in the Perc Tucker, named for the Mayor, member of state Parliament and (for a few months) Leader of the Opposition who set the cultural ball rolling by purchasing the former ANZ bank building for that purpose. It also enabled what is now one of Australia's the most successful and longest operating regional arts companies in Dance North.[48] Theatre practice since the time of New Moon has had a more chequered history, but it has not been for want of the locals trying their hand.

Tucker was a traditional Queensland Labor man with little direct interest in arts matters but he was prepared to let others like Sheila Keeffe, Mike Reynolds and later Margaret Reynolds, (no relation)[49] have their heads with it. It has been suggested that the prospect of having the gallery somewhat incongruously named after him was a factor in his backing of it. He might have been equally content with something more quotidian bearing his name.[50] Notwithstanding, both Margaret and her distinguished historian husband Henry, himself later a New Moon board member, suggest that while there was distinct support on the Community and Cultural Committee of Council which first Keeffe and later she chaired, there was also opposition.

Notwithstanding, there can be little doubt that there was a genuine desire in the Townsville Council to expand its scope of concern beyond the traditional range of local government. New social programs in welfare, housing and women's issues loomed just as large as the cultural and if the alliances across the Labor caucus were not always neat or even predictable, they were a leap forward on what had gone before. As Mike Reynolds observed: "local government in Queensland over decades and decades was about three Rs – roads, rates and rubbish – if you looked at the community there was a lot of support for sport and recreation" but much less for the arts.[51]

Oddly though in this relatively vibrant context neither was the role of tourism seen to have been a consideration. Yet the notion of cultural tourism was already quite live. Indeed, it was much on the agenda of public authorities across the country and had been since the early 1970s. When South Australia's then Premier, Don Dunstan set up his first one person arts agency in 1970 it was as an Arts and Tourism Development

Office so overt was the connection in his mind at least. If in many way SA was not the most promising territory for tourism generally, the Adelaide Festival at least had demonstrated that properly configured the arts could draw visitation from other States. The opening of the National Gallery of Victoria had similarly paved the way for linking arts and tourism. Perhaps if New Moon had begun in Cairns it might have been different, but Townsville had never been such a tourism-oriented city. And to some extent in both places the Great Barrier Reef was a powerful competitor for visitors' attention though even when New Moon moved to Cairns a touristic approach does not seem to have been canvassed. If there was ever any thought of piggy-backing the daytime adventures of the Barrier Reef and marlin fishing with a culturally-driven night-time economy there is no record of it in the Company's archives. At a State level, meter maids and surf carnivals appeared to be the extent of cultural interests in any coastal city large or small north or south. No thoughts there of the profits from a gambling Casino funding an opera house à la Monaco.

But let us look at the city in New Moon's quadrella which contrasts most strongly with the Far North. Rockhampton was and is the major population centre in Central Queensland with about 55,000 inhabitants in the mid-1980s (now around 80,000). Small towns in its catchment swelled that figure to about 60,000. It is also one of the oldest cities in Queensland being founded in 1861, a mere two years after the colony was separated from NSW and some years before either Townsville (1866) or Cairns (1876). Long a railhead for the inland grazing industry, Rockhampton's economy also relied on mining and acting as hub of state government administration. Unlike Cairns, it is not now nor was it then a tourist destination and had long had the reputation of being a tough and uncompromising place.[52] Helmut Bakaitis tells of an encounter of Paul Iles with that city. "He wore Bombay bloomers, bright socks, braces and carried a Mickey Mouse bag and that first trip, [was] the only time I began to think this is really dangerous [was] when he walked – in the afternoon – into a beer garden in Rockhampton and there were a hundred or so local tradies etc and suddenly there was dead silence. And all you could feel was 200 eyes – look at the poofters! And then I noticed there was graffiti on one of the walls, saying Southern poofters with AIDs go home. And I thought, uh oh and that was the start..."[53]

Nevertheless, Rockie did have an impressive range of cultural facilities which were quite generously funded for the times and a level of arts activity which was high given the size of its population. The Walter Reid Cultural Centre housed some 20 local groups from potters to youth theatre all under the aegis of the Council's community arts officer. The regional gallery housed a modest but representative collection of Australian works and the Municipal Theatre, School of Arts. Music Bowl and Pilbeam Theatre comprised the Performing Arts Complex with then about 130,000 patrons annually through a program that was about 90% professional and imported. In the arts Rockhampton had always been noted among Queensland towns for its music-making rather than theatre activity. This featured several choirs, a youth orchestra, three brass bands, a flourishing jazz action society and a light opera company. All these were assisted by the City Council in a variety of ways. On the face of it, it was a less promising city than its northern sisters for such as New Moon though its response to the Company's productions would at times prove to be, if anything, more feisty.

Nowhere in any of these places is there any evidence of a body of what might be loosely termed an "artistic" community agitating for such a development as New Moon became. There seems at best to have been passive support for the move to create a professional theatre company or, for that matter in Townsville, the earlier Summer Stock project. There was what today we might call a consultative process run by Lamb, Keeffe and the Steering Committee. But there is no indication of theatre advocates, individually or collectively, banging on the doors of local government for action on this front either in Townville itself or in the other cities.

However, long term Townsville theatre activist, pro-am actor and director, ultimately New Moon Board member and finally Chairman, Ray Dickson remembers only enthusiasm there at the notion that the region would have its own professional theatre company and, he adds, "pride" that it should be coming out of Townsville. "It felt like we'd become a real grown-up place."⁵⁴ We must therefore conclude that, however welcome its arrival, in no way did new Moon arise from popular demand or artistic lobby. It was unmistakably tablets handed down from the mountain and they were accompanied by a pot if not a calf of gold. Both later contributed to its ultimate fate.

Cabaret
Left to right- Valerie Bader, Gina Riley, Gillian Hyde, Deidre Chambers,
Penny McCue

3

What was the Context?

At the School of Arts, a broadsheet lies

sprayed with the sarcasm of flies

"the Great Golightly Family

of Entertainers here tonight" –

dated a year and a half ago,

but left there, less from carelessness

than from a wish to seem polite

Kenneth Slessor – 'Country Towns '

The Queensland context

As background to the creation of New Moon it is important to understand the forces that were at work in the 1970s in Queensland at the time. They were contradictory in so many ways. The State, personified to many by the long regime of Johannes Bjelke-Petersen's (Joh to his many friends but whom a former eloquent Prime Minister in 1974 designated a "bible bashing bastard")[55] is itself contradictory and nowhere more so than in the deep North. There is also so much folklore about this era, energetically propagated by a mix of media and general prejudice in the southern States, that it was easy then and to some extent still, to accept an entirely one dimensional view of it. To take a simple example: the notion of "development" above all property development was rife in Queensland – with all its negative connotations. Many observers still recall with shock and horror the late night bulldozer levelling the historic Bellevue Hotel in downtown Brisbane as an extreme case of that. Fewer reflect on the total levelling of South Brisbane with its sagging but emotive riparian buildings, tropical shops, pubs, dwellings and a few covert brothels, then reclaimed as the site for the revered World Expo '88 and later still its much-touted and now glorified "Southbank" Cultural Precinct with its theatres, museum, galleries and library. Perhaps the public saw these as a greater good or the end justifying the means. Maybe they only cared about the Hotel where the well-to-do gathered rather than the habitations of Greek migrants, Indigenous meeting places or the old Anglo working class of Woolloongabba. In this account, we must try to balance those two tendencies.

The first important part of the context of our tale was the New State Movement. However odd it may have looked from "down South", that was a very real and serious aspiration for many above the Tropic of Capricorn. Indeed, there were those who were inclined to call the putative new State, Capricornia. Its inhabitants had long been fed up with decision-making handed down (or from a geographic point of view more accurately perhaps, handed up) from Brisbane. They wanted local input and authority. Though the movement failed, one of the results was a strong trend to decentralise state government agencies and services into regional locations. There is perhaps a faint parallel in the creation of New Moon to the desire of those communities, or that part of them that cared for art, to have their own theatre company and not to be dependent forever and a day on the occasional terpsichorean forays from the Capital. One might note that the Capricornian movement is still very much alive. The hyper-active member for Kennedy, the Hon Bob Katter MHR still drags it out every so often, along with damming every river in FNQ. There have been various attempts to get the proposition up at party conferences. Some diehards still see it as just a matter of time.

Then, too, it was a time of great social change. Despite its reputation down South and the patina of conservatism that the Bjelke-Petersen government spread meticulously over its own image and behaviour, those changes were certainly affecting Central and North Queensland. Residents wanted a share of the action and that involved access to the better things in life, including the arts. They also wanted their own artistic voices heard rather than always being the recipients of imported ideas. That is not a new argument, of course, but it was one that in this context was starting to become organised in the various communities throughout the regions. Nevertheless, it was a generalised agitation and there is no evidence that it led directly to the formation of New Moon.

There were, as well, major transformations in the media which were to have a profound impact on the way local communities received their news and information and above all the diversity of those. Second TV channels had opened up in each of the towns where New Moon would subsequently perform. Prior to later networking, all those were then locally owned and operated. Until then, telecast had been provided only by the ABC with its rather restricted and, to many minds, anodyne diet. Those towns also featured thriving often daily independent newspapers which actively chewed over local affairs and took up and pushed many local causes. They also offered a surprisingly large coverage of the arts and entertainment.

There was also another issue of identity: actor, Bob Baines remembers: "Robert Arthur [one of the few Queensland actors in the original New Moon ensemble] gave me a clue about North Queensland: [he said] 'People think about it as the country. It isn't, it really is industrial Australia'. If you think about it is all heavy industry, mining, abattoirs, the military, fishing, sugar processing."[56]

It is also worth remembering that each town was much more self-contained than it is today. More businesses were locally owned. There were many fewer franchises and thus less transience. That ensured that there was in each place a body of leaders in society with a stake in the town who frequently shaped and supported local events. Even branch managers of businesses who came from elsewhere to run banks, insurance companies, government agencies and the like, tended to stay long term. The same may be said for medical practitioners, school principals and clergy. There was simply less social churn. More specifically, in the cultural domain the Queensland Arts Council was at its peak of activity with an extensive touring network bringing all kinds of product to the regions. Almost as important was the emergence of the NARPACA group founded in 1983. All its centres were, as we have noted, desperate for product. QAC and other touring sources were not supplying enough. Moreover, the local community groups were rather staid in their offerings. With these changes came an opportunity to start creating their own product. In quick succession, three brand-new venues had come on line in Cairns, Townville and Rockhampton. And somewhat later the purpose-built Mackay Entertainment and Convention Centre in 1987 would replace the aged Theatre Royal. That was the matrix for New Moon. However, there was not yet the extensive networking or regional bookings conferences of today nor a federally-funded Playing Australia that could financially underwrite regional touring nationwide.

There is one further consideration. It was what Malcolm Calder, sometime administrator of Rockhampton's Pilbeam theatre, has described tellingly as "slow country wisdom".[57] That was the spirit that supported the idea of the arts as a good thing in itself for society, much as it endorsed sport or religion, even though the individuals holding those views might not engage in or avail themselves of any of them. One might say that a city was not a city without churches, sporting facilities and a theatre. Having said that, one might add that equally they did not wish any of them to be too radical in their behaviour or intrusive in their approach. Out of all that emerged New Moon's unique model. It would be a core of five municipal councils full of such people and attitudes, co-funding a theatre company and having, in varying degrees and with various aims, their representation on its Board. It was to be a heady mix. But then, as the Australia Council's Michael FitzGerald observed: "they were heady times".[58]

One thing surprises however. There seems to have been little awareness among arts practitioners in Brisbane of what was happening in North Queensland. The new theatre developments might have been expected to have aroused either interest or concern, at various stages of its relatively short and not uncontroversial history. If either was the case, it remained well below the public radar however much it may have been talked about in private. "It is interesting that there wasn't any more formal interaction between New Moon and a company like TN that shared some characteristics", Rod Wissler observed.[59]

After all, New Moon was to receive significant State funding for activities which were, in part at least, traditionally offered by other providers, including TN's occasional regional touring. It compromised, if only marginally and in a limited district, the de facto if not de jure control that QAC supposedly exercised over most regional touring to country towns, especially of professional theatre. And New Moon's patterns of operation must have impinged on availability of dates for other touring shows in the newly opened regional arts centres in those critical provincial cities. Yet few of the operatives of QAC remember having seen its work. Fewer still, admittedly after the passage of decades, recall any sense of it being talked about at the time or any feelings as to its artistic or other achievements.[60]

Nevertheless, the ground work down South had been well and truly laid as early as 1979. John Lamb in his thorough fashion (together with Townsville Council's Town Clerk) wrote to the Director of Queensland DCA, Kevin Siddell assuring him that in his consultations he had experienced no adverse comments from the key operatives. "I have spoken to both Peter Dent [Director] of the QAC and Alan Edwards of QTC.[61]

At least in the early days, relations between New Moon and QTC seemed open and cordial. There was even a plan to share a technical trainee and a joint application was submitted to The Theatre Board for that purpose. Indeed, Alan Edwards wrote a paper about how things might work between them.[62] He even went so far as to propose that QTC tours should occur normally in the second half so as to avoid conflict with New Moon dates. Overall, Edwards had been receptive to the project in its general conception: "I think we are agreed that it is not cutting across any activity that the QTC is presently undertaking, and that this type of development is most necessary in this region. I expressed the view that the establishment of this northern and central company should not result in decreased touring activity by the QTC, but rather that this activity should be maintained or preferably increased. I think that this is desirable from the point of view of competition being conducive to rising standards and practical from the point of view that we are operating in an expanding market". He noted, however, that: "figures prepared by the QAC show that in 1981, covering all the presentations they toured throughout the State, costs have risen by 25% while audiences declined by 5%." That in itself should have raised concerns for all.

Similarly, regular exchange with Peter Dent of the QAC with respect to touring dates and product seemed, on the face of it, to be warm and collegial.[63] Dent had, in fact, expressed some initial concern that the Company might tie up the new chain of theatres for substantial periods of time, having the effect of making availabilities difficult for the Arts Council's touring attractions. However, once it was realised that the Company would be in fact be booking just one theatre for an average of four days once every six weeks, he indicated that he was quite satisfied that this would not pose a problem to the Council.[64] As things turned out, Dent's original assessment proved more accurate. While New Moon provided only a minor irritant to the Arts Council, the venues themselves were later to express great alarm that its dates, often reserved nearly 12 months in advance, were cutting across commercial hires for touring acts which were often tightly scheduled series of one-night stands. There is nothing rare or unusual about any of that. The dilemma is basic to all arts venues everywhere. It was exacerbated in this case by the frequency with which New Moon had to adjust its bookings due to outside circumstances over which it increasingly had little control. As its funding and therefore planning cycle became progressively more erratic, that factor grew to the point where at least one Council insisted that the Company bring its season dates forward into the Wet to free up dates for commercial hirers in more desirables times.[65]

Queensland is, of course, a very big state. Townsville is further from Brisbane than is Sydney. Cairns is further still. One does not have to spend very long in any of these northern towns, even today, to perceive an almost deliberate barrier of misunderstanding or ignorance even, between the two extremes of the State. How much more was it so then, especially at a time when the 'New State' movement was a hot and current topic.

We have also to put ourselves back in those cultural times which nationwide were very different from those prevailing in the early 21st century. Adelaide was still the "Athens of the South" where Premier Dunstan was seen to have reigned as a kind of Platonic philosopher king encouraging radical social experiment and funding artistic development. It was mostly "spin", but so effective in messaging that the legend endures to this day. The Adelaide Festival was without doubt the prime international showcase and almost a touchstone of high art in the country to which the cognoscenti made their biennial pilgrimage. Melbourne was still the home of commercial showbiz: Crawford, Grundy, Edgley, until recently JCW, Aztec Promotions and others, and there too was the already revered Melbourne Theatre Company, Australian Ballet and a host of preserved Edwardian theatres. There was old money as patronage and a large central European diaspora as core audience. The city boasted a splendid new Art Gallery which, despite being clearly Victoria's, was grandiosely termed "National". Meanwhile, Sydney had its Opera House barely a decade old, Joan Sutherland, the ABC, NIDA, the AETT, Musica Viva and a clutch of live privately owned theatres. Brisbane, by contrast, was the polar opposite of these. It had demolished Her Majesty's, its last traditional roadhouse theatre; the state art gallery was in a shoebox; and its museum was falling down. The Queensland Cultural Complex (as it was rather dizzyingly to be known) was not to open until 1985. Paradoxically, Townsville, Cairns and Rockhampton all had new purpose-built contemporary arts centres before Brisbane had its. For these reasons, the Queensland capital was seen as Hicksville. Wrongly, it may be, but nevertheless the view prevailed especially in the snobbish South of the country. The "optics" created by the behaviour of the Bjelke-Petersen government did nothing to dispel that impression.

So, it was not, as might have been expected, a Brisbane migration to the Tropics on which New Moon was built, but a migration from much further south. Given the reverse snobbery of the North that might well, on the face of it, have been more acceptable to Cairns and Townsville say, than if it had in fact come from Brisbane. At least it could be claimed that there was real talent in the southern capitals, stars even, whereas Brisbane remained something of a cultural joke no doubt as much among those in the theatrical know in Cairns and Townsville as in Melbourne or Adelaide. The key players in New Moon, like all five people appointed in succession as its Artistic Directors came from Sydney or Melbourne. The first two General Managers came from UK (via Sydney and Adelaide) and from Melbourne (via Paris). Few actors or other theatre workers were recruited from Brisbane. It was almost as though Brisbane chose to ignore New Moon as much as New Moon neglected Brisbane.

Perhaps inevitably the Company's Artistic Directors tended to choose those collaborators be they actors, designers or technical staff with whom they were familiar. It was not until its dying days that New Moon employed predominantly local Townsville talent or tried to engage more seriously with Brisbane-based leadership, and by when it was too late.

Even Diane Cilento, arguably the most high profile artist to be involved with the Company, although mostly in a governance role, was in a sense a "blow-in". Despite her family's distinguished Queensland credentials, her career as a film and stage actor had been in Britain. Her (then) playwright husband, Anthony Shaffer was British and her theatrical presence in Australia had been negligible before they undertook the Karnark experimental playhouse project near Cairns. They were also in their somewhat regal, high-handed manner deliberately outsiders there. (One could argue that they were outsiders of a different kind in the UK, but that is another story.) In that sense, it is perhaps not surprising that there was greater awareness (or should one say interest?) among the theatre community in southern Australia of the extraordinary New Moon adventure that was taking place in the Tropics than there was closer to hand in Queensland itself.

It is arguable too, that whereas Iles and co wanted to be recognised in Sydney and Melbourne they might not have cared less about what Brisbane thought other than via the cash cow of the State government's annual grant. All the original workers in the Company were either well known or well-connected in their States of origin. So they fed back to their mates at home "intel", enlivening even scandalous as it often was. Moreover, as they were hired on limited-life engagements averaging six months per year, all returned to their base and talked. And actors *do* talk. Word spread. The lure of the Tropics was strong. Hard work aside, who wouldn't want to spend six months there far away from bleak Melbourne's winter weather, the arctic gully winds of Adelaide or sitting by the phone in Sydney waiting for their agent to call with the offer of a TV commercial for toilet duck, a voice-over for railway announcements, still less waitressing or driving a cab? Moreover as Robert Love, then teaching theatre studies at James Cook University, remembers: "They were definitely swashbuckling adventuring in the North, bringing something to the North which these people hadn't had before. It was very much, 'we are bringing you the city'."[66]

Thus, New Moon was in effect always fly in/fly out, albeit perhaps not self-consciously. And it was always a transplanted, mainstream company from somewhere else, both in terms of personnel and mentality. Or as its last Artistic Director, David Fenton somewhat disparagingly called it "colonial".[67] It never put down roots in the community. Actor, Stephen Clark observed: "In the first year there was little community engagement [between the ensemble and the broader community]. We worked so hard there just wasn't time".[68]

One might contrast this with Dance North. No one in New Moon until the second general manager, Ruth Bereson chose to live in Townsville (say) or Cairns. It was as though their real lives were rather centred somewhere else. It is Interesting that the very idea of the company had come out of an experiment with Summer Stock. In a way, it was always that. One cannot entirely escape the Judy Garland/Mickey Rooney "let's put on a show in the barn" aspect of it all. Barns the venues themselves were mostly not, though the rehearsal premises and working conditions often came close.[69] Perhaps given the time of year "winter stock" might have been a more accurate term. By contrast, Artistic Director, Cheryl Stock and Dance North's general manager, Lorna Hempstead always lived in Townsville. From day one, Dance North emphasised community and other engagement as the basis of their worth and the source of their ultimate strength. "I think the partnerships we forged were the most critical aspect of our work", Stock says today.[70] Dance North is still alive and thriving while New Moon has long since faded and died.

The Australian context

There is something remarkable in the fact that from the late 1970s to early 1990s a handful of regionally-based, professional theatre companies emerged seemingly from nowhere, flourished in various ways and to various degrees and with few exceptions, one by one blinked out. While it manifested itself in most mainland states, its greatest flowering was in New South Wales where it peaked with arguably as many as eight exemplars, seven of them outside of greater Sydney. Strictly speaking, however, there were six which enjoyed any real stability or track record. ACT, Victoria and South Australia also produced at least one each of this ilk. It is important to distinguish these from the contemporaneous and very active Community Theatre movement.[71] That shared some characteristics with regional theatres though both were careful to distinguish themselves from the other. Murray River Performing Group (MRPG) began with a strong community theatre/community arts ethos but always associated itself with the regional theatre grouping. Mill Theatre in Geelong, by contrast, shared the concept of a regional base, but was philosophically far from the regional theatre companies in its ethos.⁷² Street Arts and Popular Theatre Troupe in Brisbane, Melbourne Workers Theatre and Theatre West adopted a more rigorous political stance, while Harvest in South Australia, not unlike New Moon, was an attempt to provide original productions in the Eyre Peninsula which would go on to service the network of four cloned regional arts venues in Renmark, Mt Gambier, Whyalla and Port Pirie.⁷³

Such a cluster of activity leads one to ask if this was all just coincidence? Each of these initiatives had a different genesis. Some grew out of past endeavours such as the Q Theatre and New England Theatre Company in NSW. Some were brand new. All at some stage were supported by their State governments and most by the Australia Council, if only in fits and starts. Some also benefitted from local government support. Michael FitzGerald recalls that: "usually there was a single driven individual, often an artist".⁷⁴ But beyond that, is there a pattern to all this and, if so, how does New Moon relate to it?

Compared with New Moon, all the other regional theatre initiatives seem modest, almost paltry in their scope and resourcing. That is not to diminish their goals or achievements. New Moon was bold and grandiose from day one. Every other regional theatre company found or arose in a city or town and established it as a base. In some cases, they defined a region around it or found one already made e.g. the Riverina, the Albury-Wodonga catchment, Hunter Valley, New England or the Illawarra and took that as their wider, albeit immediate, constituency. New Moon scoped an area roughly the size of the British Isles as its territory (and boldly aimed for more) and sought to tour not just the occasional production across it, but annually to service, at the very least, all of its main centres with a multi-play season. What's more, it aimed to do so with a company based around a salaried ensemble of actors, resident designers, initially two Artistic Directors, management and technical staff.

None of those other regional companies had anything like New Moon's funding base with State and Federal matching grants and, above all, five collaborating LGAs. As we have seen, it had started in North

Queensland with around $300,000 confirmed funding (depending on how it is calculated). In 1978 RTC received start-up grants of $35,000 ($20,000 from the Theatre Board and $15,000 from the NSW Ministry for the Arts). Only Hunter Valley Theatre Company (HVTC) at its height came within cooee of New Moon's support from the private sector. So, for a couple of glorious seasons the New Moon glowed exceptionally bright and blazed a trail well beyond anything its peers could match, even though some of them had been established five years earlier. To be fair, most exhibited less extravagant aims, arguably better and more diligent planning and, above all, less wilful leadership. As a consequence perhaps, they lasted longer and left, in some cases, more tangible legacies.

Of course, each has its own history reflective of the region and the wider cultural and other circumstances of the times. Each has its own genesis and while there may be some broad similarities, no two are exactly alike. For example, Q Theatre (QT) in Penrith was transposed to Western Sydney in 1977 from the lunch-hour company founded by Doreen Warburton and Ben Gabriel that had played the boutique AMP theatrette in Circular Quay from 1963 onwards. HVTC started as an initiative of the Arts Council of NSW in 1976. MRPG in Albury-Wodonga emerged from a community theatre/circus initiative by a group of hot-to-trot Victorian College of the Arts (VCA) graduates.

While the NSW story has been told a number of times, most comprehensively by Des Davis in his doctoral thesis,[75] no one has so far outlined the wider national story of those remarkable 20 years which enfold the waxing and waning of New Moon though Meredith Rogers[76] covers the community theatre dimension of the times and as does Jocelyn McKinnon.[77]

To provide some context and comparison with New Moon, the following summaries may be helpful. The history of HVTC has been recently and comprehensively covered by Julian Meyrick[78] but in the interest of completeness here, one can note that it began as part of a "grand vision ... for a network of companies around the state and arose from a plan of administrator, Tony Trench and energetic director and Novocastrian, John Tasker at the Arts Council of NSW.[79] In the event, funded in part by the Joint Coal Board which curiously was the very body that had funded the Council's original touring theatre initiatives back in the 1950s, this led to the establishment of the Newcastle-based Company in 1976 with Terence Clarke as its first Artistic Director. It opened with John Romeril's 'The Floating World' and over the next two decades and four Artistic Directors in succession endured a see-sawing history of impressive highs and desperate lows, of brave new works and well-worn classics, of up-and-down funding support from State and Federal sources but never quite enough of either to balance the books and a variable audience and thus revenue response. All those were characteristics of the regional movement everywhere. For most of that time, HVTC was housed in the intimate Playhouse, a converted ballroom attached to the Civic Theatre, situated in the heart of the business district and ideal, one would have thought, for a small resident company in a medium-sized, post-industrial city. But somehow the whole enterprise failed to take root. Various programming schemes came and went. Its height was probably during the term as Artistic Director of Brent McGregor who for the most part steered a steady course between the familiar and pushing the theatrical boundaries. In the end, by the mid-1990s the Company simply ran out of goodwill and funding. That, too, was to become the pattern of demise of much if not all of the regional theatre phenomena.

From 1980 to 2003 Theatre South (TS) in Wollongong produced and presented plays in the Illawarra region of NSW. For most of its existence the Company was funded by the Australia Council and the NSW Ministry for the Arts with occasional support from local government. Here the local University played a critical role in its establishment and to some degree in its continuance. Among all the regional companies considered in this story, it is the only one to be led by a single Artistic Director throughout its life. On returning from Canada, Des Davis had been appointed to the University of Wollongong as Lecturer in Drama. He presented a plan to the Vice-Chancellor and with that support began in 1981 with a small "permanent" company that lasted for the first three years. It offered a combination of adult main-stage Australian and other 20th century works, together with theatre-for-young people productions and toured the region with both. Above all, TS told stories of relevance to the local communities. In all, it produced an amazing 38 original works of which 22 were regional stories with a strong commitment to those of the culturally diverse population that had settled in and around Wollongong. That was perhaps the Company's great achievement and it may be the greatest achievement of the entire regional movement. But, of course, it also did a scattering of classics and established plays. TS operated for most of its history out of the Bridge Theatre, though there was a later move toward the Illawarra Performing Arts Centre for larger cast pieces. Gradually however, the purse strings were tightened. By the 1990s the concept of regional theatre had gone out of fashion federally and there was also a sense that Davis's long occupancy of the job had run out of steam. By 2000 all funding had been withdrawn. Only a three year sponsorship from BHP kept it going a little longer.

Q Theatre (QT) had a markedly different trajectory. It was very much an actor-driven initiative of a group led by the redoubtable Doreen Warburton. They had begun in the early 1960s producing one-act plays in lunch-hour slots at Sydney's Circular Quay. Before the days when bright young things pounded the city pavements at noon in their quest for a better body, the idea of a show at midday was an attraction. For a modest ticket price one could buy a sandwich and a coffee, see a play and return refreshed and uplifted to the office. At some point, nearly every actor in Sydney was pressed into service for this boutique enterprise. Ms Warburton was not easily refused. Nor did QT confine its efforts to downtown. It undertook extensive tours in the 1960s across the State and later even interstate. Gradually, it came to focus on outreach to Western Sydney and in 1977 it made the break. QT moved to Penrith where the local Council had made an old Railway Institute building available which they converted to a 120 seat theatre. With a diet of a five-to-six-play annual subscription season of roughly a third British, a third Australian and a third "classics" with a sprinkling of musicals and other international works all under Warburton's direction, it built a robust constituency and a strong local reputation. Warburton retired in 1988 and after a brief and undistinguished inter-regnum, Helmut Bakaitis took over and remained for a further eight years producing a choice of plays not substantially different from that in Warburton's time. But there, too, was a slow bleeding to death. As part of the wider loss of official nerve about regional theatre and in the belief that there might be a better way to arrange things (even if that was never really stated or planned for) in 1997 the Australia Council withdrew its funding. The NSW Ministry brokered a merger between QT and the equally struggling New England Theatre Company (NETC) to form a new entity with the less than alluring brand "Railway Street Theatre Co" and designated the combined entity as the State's major touring company. Perhaps the reference to Railway was intended to suggest travel and thus networking. If so, the allusion fell on deaf ears. By 2000 that company too was on the skids and by 2003 was to all intents and purposes defunct.

The Riverina Theatre (originally Trucking) Company (RTC) shared some features of the other bodies but exhibited some of its own. Its early history was characterised by the support and active involvement from the local tertiary education institutions, notably the Riverina Collage of Advanced Education (later to become part of Charles Sturt University) which enabled it to obtain as its base the Riverina Playhouse on its former campus. It was started by Terrence O'Connell who had gone to direct a couple of amateur productions in Wagga Wagga under the Arts Council's Visiting Director Program. In due course, he became its first Artistic Director and in many ways what he did there was a foretaste of what he was later to do at New Moon and elsewhere: a touch of burlesque, a lot of music, high energy and a bit radical. He had started with local amateurs gradually introducing professionals and built up a team supported by lots of volunteers. It is as good a place as any to observe that had he pursued that same rubric with New Moon in Townsville (or indeed in any of the North Queensland cities) it might have been a more successful formula than plunging straight into the fully professional imported ensemble style with which in a way he was lumbered there. Coincidentally, Peter Barclay became the third artistic director of RTC for about 18 months and it was during that time that he worked with O'Connell on a production of 'The Rocky Horror Show'. As it happened, the mix of work established by that combination was to continue under various of his RTC successors but rarely as successfully. Among them, John Saunders for six years from 1991 was the only one to enjoy a substantial tenure. Rapid changes of theatrical style and content and the fact that actors and other creative personnel tended to come from Sydney and thus failed to put down roots in the Riverina, meant that the Company never quite belonged. Moreover, unlike Newcastle or Wollongong – or indeed Townsville and Cairns – even with a growing student population, Wagga Wagga lacked the critical mass of catchment to maintain successfully a resident body of performing artists, let alone provide a substantial audience for its productions. Again, a long slow decline with something of a revolving door of leadership led finally to a complete loss of funding in 2005. Nevertheless, the fire had gone out well before then.

The Armidale based theatre company (NETC) shares with QT one important characteristic: both are essentially the story of a fiercely determined woman who led, shaped, cajoled and dominated their respective scenes for decades. In NETC's case it was Anna (aka Bunty) Glover. The two women could not have been less alike in personality or background, though curiously both were transplanted Brits. Both had a fierce passion for their regions and drew on every available human and physical resource to realise their visions. There the comparison ended. The other interesting aspect for our New Moon story is that like the North Queensland venture, NETC was always a touring company. "I am vitally concerned with the region", Glover would declare loudly.[80] It grew out of her background as a regional organiser for the Arts Council in Northern NSW which was always predicated on ribbon tours of theatre, dance and music passing through caravanserai-like from Sydney to the bush. The concept of developing something specifically in the region was tested and refined through a collaboration with the Australian Theatre for Young People (ATYP) in what was called the Armidale Project in 1977/78 and in 1981 led to her establishing NETC with Murray Foy as is first Artistic Director, a role in which he remained for 8 years. Its programming was largely mainstream and its work was constantly on the road in a circuit which ran in a broad swathe across the State from the Northern Rivers to the black soil plains of Moree. It was a huge backyard to mow where no one town was sufficiently large to adequately sustain it. On average, NETC presented four or five plays a year with a fair presentation of Australian work of which local playwright Bob Herbert's 'No Names No Pack Drill' was perhaps the most notable success. The University of New England was always a crucial factor in NETC's establishment and survival as was the funding of the NSW Ministry. Glover retired in 1995 and eventually the Company was folded into the Railway Street merger and effectively died in its embrace.

MRPG has the most complex origins and history of any of the regional companies and in some ways the most solid legacy. First, it sat in the twin towns of Albury-Wodonga on the border of our two most populous states once touted by the Whitlam government as the beta site for the growth of new inland cities. Founded by three graduates of the VCA eager to demonstrate a new way of doing things, it was launched in 1979 with funding from the Theatre Board and the NSW and Victorian governments. As in Queensland, tripartite arrangements were in vogue that year, but this time there was no local government component. However, the aim there was not the theatre of pre-existing or even conventional plays but rather group-devised work using a mix of skills which most actors did not at that time command to any great degree. There were many aspects of community cultural development practice in their philosophy and output. As well, unlike all the other regional companies, because of the nature of their product and process, MRPG was able to maintain shows in its repertoire for long periods. It was thus able to revive and tour them on demand.

Gradually, one side of the Company morphed to what we know today as the Flying Fruitfly Circus – the training ground and performance platform for young physical theatre artists. The other side of MRPG began to produce what today is known, somewhat lugubriously, as text-based work. These were original and existing scripts, though still with a radical edge and purpose. By the late 1980s, that Company had adopted a more conventional structure and through a succession of leadership experiments with different forms of operation including a collective directorate, gradually became more mainstream. By the mid-1990s, the bifurcation was compete with the emergency of the Hothouse Theatre Company when to all intents the two descendants of the MRPG went their separate ways.[81] That Company has had its ups and downs and a number of false restarts, but it continues to this day to produce and present work and to service its region and sometimes even beyond.

It is interesting to note that there are some curious overlaps of personnel among these companies. They are enough to suggest more than chance but not enough to indicate a pattern. For instance: both Terrence O'Connell and Peter Barclay had a background with RTC. In O'Connell's case as founding Artistic Director of that company it was perhaps not surprising that he should have been a prime candidate to take on another regional start-up, albeit one much better resourced and which appeared to enjoy better prospects. As we have seen, Helmut Bakaitis went on from New Moon to become a long serving Artistic Director of Q Theatre. His track record as actor, director in both adult and youth sectors and his regional credentials made him eminently suitable for that purpose. By a curious reflex action David Fenton briefly New Moon's last Artistic Director in 1990 went to RTC in 1997 and Gary Down who, though never Artistic Director of New Moon as such, subsequent to his stint in North Queensland went on to become Artistic Director of NETC.[82] One can put all of these down simply to the individual talents of the artists in question and claim no more. One might also attribute it to the relatively paucity of practitioners with the requisite grassroots experience that they should have circulated in this way or one can simply note an interesting set of co-incidences that in reality signify nothing.

But what, in a wider sense, drove all of this seemingly frenetic activity? Three things stand out. Above all, was the desire of local activists to take greater control of their cultural circumstances. One can see this most noticeably in the progressive devolution of planning and decision-making in the arts from the old top-down Arts Council model with its "head office" and branch structure in most States to a more demotic practice of regional initiative and down-up process. The Arts Councils everywhere had been the main source of professional theatre touring to the regions since the early 1950s. The model started in NSW spread to Queensland and Victoria and thence to other states and by the mid-1960s was pretty well the norm all over. Touring productions were chosen in the capital, offered to (or in some cases foisted on) branches with a lot of the leg work left to the local volunteers. Allied to this was a progressive rejection of the idea that art (of whatever genre) was something made in cities and taken to the bush but never vice versa. But just as the nation was changing and people everywhere were demanding more local control of their lives and economies, so in the arts concerned citizens wanted theatre that was made where they lived even if it did not necessarily as yet reflect who they were. Remember the Whitlam government's Department of Urban and Regional Development (DURD) had injected fire into the idea of new growth centres in the bush. Albury-Wodonga was to be its showcase and not surprisingly the site of one of the new theatre ventures and arguably the one which most demonstrated the virtues of local engagement and reflection. Perhaps that is why its descendants, though of a very different ilk, survive to this day. Or again, is that mere chance?

That aspiration for local self-determination has not gone away and it should not be thought that the gradual demise of most of these companies necessarily represented a failure of the dream. It showed, too, that the conventional regional theatre model with full-time Artistic Director and General Manager, an annual season of plays drawing on a mix of local and imported actors engaged on a per show basis was not the only possible way of doing things.

Second tier cities like Newcastle and Wollongong were offered resources by DURD to renew themselves and if it all fell in a heap with the Dismissal in November 11, 1975, the spirit of self-assertion lived on. Part of this was also manifested in the shooting up of new regional arts centres to replace the dusty town hall and Schools of Arts of yesteryear which had long done duty as venues for the touring shows. We've already noted the impact of these in Central and North Queensland, but it was equally true in other States. Sometimes they arose from individual local government initiatives usually after intense community pestering (another instance of the new local cultural assertiveness) sometimes, as notably in South Australia by a State government which somewhat Napoleonically, Premier Dunstan in his "Tuileries by the Torrens", decreed that four regional towns would each have an identically-scaled theatre so that his favoured State Theatre company could tour all its productions without modification. (So much for regional democracy there!).

But whatever the driver, the results were similar. New venues needed more product and at least some part of that had to be generated locally. In the event, other than those in Queensland and South Australia none of the new companies ever really occupied these purpose-built *maisons de la culture* or did not do so consistently. That is yet one more irony in this story, not lacking in irony. However, it is clear that as the central planning model of the Arts Councils declined, so the regional theatres grew and took on energy to service their base towns and immediate regions more frequently and, it was hoped, more coherently than city-based tours ever could. There was, too, always the hope that this would offer opportunity to locals to train and perhaps gain experience and employment. Undoubtedly that happened in some places more than others. It's no surprise that the bigger centres like Newcastle and Wollongong were more successful in that endeavour and that the most remote places were more reliant on imports, though RTC was probably a good example of a mix, albeit a spasmodic one.

None of this is to suggest that the Arts Council model was of itself a failure. Indeed, Australia continues to struggle with the search for the touring format so that sometimes it seems as though the wheel is reinvented every year. No one person or agency has yet come up with a satisfactory scheme still less one that adequately showcases regional work to the cities (and other regions). As a result, to this day most performing arts product toured across the country originates from capital city-based producers. Names and rhetoric may change, but the pattern and the essential dilemma remain the same. As it happened, while the other Arts Councils eventually devolved themselves out of business or turned into a very different beast known as Regional Arts Australia and its various suffragans, the old model survived in Queensland latterly under the name ArtsLink until very recently when it went into voluntary liquidation.[83] That longevity was due no doubt to the particular demographic distribution of the State in which uniquely in Australia the majority of the population live outside of the capital. Thus, there was not only an extensive regional audience base, but a significant body of political weight to be recognised and satisfied.

However, in all of this it is clear that among those governments local, state or federal which came in various ways and to various degrees to fund and sustain these feisty little regional theatre enterprises, there was never an overarching strategy. Each company had come into the world as a squalling infant welcome or not as the case may be, Yet even in New South Wales the then Ministry for the Arts never evolved a coherent plan about them. It had views, it had tactics, even occasionally policies which encompassed them. It commissioned studies which touched on them and from time to time it re-arranged the deckchairs around them. But it never really planned for them. So, in a sense they were always orphaned, grew willy nilly and like an untended garden one by one shrivelled away.

Other States had too few genuine instances to derive a pattern like NSW's. South Australia's Harvest Theatre Company which ran from 1981 to 1991 and Queensland's New Moon were one-offs and were dealt with as such. It is interesting to speculate as to whether, if New Moon had succeeded, the Queensland government might have been tempted to replicate the model elsewhere in the State. It's improbable that that could have happened with Harvest, however successful. The State's population outside of Adelaide was and remains too sparse to sustain more. As it transpired, even one company could not last.

In a way, by basing itself seriatim in different cities, New Moon was its own regional theatre network. Where New South Wales had half a dozen companies in six towns and at their death knell tried amalgamating two of them to make a state-wide company, New Moon looked for economies of scale by being its own umbrella, albeit a peripatetic one, servicing four or more centres in a cycle and variously laying its scene, or what appeared to be its scene, in one or other of them. In the long run, that model was no more successful that the New South Wales version, yet it was infinitely more radical and but for other factors might have succeeded.

In a number of ways Harvest Theatre Company in South Australia is probably the most interesting comparison with New Moon. To date, it has been the least anthologised. First, beginning in 1981 and ending 1990/91 it covers almost exactly the same period. Second, both had a succession of Artistic Directors each in turn bringing or aiming to bring different philosophies and styles to their respective companies. Whereas Harvest began, unwisely as it happened, with a more intimate, community-focussed approach and switched to a more mainstream/main stage program,[84] New Moon began with an ensemble and works of scale in the popular vein and over time shrank back to smaller casts ending with a decidedly community-oriented, if short-lived, director. Third, both ventures were originally driven by an unusual combination of a locally based advocates: Lamb in Townsville and Don Winton of the Eyre Peninsula Cultural Trust in Port Augusta; and enthusiastic state government arts officials: Kevin Siddell in Brisbane and Chris Winzar, Director of Arts Development in Adelaide.

Both companies were unusual in the regional theatre movement in not having a principal theatre base such as HVTC, TS, RTC and QT each enjoyed. Both were intended to service a chain of newly constructed, purpose-built theatres as well as roping in smaller towns and districts. Both had multiple support from local government entities though Harvest's came nowhere near the symmetry of New Moon's municipal partnerships or their scale. Both enjoyed strong State government support aimed at servicing far flung regions. Each enjoyed the leadership of two men of considerable vision and entrepreneurial drive, both as it happens Brits: Iles at New Moon and Brian Debnam at Harvest. However, there the comparisons end.

Harvest never enjoyed the tripartite funding base like New Moon's at its apogee. Queensland's regional cities are its strength and its glory giving them, especially at the height of Joh's National Party ascendency, an influence on State policy certainly unrivalled at that time and probably unparalleled in the history of the Federation. South Australia, by contrast, was a city state with 80% of its inhabitants clustered in the metropolitan area and just a fringe of towns which are small-to-tiny by Queensland standards. Tropical Queensland was experiencing population growth and an economic boom driven by agricultural expansion, tourism and new mining industries. The older smelting and ship building industries of Port Pirie and Port Augusta and the Iron Triangle were entering their slow and inexorable decline from which the reforms of the Hawke/Keating governments were about to pull the last economic plug. Whereas Iles had plunged into North Queensland with no experience of that arcane world and as it turned out little feeling for it, Debnam had an extensive background in country South Australia having worked as touring co-ordinator for the SA Arts Council as well as a decade of making productions and dealing with regional presenters and audience taste in that State, the Northern Territory and Western Australia.

Outside of NSW there is no evidence that these companies had any great consciousness of each other beyond what they might have had of the theatre spectrum generally. Nor even, as late as Davis's 2007 thesis, is there any sense of New Moon in that wider context.

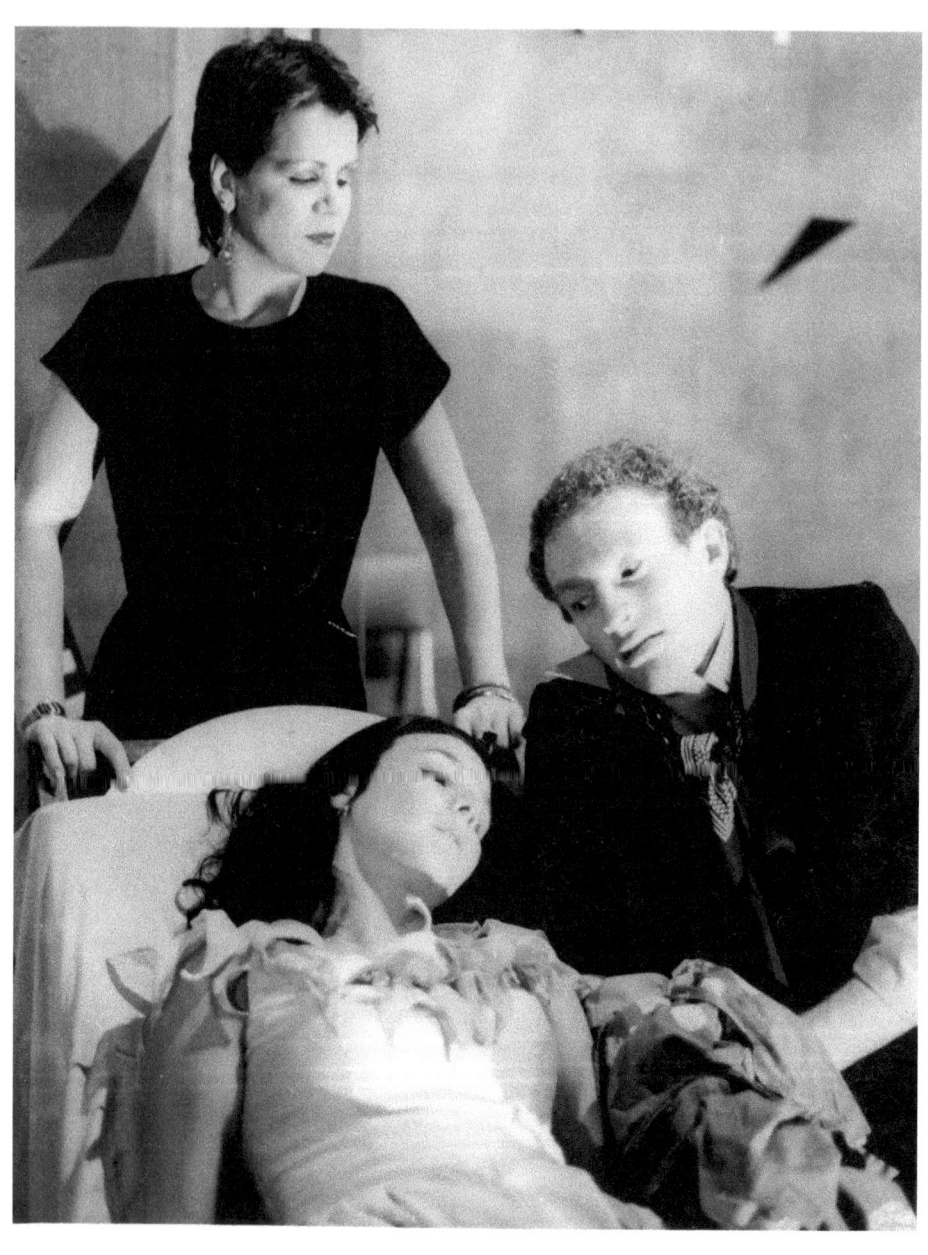

No Orchids for Miss Blandish
Left to right- Valerie Bader, Margaret Moore, Wayne Pigram

4

Who were the characters?

There was an Old Man with a beard,

Who said, 'It is just as I feared!

Two Owls and a Hen,

Four Larks and a Wren,

Have all built their nests in my beard!'

Edward Lear

Prime Mover

There is such a huge cast of characters in the New Moon story that it is simply not possible to do justice to all, even if that were desirable. Some were well-known in the arts or the political scene at the time. However, here and there, other kinds of intrusions – anecdotes even – will arise at the appropriate moment in the telling of this tale. Some will be overarching matters and in those cases an attempt is made to bring both personal and professional histories into a little more focus. But there are players whose parts might be less visible – for all that they might have been acted out on stage – and others still who fulfilled vital roles behind the scenes as workers, in management or governance or as activists in the cause whose contribution is no less significant than that of those who stood out front. Our narrative offers a sampling of those as well.

John Lamb was, of course, the prime mover of New Moon at its beginning and he was there at the end fighting to keep it afloat ten years later. It is probable that he came up with the concept of the Company though at no point did he appear to claim it as his own and demonstrably others, like Ric Nelson and Rod Wissler, contributed actively to its evolution. Certainly, Lamb secured the base funding from the State and Federal governments though one must acknowledge the role played by Kevin Siddell as Director of Queensland Division of Cultural Affairs in championing it at all three levels of government. It is likely that Lamb devised the tripartite financial deal with the city councils although others, like Sheila Keeffe, were arguably more instrumental in finalising the specifics and nailing the "deal". There is, too, a hint that Paul Iles may have been the great architect of the whole scheme.

Nevertheless, as broadcaster and actor, Margaret Bornhorst states: "John Lamb was pretty impressive. I wouldn't be surprised if he'd been responsible for my being in the company." [85] More broadly, Lamb was all over the arts scene. He was the inaugural director/manager at three regional arts centres in Queensland and the Northern Territory: Cairns Civic Centre from 1974 to 1977, Townsville Civic Centre from 1977 to 1983, and the Darwin Performing Arts theatre from 1983 to 1987. After the last, he returned to Townsville where, he consulted with and was board member and chair of New Moon in its dying days while serving as a senior manager at the 5th Townsville Pacific Arts Festival which became a centrepiece of the 1988 Australian Bicentenary commemorations in that city. Thereafter, finally until his death in 2017, based in Melbourne he pursued private import-export Australia-China business interests.

During his time at Townsville he was instrumental in the establishment of NARPACA and also became a member of the Confederation of Australian Performing Arts Centres. This was the grouping of capital city venues (and ultimately festivals) and his was the only "regional" Arts Centre to be granted the privilege of joining it at the time. While in Darwin, Lamb saw the need to establish a wider national body incorporating capital city and regional arts centres across Australia.

The opportunity arose at a Confederation of Australian Arts Centres meeting held in Darwin, where it was decided to convene a national meeting of all such centres. A motion was put forward at that meeting to establish the Australian (later Australasian) Performing Arts Centres Association (APACA) now known as PAC (Performing Arts Connections) Australia. For those initiatives he was recognised as a life member of both bodies.

After his death in 2017, NARPACA paid tribute to his work for the Australian performing arts industry noting that: "He can well and truly rest assured that the work he began and delivered in his lifetime has been truly part of the bedrock that makes our Performing Arts Centres across Australia stand strong as true leaders of our communities."[86]

The might-have-beens

While they were never part of the story proper, it is interesting to reflect both on those whom the New Moon founders and their advisers had actually appointed and on who *might* have been its inaugural Artistic Director. It is noteworthy that from the outset there was a kind of stumble. Well known, hyperactive, independent theatre/opera director, John Milson was selected for this role from quite a strong field; was offered it;[87] and announced with a blaze of publicity in the regional press.[88] Just as suddenly he withdrew, citing physical and mental exhaustion. He had been directing for the Queensland Opera Company (QOC) at the time and pulled out of that commitment as well. Milson was a chain smoking, roll-yer-own bloke and a workaholic. He was at that time essentially free-lance, so he would not have lightly walked away from permanent employment. That said, in August he had written a long letter to the Steering Committee setting out his ideas for the Company and at the same time expressing reservation about some of its elements.[89] They included the proposal that the General Manager should be the CEO. He observed that he was used to a situation where the artistic director and general manager were co-equal. While he favoured both being on the Company's board, he saw no need for a hierarchy between them. Milson was also a risk taker. "Give it a whirl" was an expression never far from his thinking or his lips. During his extensive career, he ran Perth's Hole in the Wall theatre company, directed for Opera Australia and various state companies and initiated the highly regarded musical theatre course at the WA Academy of Performing Arts (WAAPA) which program he went on to head for 12 years.

Sydney-based at that time, Milson had won the New Moon job from a strong field and against two notable Queensland competitors. The selection panel of Rod Wissler, Paul Iles and Twelfth Night Theatre's Joan Whalley was far from loaded against Queenslanders. Milson was a regular guest in Brisbane and was that year directing for both the QTC and QOC. So it was clear that there was no intention at that stage to appoint a rank outsider. Indeed, why would there have been? Well-known local producer/director and leading light, Bryan Nason was the fall-back position when Milson withdrew, but he had meanwhile been appointed to TN Theatre. Brisbane-based, Rick Billinghurst also on the shortlist was approached but had recently concluded his term as the first salaried director of that city's La Boite theatre and chose to pass on North Queensland. So the position had to be re-canvassed and at that point the decision emerged to go for the joint role (one hesitates to call it a partnership) of O'Connell and Barclay.

The winners

O'Connell had begun his career as a company member of the National Theatre at the Playhouse in Perth. During his three years there he played a variety of roles in work spanning the classics, musicals, pantomime and modern drama. In 1975 he took the directors' course at NIDA where he directed three productions two of them by Australian writers. He then went on, as we have seen, to found RTC and became that company's first Artistic Director. As mentioned, his choice of work there was judicious mix of local and imported performers covering a wide and elective range including company-devised shows.

Since 1979, O'Connell had been working as a freelance director. As a measure of his versatility, a recent production before taking up the New Moon position had been 'Fairground Snapz' at the famous Last Laugh theatre restaurant in Melbourne. However, his very last artistic engagement before moving to North Queensland had been as an actor playing the lead role in 'The Rocky Horror Show' directed, as it happened, by Peter Barclay. Though they had shared successively the directorship of RTC that was the first time that the two had worked together, but the role reversal of acting and directing did set something of a pattern for their plans for New Moon, since as co-directors they undertook to alternate between the two functions. "That was, how it worked out. We played minor roles but I was no great actor. I wasn't even a good actor but I loved doing it, so it was."[90] Given the intimacy with which they were going to have to operate in new context, the Company's Board, and especially Lamb, might have considered more deeply how little genuine, collaborative experience the two had had as a team. Despite their overlapping talents, there was a significant philosophical gap between them which was to widen rapidly and, in the end, undo the experiment of dual leadership.

Nor was it something into which O'Connell had simply leapt: "I was being offered quite a few potential regional theatre projects or possibilities of creating new ones, on the back of the success of RTC. People were keen to have their own version of it... New Moon was another regional project (in a beautiful part of the world) but one that was to be fully professional which was an attraction". The difference between the two starting points for these companies was stark: "RTC was, in essence, a community theatre project (led by a small core group of minimally paid people) with a very professional image and work ethic." New Moon seemed like a big step forward. "I think I was relatively naive in my expectations. I probably expected that I could largely continue, artistically and philosophically, in a similar manner to RTC. Ha! This was not to be... I was extremely optimistic. I was young! And not all that experienced at running a company outside of the very special circumstances of RTC." [91]

By contrast, Barclay's background was both narrower and, in a sense, more focused. He was about the theatre of ideas rather than of sensation. A graduate of Sydney University in 1977, he had co-founded The Rocks Players in Sydney where he was both actor and director of three Shakespeare works as well as a variety of community entertainment. "I think Peter was too smart" reflected Anthony Babicci one of the two designers in the original New Moon ensemble. "He was too good a director and too smart in terms of the literary aspect of theatre."[92] After the Rocks experiment, Barclay went to the Nimrod Theatre in 1978, first as assistant director and then as a resident director. There he was very much taken under the wing of Paul Iles and inducted into a range of administrative experience and procedures. "I really loved Paul... and whatever I know about theatre administration I got from him"[93] Such an approach was unusual at that time (and still to this day) for young directors who tended to be quarantined in 'creative' areas. Iles was well ahead of his time in Australia in considering that it was important for those who worked as directors, and in particular aspired to be artistic directors of companies, to learn as much as possible about the broader practical workings of the theatre, its management, lobbying functions and governance not to mention technical and organisational aspects. It is curious then to reflect that when it came to New Moon successive artistic directors reported that he hardly involved them at all in administrative matters.

At Nimrod, Barclay got to choose programs and directed some productions. He also became a committee member of the Australian National Playwrights Conference and organised readings Australian of scripts and practical workshops. As well, he worked with the Goethe-Institut producing readings of modern German plays and had been a guest director of the HVTC for a production of 'Treats' by Christopher Hampton. In 1980, following Nimrod, he had become Artistic Director of RTC and it was from that post that he went to join the brash, new tropical Queensland venture. He was about to do the production of "The Rocky Horror Show" mentioned earlier when "Paul rang to keep me up to date with the progress of the New Moon project and letting me know that the position of Artistic Director would soon be advertised and I suppose it got to the point where Terry and I thought that we might put in a joint application for the position... and so Terry said: look there are four shows in six months at this new theatre company and I just don't know if I could go bang, bang, bang, bang so how's about we put a combined application and we'll cast each other in minor roles in order take to get the actors' wage across the line so that was the logic. He does one and I do one; he does one and I do one ... I thought that would be easier. Terry and I had worked well together before, though we didn't get on so well up there".[94] There was no suggestion that they would automatically get it just because of Iles's intervention and there was no suggestion at that time that Iles himself would become the general manager.

Certainly, one of the bonus points, on paper at least, of this devised co-directorship was that the pooling of experience of the two directors would enable them to cover a wider range of work given their respective specialist areas. They were, after all, two young directors with between them an interesting mix of experience in the professional theatre and at a scale and in locations that for the most part were valuable in the new venture. With these two at the helm the Company seemed set to secure a successful and exciting future. What could possibly go wrong?

Higher up the tree, so to speak, formal choices were also being made of those who would guide the progress of the new enterprise. At the first Annual General Meeting held auspiciously on February 28, 1981 at Townsville's Civic Theatre, the new board listed earlier was created for the Company. Its changes of personnel and, it could be argued, coherence will be traced through this chapter. The shifting sands of New Moon's governance scattered over such a huge geographical area proved a poor foundation for the infant venture. It is no reflection on the individual capabilities of the many people who served that they failed ever to achieve a corporate identity or were able to formulate any consistent oversight of it. There is evidence that Iles was more than happy to take advantage of that situation, enabling him variously to divide and conquer or simply confuse with avalanches of reports delivered late or tabled at meetings.⁹⁵ If so, we can see how that came to be a weakness that unravelled everything.

Since he is central to this narrative it is time to pull together the story of Paul Iles himself and to make sense of who he was, where he came from and indeed where he went afterwards. In commencing, one should observe that despite the eccentricities of his behaviour in North Queensland and, for that matter, elsewhere, all who knew and dealt with him in Australia and the UK regarded him, rightly, as a vastly clever and knowledgeable person of the theatre who ran his various enterprises with a shrewd combination of passion, chutzpah and pragmatism, always remembering that it was what went on stage that was paramount.

Iles was born in 1952 and learned his trade quickly at a variety of UK regional theatres in the early seventies, including the Northampton Repertory Theatre, the 69 Theatre Company, Manchester, the Oxford Playhouse and the Watermill Theatre, Newbury. He applied for the job of Secretary and General Manager of Sydney's Nimrod Theatre as advertised in *The Times* of London in 1976 and was interviewed on their behalf by telephone by Helen Montagu, the Australian producer then Managing Director of the West End group, H.M. Tennant Ltd. He was just 24 and within a short time in Sydney had more than made his mark. He became an Australian citizen three years later, moving to be General Manager of the State Theatre Company of South Australia in 1979 having declined to follow Richard Wherrett from Nimrod to the newly formed Sydney Theatre Company. Then came the New Moon adventure.

After North Queensland and returning to Britain via Perth, Iles was successively general manager of the Grand Theatre, Blackpool from 1988 to 1992, and the Festival Theatre, Edinburgh from 1992 to 1996 where he oversaw its £22 million refurbishment from the former Empire Theatre. In those roles, he fashioned seasons that successfully combined high art and popular entertainment and enhanced the theatres' profiles, never neglecting the importance of a good night out. But even there his work was not without its controversy. Among his private memorabilia was a letter from the former Lord Provost (Edinburgh's equivalent of Lord Mayor) complaining about receiving an invitation addressed to him and his "partner" rather than his wife. The communication was thereafter proudly displayed on the door of the lavatory of Iles's flat. His attitude to officialdom had not softened with the passage of time. After a scarcely surprising dispute with the Edinburgh city authorities, Iles left the Festival Theatre and set up a theatrical management consultancy, The Laughing Audience.

Iles often inspired great commitment from his staff, who respected his deep knowledge and his passion for the theatre. But even his obituary writer acknowledged: "he was a difficult man to work with, and there are to this day touring theatre producers who would be unlikely to have anything good to say about him".[96] Many denizens of North Queensland could have echoed those sentiments. And it was not only the recalcitrant officialdom of Bjelke-Petersen's state that saw it that way. Closer to home, some company members also took a wry view: Babicci observes: "Paul was not really an intellectual. He was a very good manager and [good at] social life. He could manipulate people and he loved the whole game-playing and all of that to such an extent that people didn't even know they were being played... he was like the Cheshire Cat. He always had this big grin and this thick English accent and this [way] of always snorting and pushing his glasses back and you always felt you were in the presence of someone who was kind of devious but at the same time he was very effusive and very clever." [97]

In later years, Iles was active in many UK public arts bodies. He served for nine years on the Theatres Trust, the British national advisory body for theatre buildings; he was a member of the Scottish Arts Council for three years; and at the time of his death was chairman of Northern Broadsides Theatre Company, a trustee of the Grand Theatre and Opera House, Leeds, and associate director of the Georgian Theatre Royal in Richmond.

Interestingly, although he wrote voluminous reports for New Moon on programming, casting, organisation and finances almost none of them reveals any opinion of the work itself or what he thought of the Company's theatrical (as against its promotional) achievement. For someone who so loved the genre and so ostentatiously placed himself in the public eye, his views are curiously private. A small, oblique glimpse may be obtained in retrospect. Although written 17 years after leaving Nimrod and a decade after New Moon, in a later comment Iles singles out what to him were the key features of Nimrod: "I think the most exciting aspects of the Company were the boisterous acting style [and], the pseudo resident ensemble where the core of actors became identified with the work".[98] They might well have applied to New Moon. Paul Iles died of cancer in 2011, aged 59.

On the board

Meanwhile, New Moon's governance was also slowly morphing in line with the comings and goings of elected local officials and by December 11, 1981 Directors listed are: "Snow" Wright (chair), Peter Barclay, Terrence O'Connell, Paul Iles, Executive Director (Described as "consultant to the Steering committee" prior to appointment as ED) David Berker, John Lamb, Margaret Cossins, Bruce Shepherd, Tom Bencke, Val Hardman, Carmel Daveson, Robert Randle and Ian Satchwell.[99] Shortly after the March 1982 Board meeting, Sheila Keeffe and John Lamb resigned. The Townsville City Council appointed Ald. Margaret Reynolds and Ald. Des White and Pioneer Shire appointed Cr. Alex Dawson to replace Wright. Cairns reappointed Ald. Cossins and Mackay City Council Ald. Daveson. Bencke resigned as did member-elected Val Hardman.[100] How ill-coordinated a board this would be is clear from such diverse and scattered membership over so great a territory. How complex it would prove to create a plan or even consensus out of such diversity time would show.

Even so, there were outstanding examples of great commitment to the cause and rare talent being brought to bear on its leadership. Mackay-based businessman, Bruce Shepherd is a prime instance of those who worked quietly, often in the background, to make the new company a success. He had been a member of the Steering Committee prior to the Company's incorporation, then chair of its Board from June 1982 to February 1984 and thereafter deputy chair in 1984 and 1985. Shepherd came from a distinguished pioneering Mackay family. His father had risen from office boy to Managing Partner in James Crocker & Sons (later Crokers Fuel & Oils Pty Ltd) a distributor for Texas Co (Australia) which Bruce later came also to run. It was instrumental in establishing the first Caltex Oil Bulk Ocean Terminal at the Mackay Harbour. Working for the company since the 1970s, Shepherd guided it through its continued expansion to service a 55,000 km2 area of central Queensland, from St Lawrence (to the south) to Bowen (in the north) and west to Alpha.

The Shepherd family were also active members of cultural ventures including the local School of Arts and the Mackay Choral Society. Bruce was the chairman of the fundraising committee to replace the venerable Theatre Royal with the new Mackay Entertainment Centre which he described at the "most important public building ever built in the region."[101] He was a "fantastic chairman... [and an] extraordinary man," Bakaitis declared[102] As chair of New Moon following Sheila Keeffe's departure, he led and cajoled and at times invested his own funds to hold its fractious elements together and keep it on track while never, it seems, losing faith in its essential goal of bringing quality professional theatre to the North. A fine example of this thinking in these roles might be had from the record of a meeting at the Townsville Travelodge, at which he quoted Isaiah Berlin in saying what was needed on a board was a group of people who: "go on nagging and nibbling in an effort to correct faults, to prevent complacency from creeping in, to anticipate criticism, to sense trends, and to do that in a friendly and helpful way, designed to ensure that public money is being properly spent, endeavouring to promote the efficiency of the administration and to assist the artistic director". [103] It would be hard to think of a better or more succinct rule of thumb. Soon after that time, he moved to

Brisbane and while he was happy to remain on the Board he felt he had to surrender the chair. That did not put an end to his generosity. When in late 1984 Iles was frantically putting together a shareholding deal for the interstate tour of 'Beach Blanket Tempest', Bruce Shepherd had no hesitation in putting his hand in his pocket to contribute.

On the boards

But there were other kinds of participants in New Moon who had a stake in North Queensland from a very different angle and in ways that did not always turn out quite so happily. Margaret Moore (née Bornhorst) was one such. She had the distinction of being the first and for some time only 'local' acting recruit to the new company, with mixed fortunes as it happened. She'd been a student at the University of Queensland in Brisbane in the late 1960s when it was a hotbed of radical anti-Vietnam and other protest activity and also came to New Moon from a more complex Queensland background than most in the Company: "Mother was a war bride and father American. We came back to Australia when I was 13." Being in one sense a "foreigner" and at the same time indelibly a local, also set her apart. "I was on tour in North Queensland with the Popular Theatre Troupe (PTT) and I fell in love with a Townsville journalist and stayed there. [Earlier] I had taken a job with the Queensland Arts Council as a tour manager which is where I became excited about the idea of acting. I got into NIDA spent a year there and went into QTC, did three adult plays and then schools shows." She then moved into PTT with which she toured across the State. And at various times while in the North Bornhorst had been a supply teacher on Mornington Island and a griddle girl on the railways. "I did front-of-house at the [Townsville] Civic Theatre and acted in local plays and by the time New Moon came along I had my own ABC afternoon radio show".[104]

Yet in spite of all that – or maybe because it – she always felt uncomfortable in the newly fledged venture: "I was the only local [actor] and I think they thought it would look bad if there wasn't one in the Company. It was a very strange experience. I had been a founding member of the cooperative Popular Theatre Troupe and frankly that was more me. It was political and about ideas and I had a major input into the content of the shows. In New Moon I was a fish out of water with everyone else". But it was not the first or the only time that someone closely connected with New Moon felt that it was rather conventionally structured in a standard top-down directing style. Interestingly, today Stephen Clark considers that at first it felt uncertain and tentative and only "in the second year we loosened up as the actors became more comfortable in the ensemble".[105] Notwithstanding all that: "They were all incredibly talented" Bornhorst remembers, even though she had other reservations: "They were all musicians as well as actors and I was not as proficient in singing. There was a whole coterie who knew each other before they came to Queensland. But they had no feeling for or awareness of North Queensland. Here's me an American immigrant – but also a 5th generation Queenslander – who loved Queensland and knew all those cities from travelling and touring. I loved watching the geniuses in action but they weren't connected."[106]

Aside from this, things artistically did not run so smoothly: "They cast me as Lady Macbeth and then wanted to throw me out, but I said no. One of the things about acting is that you have to feel you are working with people who like you and respect you. I kept a diary which started in February,1981 while 'Macbeth' was happening until May that year. I suppose I was a very neurotic young woman and diaries were my way of trying to make sense of things." Nevertheless, there was an upside for her: "I liked the musicals best. And yet that was where I was least blossoming". However she also recalls that the venture of New Moon itself at first had wide support: "I remember people being very enthusiastic about everything."[107]

In the end, however, and for quite different reasons it was a turning point of different kind in her life: "New Moon was what convinced me that I didn't want to be in theatre because there you have no control over the content or the message. You're a prostitute really." Bornhorst later went to Sydney into various aspects of training in which having returned to Brisbane she still works as a consultant.

Curiously, experienced professional, Stephen Clark, also in the first New Moon ensemble, came eventually, though by a very different and more positive route, to a surprisingly similar conclusion: "[At the end of the second year] I felt I wanted to move on and grow out. I felt that I had exercised the creative path of my life. And New Moon had allowed me to do that. It really allowed me to exercise my creativity, in a way I had never had an opportunity to do before. It was then that I realised I was a very creative person. It really allowed me to exercise that to the point that I began to feel a very strong, cognitive drive. I wanted to move on [from the performing arts] to develop the other side of my brain basically." [108]

Initially, however, his feelings were very different: "for me it was a great adventure. Little did I know that it was the start of the rest of my career. So, it was all very, very exciting and all extremely brand new. I had never been to Townsville before and I remember landing in Townsville and hurriedly trying to find somewhere to live and then we got underway with the first production. I also remember the first communal, social gathering that Terry [O'Connell] held at his house up on the hill there in Townsville and that was where we met everybody and it was just a big new adventure really."[109]

Behind the scenes

It would give a very unbalanced picture of those who formed part of that initial feisty band not to feature those who worked equally at the coalface, albeit behind the scenes. Kerry Saul was one of the many people whose lives were changed by association with New Moon. Plucked out of New Zealand where he had been working as a carpenter building modular homes, Saul landed in North Queensland and found there the makings of a theatrical career in which he has remained in ever since. "I always thought I'd end up in Australia", but more probably in the construction industry.[110] Yet after a peripatetic life in the technical areas of Queensland theatres, today he is the respected General Manager of the heritage Empire Theatre in Toowoomba and, ironically perhaps, a key part of the national regional touring world where he cut his teeth.

Saul had been working in the far north of his native New Zealand when he got the call. The new theatre company in North Queensland needed a set builder. A mate in Tasmania had sent him an ad. It was actually for QTC. He applied and heard nothing. Then in late in November, 1981 he got a phone call from Paul Iles. Was he still interested? "It was not long after Australia had decided Kiwis had to have passports". It took him just under fourteen days to get one, pack his gear and land in Townsville. He arrived on December 9, 1981. "December 10 was my 25th birthday ... it was 37 degrees on the tarmac... You could get a direct flight from Auckland to Townsville at that time and no-one met me".[111] The first show was due to go out on January 20. Like most of the new recruits, he had no idea what he was getting into though he remembers thinking that the touring circuit from Cairns to Rockhampton was the length of the whole of New Zealand.

There was nothing to begin with: no workshop; no materials. They ended up in a derelict department store in Sturt Street. He recalls: "There was beautiful double staircase as you went up... The rain had been coming in the room for so long that the floors had rotted through in the centre of the building, right down to ground level. My workshop was on ground level and they roped off the area and the rehearsal areas so the people didn't fall down the holes... and we actually moved offices to downstairs. So that was our home for the first six months..."[112]

'Ned Kelly' was first cab off the rank. David Bell's design proved a challenge. "Nimrod had been using steel... Well, I was a carpenter and I went okay, I can do that. So I ended up teaching myself to weld within two or three days really. We got the steel up from Sydney and we built a steel set ... which was absolutely [expletive deleted] enormous. It was a hard set, full hard legs, all six metres high with a hard back wall and in hindsight there was a yellow wall behind it which was just a straight painted yellow thing and we got it into Cairns and Terry came in and... said what's that and we said that's the yellow wall and he said it could have been cloth, you know… That was a tough ask. I can remember standing on top of a ladder in Cairns at 3am in the morning welding things. We actually slept inside the Theatre. We used to get the key from the Car Sales guy. But that was where we started and Jimmy Mann was Stage Manager. I wasn't playing budgets. I was the set builder. I just went out and got stuff and said: yes I can do that because that's what I do. So I reckon by the end of it, we'd actually spent, on that particular show, probably four show budgets to get it up and we figured that out, eventually. It was great. 'Ned Kelly' was a really great show. I think…"[113]

The second production was 'Macbeth' also designed by Bell. The set "had a raked 5 metre radius with tapered walls and tapered curves walk-offs in all sorts of directions and … they asked me to cost it … and I went for it and did what I could to figure out and … it was way, way over the budget and David [Bell] got really angry at the meeting and broke all the bits off and said how much will this cost? But we did it and I've got to say it was a good lesson learned".[114]

So it rolled on for another two productions that year, though when Antony Babicci came the designs became lighter and more tourable. When the last run closed, Saul went down to Brisbane following employment with the Warana Festival, QTC and others. Meanwhile, he'd met his future wife Sandra who was also to work in New Moon's administration. The Company's base by then had shifted to Cairns. There they had a decent workshop and just one Artistic Director to please: "I never knew why they moved from Townsville", but there's no doubt that year was much easier. However, "it rained the whole bloody time I'm sure. The house that we lived in, the grass went rotten out on the front lawn because it was under water for so long. It was the worst time to live in Cairns. January through to June…" [115] Saul didn't return for the third season though Sandra continued to work for the Company right into Bakaitis's time. He worked on set building in Townsville and as a mechanist for the Civic Theatre and kept an eye on the New Moon as it waxed and waned.

Through all this the revolving door of governance continued to bring in fresh faces and new though not always helpful ideas. As a measure of the rate of change by June 17, 1982 the board is listed as: Shepherd (chairman) Cossins, Daveson, Dawson, Berker, Iles, O'Connell, Des White (Townsville), Margaret Reynolds (Townsville), Randle, Satchwell and Hardman. On November 12 that year Diane Cilento, Stan Marsh and Paul Brady (a Rockhampton lawyer) joined. Simultaneously private sector support leapt to a remarkable $59,600. That was proportionately as good as if not better than what was being raised by those organisations that were coming to be designated as state theatre companies in capital cities.

Moon and star

It was a curious set of circumstances that brought Cilento and New Moon together and one which if better managed could have been a powerfully winning combination. Although a minor player on the world stage, in Queensland Cilento was a celebrity. In the rest of the country she was a "name". Before the plethora of world-famous Australian movie stars to which we are accustomed today, who pop in and out of Australian film, stage and TV, no other all local theatre company would boast anyone quite so famous. Frank Thring at MTC would have been the closest at that time. As a consequence, her star shone more brightly back home than it would today. That she had chosen to live and work within New Moon's catchment was beyond co-incidence and that she chose (or was inveigled into?) becoming associated with the Company was remarkable.

At all events, as we've seen, she joined the Board in 1982 and remained until December 1985 during which she was chair for 1984 and part of 1985. Cilento starred in and toured with 'Agnes of God' in 1986 not only for New Moon and but also for Gary Penny Productions to Brisbane, Sydney and Melbourne in association with theatre companies there. After leaving the Board she continued to consult, not always in a helpful manner, notably in the skirmish over the John Lennon/ Yoko Ono's rights for 'Imagine' and the Doplo affair, of which more later. As with so many aspects of the Company's history, what might have been a boom largely turned to bust.

Cilento was born in Mooloolaba on Queensland's Sunshine Coast. Her parents, Sir Raphael and the notoriously homophobic radio personality Lady Cilento (née Phyllis McGlew) a.k.a. "Medical Mother"[116], were both well-known medical practitioners. At an early age, Diane decided to follow a career in acting and, after being expelled from school in Australia, was educated in New York while living there with her father. She later won a scholarship to London's Royal Academy of Dramatic Art (RADA) and moved to Britain in the early 1950s. After graduation, she found work on stage almost immediately and was signed to a five-year contract by distinguished producer, Alexander Korda. Her first leading role in a film was in the British movie, 'Passage Home' (1955), opposite fellow Australian, Peter Finch. She soon secured other roles in British films and worked steadily until the end of the decade. In 1956, she was nominated for a Tony Award for Best Supporting or Featured Actress (Dramatic) for Helen of Troy in the New York transfer season of Jean Giraudoux's play 'Tiger at the Gates' (aka 'La guerre de Troie n'aura pas lieu').

She was also nominated for the Academy Award for Best Supporting Actress for her performance in 'Tom Jones' in 1963 and appeared in 'The Third Secret' the following year. However, she allowed her film career to decline following her marriage to actor Sean Connery, the second of her three husbands and to whom she was married from 1962 to 1973. She starred with Charlton Heston in the 1965 film 'The Agony and the Ecstasy', and with Paul Newman in the 1967 western film 'Hombre'. Later she was known to remark, sardonically, that she used to get the roles that Susannah York turned down.[117] In 1985, Cilento married playwright, Anthony Shaffer, author of 'Sleuth' and the script of 'The Wicker Man'. She met him when she appeared in that film in 1973, and he joined her when she returned to Queensland in 1975. Cilento continued working as an actor, in films and television including 'Agnes of God'. In the 1980s, she settled in Mossman, north of Cairns, where she built her own outdoor theatre, named "Karnak", in the Daintree. The venture allowed her to participate in experimental drama. In 2007 she started preparations for a one-woman theatrical tour of Australia based on the life of Peggy Guggenheim. The tour never took place. Cilento died of cancer at Cairns Base Hospital on 6 October, 2011, the day after her 78th birthday.

Changing the guards

in April 1983 the Board is listed in detail as: Bruce Shepherd, Chairman – Mackay, Managing Director James Croker & Sons Ltd and Public Accountant; David Berker – Townsville, Management consultant, Paul Brady – Rockhampton, Solicitor, Diane Cilento – Cairns, actor, Margaret Cossins Deputy Mayor Cairns City Council, Carmel Daveson Deputy Mayor, Mackay City Council, Alex Dawson – Pioneer Shire Surveyor and Councillor, Paul Iles, Executive Director, Stan March – Councillor, Mulgrave Shire, Terry O'Connell Artistic Director, Ian Satchwell – Rockhampton, Des White – Townsville, General Manger, Copper Refineries Pty. Ltd., and by June 1983 Ald. Terry Moore, Dentist, Rockhampton City Council and Ald. Mike Reynolds, Mayor of Townsville and educator joined, while actor, Gillian Hyde was noted as the "staff representative" though there would appear to have been no legal basis for that designation. On February 4, 1984 Kerry Williams from Rockhampton joined the Board and on the 17th of that month Diane Cilento fatefully became chair. By April 26, 1984, rather weirdly, Brian Sweeney and Harry Miller were appointed "Associate Directors". Needless to say the arrangement did not last. Miller, in particular, coming from a hard-edged, hands-on, commercial world thought it absurd that he should have the role but be required to exercise no real influence. Sweeny, however continued to be supportive from the sidelines.

In June 30, 1984 Margaret Cossins resigned from the Cairns City Council and Ald. Peggy Forsberg became her temporary replacement; Fred Thompson who had a long association with a variety of arts enterprises including the establishment of the Townsville Community Music

Centre, was appointed also pro tem to replace David Berker; while Ian Satchwell who had resigned from the Pilbeam to take up a position in Tasmania was replaced by that theatre's new manager, Malcolm Calder. As a consequence, there remained only one Director, Carmel Daveson who had been on the Steering Committee and together with Bruce Shepherd one of only two Directors with three years' experience in the governance of the Company. It is an extraordinarily rapid rate of turnover and would be cause for alarm in any circumstance, still less in that of a brand-new organisation operating in untried territory. That discontinuity was to prove a critical weakness. However, it did not seem to be reflected in support from private donors and commercial sponsors which in 1983/84 remained steady at a remarkable $54,400.

Yet barely a year later, by August 1985 in fact, things have changed again and the Board is listed as: Ald. Terry Moore (chair), Helmut Bakaitis, Artistic Director, Malcolm Calder, Diane Cilento, Cr Alex Dawson, Ald. Peggy Forsberg, Paul Iles, Ald. Elaine Martin, David W Semler, Fred Thompson, Ald. Valerie Valentine (first meeting) and Kerry Williams.

A second wave

Together with Iles, Helmet Bakaitis may fairly be regarded as the other pivotal personality in the New Moon history, already crowded with personalities. He was born in Lauban, Lower Silesia, Germany (now Lubań, Poland), to Lithuanian parents. He was educated at Fort Street High School, Sydney, where he even at a young age he made a startlingly strong impression with the title role in 'Hamlet; in a school production which was performed on the steps of the Sydney War Memorial, later at the Elizabethan Theatre, Newtown and then filmed at the Movietone studios. It was by no means his last encounter as actor with the Bard: "I did a 'Lear' with George Ogilvie directing at the Sydney Theatre Company – also way back played the Fool in Jim Sharman's 'Lear' at the MTC."[118]

He graduated from NIDA in 1965 and from 1966 to 1971 was a resident actor and playwright with MTC and later working as actor, dramaturg and assistant director at Old Tote Theatre in, Sydney. From 1972-76 he was Director of Youth Activities at the South Australian Theatre Company (SATC) while also a member of that company's Artistic Directorate together with George Ogilvie and Rodney Fisher. There he set up SATC Youth Team – to establish and support integrated drama programs in South Australian upper primary schools as well as the Saturday Company – a youth theatre ensemble of some 100 teenagers which gave regular performances at The Space in the Adelaide Festival Centre, the Stables Theatre, and at outdoor venues. In addition, he became Director of Youth Programming for the Adelaide Festival of Arts and was founding Artistic Director of Carclew, a drama resource centre for South Australian teachers and a youth performance hub. During that time, he wrote and directed 'The Lady of Sir Orfeo' for a cast of 80 teenagers in The Space and 'Carlotta and Maximilian' featuring a cast of 200 teenagers. He conducted regular teachers' drama-in-education workshops in Northern Territory and South Australia and co-founded (with Chris Westwood) the Come Out Festival, Adelaide's biennial youth arts jamboree. After leaving SATC he undertook post-graduate studies in drama-in-education at Newcastle-Upon-Tyne University and worked on youth theatre projects at London's Round House and Jackson's Lane Centre. Returning to Australia in 1978 he became the founding Artistic Director and CEO at St Martin's Youth Arts Centre, Melbourne. Then came New Moon.

After leaving North Queensland in 1986 Bakaitis freelanced for a year at Belvoir St Theatre, the Sydney Opera House and the QTC before becoming – as mentioned earlier – Artistic Director of the QT, Penrith. Following that he joined NIDA as Head of Directing in 1998 and there he remained until 2007. Among many distinctions he was awarded the Gloria Payten Fellowship for extended study period in People's Republic of China (Shanghai, Hangzhou and Shaoxing) and conducted developmental drama workshops with Gifted Children at the National University of Singapore and Classical Western Drama workshops at Ho Chi Minh City Theatre Academy, Vietnam.

Since 2007 Bakaitis describes himself, somewhat understatedly, as "a semi-retired Leura resident in the Blue Mountains" although he continued as Senior Tutor in Film Studies at NIDA and at Actors Centre as well as senior Directing Tutor at the Australian Academy of Dramatic Art from which he resigned 2014. He continues to appear in film, TV and stage productions in Australia and elsewhere. Such are the times, that despite such a long, distinguished and productive career as actor, writer, director and teacher, a popular website which shall be nameless, writes: "He is best known for his role in 'The Matrix Reloaded' and 'The Matrix Revolution' as the character, the Architect". Tempora and mores etc ...

Since his friend and colleague Rodney Fisher played such an important role at critical moments in New Moon it is only right that Bakaitis should have the last word on that: "George (Ogilvie), Rodney and I have been interlinked for most of our lives. Rodney initially came up to Far North Queensland while he was shooting the mini-series of 'Melba' and as he had once lived in Townsville (as well as Toowoomba etc) he was someone whose judgement about the place and its culture I could rely on. I still value his advice today."[119] It is fair to say that Fisher made some of the shrewdest observations about New Moon's strength and weaknesses at the time which, had they been followed, might well have meant its salvation or at very least a longer life.

By December 4, 1986, just as Bakaitis was departing the Company its Board stood at: Ald. Valentine (chair) Bakaitis, Calder, Cilento, Bill Langdon, Ald. Martin, Semler, Rob Spencer, Wright, Dawson, Forsberg and Moore. The departure of Iles over a year earlier had ushered in both new board members and a new general manager, Ruth Bereson who also found herself a stranger in a strange land and, as with others we've noted, it proved to be a career watershed: "New Moon turned out to be a significant moment in my professional life".[120] Prior to taking up the position she had had skirted the arts world in various capacities: assisting a classical music producer in Paris, hovering on the periphery of the école d'art lyrique at the Opera Comique and on her return to Australia working as an administrator of Community Arts at the

Victorian Ministry for the Arts and as coordinator of Continuum '85. a visual arts project involving public and private galleries in Japan and Melbourne. "My preferred art form had always been theatre and when I was approached to join New Moon, I knew I was not entirely qualified to take up the position but I seized the opportunity. I had so much to learn and the energy and perhaps naivety to think I could undertake it".[121]

From the start, it was a complex, uphill and, to mix the metaphors, deep-end experience. Her first visit to Queensland was a whistle-stop tour with the Cultural Affairs Division in Brisbane, to address both the funding issues and the need to manage what today we might call the "optics" of the Company which had taken something of a battering. That was followed in rapid succession by a trip to Mackay to engage with local groups and meet local board members and a car journey to Townsville where Bakaitis briefed her urgently on as much as she could absorb. "Arriving in Townsville on a Friday, I was informed we had to finalise our proposal for the Australia Council funding by the following Monday. And so the baptism by fire began".[122]

Nevertheless, there was knowledge and support from various parties: "Helmut very much wanted to redress the issues at hand and mentored me through the process. The CFO of the Australia Council, Bob Taylor worked with [local accountant and auditor] Ian Jessup who was yet another unsung pro bono New Moon hero, to develop a viable financial plan and Dona Greaves and Kevin Radbourne at the Queensland Ministry offered invaluable assistance and some funding assurances".[123] With that basic structure in place a program was devised for the following year.

"My memory of this time was of constant work, learning the business and operating at the same time."[124] That meant threading their way towards some degree of financial stability along the rocky road in an ever-changing landscape while simultaneously trying to affect a balance between the, by then, somewhat alienated municipal councils, a nervous state government and a very sceptical Australia Council. There were local issues to be addressed as well: calming old nerves, making new allies, working in the arts sector in each of the towns and, among all of that, trying to create and support a theatre product of genuine artistic quality. "My sense is that once Helmut was assured that all was on track, he pulled back and I was left, with the Board, to try to keep the momentum going".[125]

But New Moon became a learning experience of a different kind for Bereson and one that in the event was to take her in a radically different direction, as it did for others we've already noted: "I became increasingly interested in the politics of funding and governmental policy at all levels concerning the arts. My experience showed me that if one were to really work in the area it was not through strict adherence to governmental procedure but through the development of spheres of influence which would help one through the process. During this time, I received a call from the [federal] Department of Arts, Territories, Environment etc in Canberra that a British academic would be visiting town and would I arrange a lecture for him at the [James Cook] University and look after him? ... what unfolded was a life changing three-day conversation with Professor John Pick, who demonstrated to me the power of research and who offered me a doctoral place at his university."[126]

She declined the offer muttering something about being too busy at the 'coal-face' but the questions he posed and the opportunity to really try to get to the bottom of all she was experiencing in more than a knee-jerk, reactive fashion proved in the end too alluring. So, a few months later: "I called him and gingerly asked if the offer was still on the table. I also visited one of our board members, Henry Reynolds at JCU and discussed my interest in pursuing this and he kindly wrote the letter of reference I needed for my application for doctoral studies".[127] About a year later, Bereson left New Moon and worked first as logistics manager at the Festival of Pacific Arts, which greatly enlarged her scope of knowledge of Federal government agencies and then left Australia in 1989 to pursue her studies, not to return until 2015 after an academic career which led her to the United Kingdom, France, Singapore and the United States. "It was a heady, adventurous time: both brave and naive. My overriding memory of New Moon is that despite the many and varied vicissitudes during my tenure there, the work was always of a high quality and something one was proud in a small way to have enabled."[128]

Closing acts

As we move closer to the waning of our Moon, it's important to record yet another set of changes to the governance of the Company and to remind ourselves that these tedious recitals are offered not out of some Gilbertian obsession with making little lists, but rather to highlight the dangers which this constantly changing assembly of notables posed in the oversight of an already fragile enterprise and in particular as it became year by year more debilitated. So then at the annual general meeting on April 11, 1987 the following new board was elected: Ald. Valentine, appointed Townsville City Council, chair. Cr Dawson, appointed Mackay/Pioneer, Robert Spencer. Bill Langdon, Ellen Brown, Ray Dickson, Sylvia Sarinos and Prof Henry Reynolds. Note how the local government sector has shrunk in line by then with the progress of withdrawal of their financial support.

However, other than Board members, until almost the end there were not many in the New Moon cast of characters who might reasonably claim to be "locals". Kirsty Veron doesn't quite qualify, but she comes closer than most. A Bachelor of Arts from New England University to which she later added the Associate Diploma, Performing Arts and later still a Master of Creative Arts from James Cook University, Veron is typical of the multi-tasking, multi-skilling activists often found in the arts in regional centres in Australia. "I have been a lover of theatre all my life, an interest fostered by my family – my grandmother used to produce Gilbert & Sullivan musicals in my home town, Glen Innes, I think in the 1920s and '30s".[129] With those interests and if someone has an aptitude at all or sometimes just stands still long enough, they are bound to be thrust into many roles. Veron's succession of functions as administrator, board member and actor with New Moon in its later years was followed by, even possibly shaped, all those other responsibilities she has taken on in Townsville and elsewhere in later life, mainly in the cultural sector.

"I arrived in Townsville in 1972, in the wake of my marine biologist (now ex) husband and very soon became involved in Townsville Little Theatre. I also pursued my love of music, playing violin and singing in local music groups. My administrative career really began when I was handed the role of organising activities for the Townsville Community Music Centre (TCMC) in the mid-1980s. It happened pretty much by default, because others who had been involved were no longer available, for a variety of reasons. I credit what skill I have in this area to the mentorship of Fred Thompson, a dear, kind man who was the first President of TCMC and who skilfully guided my early administrative development."[130] She had also encountered Rod Wissler when he first arrived in Townsville as one of the lecturers in her Associate Diploma course. And her recollection is that by a twist of fate it was he who employed her as New Moon's local administrator in 1989, while he guided the Company at a distance from Brisbane.

"I have had an interesting and varied career as an arts administrator and manager over many years, for which I can thank my years in Townsville, where I had opportunities that would not have been available in a smaller town or a bigger city"[131] Her time there coincided with the expansion of Townsville's professional arts life and thus her experience was able to expand with it. Immediately after New Moon, Veron went on to be variously publicist and tour manager for Dance North, General Manager of the Darwin Theatre Company, Manager *On tour by Request* at the Queensland Arts Council and Manager – Cultural Services for the Redcliffe City Council in south-east Queensland. Latterly, she worked as Executive Assistant and Office Manager for the Queensland Minister for Science, Information Technology, Innovation and the Arts in Brisbane. That is to mention just a few stops in a busy and productive career of which New Moon was but one interval along the way, but a crucial one – as it was to prove for many.

In February, 1989 Lorraine Bird from the Pioneer Shire and later MP for Whitsunday joined the New Moon Board and in July that year Ray Dickson stepped down as chair to be succeeded by John Lamb who had now come full circle. At the same time, Townsville business owner, Leah Bryant was co-opted and Associate Prof Elizabeth Perkins from JCU also joined. Again, it can be seen how rapid turnover of membership and the frequent acquisition of new board members with little background in the Company at the very moment when critical and level-headed decisions were needed continued the fraying of its oversight.

But harking back to a slightly earlier set of governance changes, we return to Robert Spencer, one of the longest serving board members of New Moon who was not an elected official or manager of a municipal venue. Today, he still describes himself as a New Moon groupie: "I've always been disappointed that its story wasn't better known and the history better remembered, because it is an important part not just of theatre history but of Queensland history"... "I went to Mackay in July 1980 as a locum to a firm of solicitors and not long after was offered a position with them. I suppose it was around the time New Moon was being dreamed up". He had no theatrical background but soon found himself involved with the Athena Theatre, a youth company run by a dynamic local woman, Anna Marie McGregor. "I guess I'd always felt that it was important to involve young people in theatre and soon became active, particularly on the organisational side."[132]

At some point he was approached to be on the Board of New Moon. While he doesn't now recall who broached the subject, he still regards it as a happy event. In due course, he was appointed formally by the Mackay City Council as its community representative alongside whoever the selected Councillor was from time to time. "I actually regard that as one of the real weaknesses of the Company. The constant turnover of Directors as a result of local government elections meant that there was little continuity and no one ever learnt enough to act effectively". But it was far from the only serious matter. Personalities also loomed large and not always very productively. "In all honesty, I would have to say that another issue was the way Diane Cilento as chair dominated proceedings. She was not generally receptive to ideas from others. Of course, she was an experienced theatrical personality – an actress as she would have said back then – and a name in Queensland. I think the local government people were a little overawed by that and she certainly took advantage of it. There was always a degree of – what shall I call it? – tension between her and the other directors, the creative people in the Company and of course the management especially when Ruth Bereson took over who Diane regarded as a novice from Melbourne. Diane's ideas tended to be centred on herself [rather] than on what the community might have wanted". Also, Cilento came from a prominent and exceptionally conservative Queensland family. That too would both have impressed and maybe appealed to many in the equally conservative local government world. "She also had a tendency to regard herself as the voice of North Queensland and not everyone was prepared to contest that." [133]

Spencer's first encounter with New Moon was seeing 'No Orchids for Miss Blandish' in Mackay and admits to being astounded. "Seeing that quality of acting and production in the old Theatre Royal, which was frankly a dump, was a light bulb moment for me. Suddenly, it seemed that it was really possible to have locally-produced theatre of that quality right in our midst. It was exciting. The contrast between what it did and what the public was used to from the local amateur groups could not have been greater." [134]

From a Mackay point of view, Spencer considers that New Moon also had a positive effect on the drive for a better venue there. "I don't say it was *the* catalyst for that, but was certainly a factor in it. So many shows used to just pass by Mackay and the coming of New Moon helped to galvanise the community to argue for a new theatre and ultimately a fund raising campaign which in turn put pressure on the authorities." Spencer believes, however, that it had a wider impact. New Moon was like a time bomb that set off a whole explosion in the arts. "I wouldn't claim it did so on its own, but it made people think and act. Dance North for instance took off soon after and people in general became more interested in cultural matters. I think the controversy helped all that."[135]

He recognises that inevitably there were problems: money or the lack of it was always an issue and that just got worse as time went by. The constant touring and keeping a large company on the road was expensive and there was a feeling that the government officials in Sydney and Brisbane really didn't understand the conditions or the challenges in North Queensland. "I don't say that's right, but it was a strongly held view not just about New Moon or the arts but in general". Moreover, it was a time of great political turmoil in Queensland which did not serve to make the Company's path any smoother. Yet despite the ups and downs, Spencer continued to believe in its value and during his time on the Board considered that under successive artistic leaders it was always committed to quality. "And my recollection is that it was always well received. Sure, there were some who didn't care for this or that show. But that's normal." Overall, the public looked forward to the visits to Mackay at least, and appreciated New Moon when it was there. His other two light bulb moments for very different reasons were 'Beach Blanket Tempest' and 'Away'. "'Beach Blanket Tempest' was a genuinely original, whacky idea by the team that had made 'Dingo Girl' down in Sydney. It could have been an interesting path to follow, but for some reason it wasn't pursued."[136]

Spencer went off the Board when Mackay/Pioneer councils stopped funding the Company. But right to the end he kept an interest and was devastated when it finally folded. "Nothing has really replaced it. There are local companies in Townsville and Cairns that struggle on and do good work but nothing of the sheer scope or ambition of New Moon. Its loss was a tragedy". Spencer remained in Mackay until 2003 when he was appointed as Magistrate based in Cairns from which he presides in a remote circuit that brings him into regular contact with what it would be fair to call the real and at times raw deep North. "But no doubt New Moon changed my life and outlook. I missed it terribly and still do". [137]

At the time of its final production, "The Summer of the 17th Doll" in early 1990 the New Moon Board had changed yet again: John Lamb (chair) Ray Dickson (deputy Chair) Lorraine Bird, Leah Bryant. Stan Newman, Townsville City Council, Elizabeth Perkins and Henry

Reynolds, JCU and Robert Spencer, Cairns with Rod Wissler, Artistic Advisor/Director.

One could in fairness claim that New Moon began with an idea of John Lamb and a committee. Committees are not the worst way to launch a venture. At their best they can garner collective strength, safety in numbers, and a network of contacts. What in fact they represented when New Moon first rose was a group of investors. To all intents, the five LGA's were shareholders: they put their money in hoping for the dividend of regular shows in their theatres and cultural benefits to their communities. They were also, in that sense, stakeholders, as we would likely say today. But there was a genuine investment in the idea and its outcomes. When that failed to materialise, the shareholders peeled away and were replaced for the most part by people who believed in the enterprise but who had little power either of the purse or politically to save it, least of all when the Board was charged with making that fateful decision to pull the plug on the last production significantly enough titled: 'Can't Pay, Won't Pay' in early 1990. And so, beginning with a group of concerned community representatives and John Lamb it could be said to have concluded the same way: John Lamb (chair), Lorraine Bird, Leah Bryant, Ald, Stan Newman, Chair of the Arts & Cultural committee of Townsville Council, Prof Elizabeth Perkins, Prof Henry Reynolds, Robert Spencer, Cairns, Rod Wissler and Jane Pirani, Artistic Director Extensions Youth Dance Company.

A little less than 12 months later filled with frantic activity the wind-up minutes of the Board meeting of December 10, 1990 show yet again a change of cast. It is worth noting that James Cook University which for a variety of complex reasons had chosen never to become one of those critical investors should have been so heavily represented at the end: Colin Campbell playwright, Chris Cottrell. Accountant, Melanie Guiney. JCU, Pam Lythgo. JCU, Elizabeth Perkins JCU, Andrea Phillip. Director of Townsville Aboriginal & Islander Media Association (TAIMA), Kirsty Veron, Rowan Silva lawyer, Townsville and Ald. Stan Newman. The TAIMA link was a close as New Moon ever got formally to an Indigenous connection. That was not rare for Australian theatre at the time, but given its location is nevertheless revealing.

In addition to this revolving door of directorships, in conclusion one should also note that the Company had eight chairpersons in just nine years of operation. To reiterate they were: Ald. Sheila Keeffe Townsville City Council; Cr Walter Percival "Snow" Wright, Pioneer Shire Council, Bruce Shepherd, businessman, Mackay, Diane Cilento (actor) Cairns; Ald. Terry Moore, Rockhampton City Council; Ald. Val Valentine, Townsville City Council, Ray Dickson, media Townsville and John Lamb, arts manager, Townsville.

Agnes of God
Photo: Sheena Dunn
Left to right- Cornelia Frances, Kaarin Fairfax, Diane Cilento

Gentlemen Prefer Blondes
left to right- Vanessa Downing , Deborah Kennedy

5

What was the Tale?

You cannot build bridges between the wandering islands;
The mind has no neighbours and the unteachable heart
Announces its armistice time after time, but spends
Its love to draw them closer and closer apart.
A.D. Hope – 'The Wandering Islands'

Triple Helix

The tale of New Moon is a triple helix: three strands entwined by wild ambition, force of circumstances and the bizarre denouement of a Queensland government drama. While, even to the informed observer, the political background might have seemed largely irrelevant, to a small, regional arts enterprise like New Moon, it is clear with hindsight that it was a significant element in its rapid rise and slow painful decline.

For that reason, largely without further comment, the author has chosen to thread through this chapter some odd and, at the same time, outstanding moments in the State political saga. It is not suggested that there is a direct link between the Company and any of the often sensational events chosen for inclusion. It is merely to indicate that hubris was in the air; that going "troppo" was not confined to thespians in the far North, but was a wider social phenomenon; and that in both cases fate (by whatever name), played a leading role.

The ambition is manifest. In New Moon's case it was characterised by trying to build a permanently touring theatre company from scratch with a group of artists and management who had hardly worked together, let alone in those territories and launching it with an intensive four-play season over four cities, all within six months! Its wider claim was to be *the* permanently touring theatre company servicing, at the very least, Northern Australia. In a moment of candour, Paul Iles acknowledged that he might well be accused of "gigantism" in his thinking along these lines.[138] But remember: the QTC had sought successfully to anoint itself the *Royal* Queensland Theatre Company. Even the AETT back in 1954, at the height of Australian royal visit fervour, had opted for a less extravagant title than that. Not long after, Iles's old stamping ground had cynically rechristened itself the Nimrod *National* Theatre Company. (There was talk too of Musica Viva Galactica, but that was deemed to be an exercise in rare chamber music humour.)

The force of destiny or circumstance (if preferred), as in Verdi's opera so in life, lies somewhere between fate and sheer bad luck. New Moon had its share of both. Yet one factor is inescapable for any enterprise, be it artistic or otherwise, in regional Australia: that is to say, attracting and retaining skilled personnel. This is especially the case in Northern Australia where climate exacerbates the problem. Prospective settlers arrive or visit in the Dry, find it exciting and agreeable; then they hit the Build Up and then the Wet. The Further North one goes the more acute this factor becomes. In Year Two of New Moon i.e. 1983, Iles opted to relocate the base of operations to Cairns: hotter, wetter and stickier by far than Townsville, which rather perversely for its geographic location lies a rain shadow. Cairns being more "fun", it is possible that the move frayed the Company's work ethic and also the basis of its oversight by the critical Townsville interests, including the supportive city council that had set the theatrical ball rolling. It also sidestepped the prospect of growing an involvement with James Cook University which could have been a prime associate in stabilising and sustaining New Moon, as well as in providing a source of locally trained actors and other theatre workers. Fatally, that link was never to be made.

But whether in Townsville, Cairns or Rockhampton, New Moon artists and staff were always, as we would say today, fly-in/fly-out. In that, too, they reflected another fact of life in the North: many seasonal workers leave their real lives behind elsewhere for short-term, intensive periods of labour be it in art, mining or back in the day mustering, cane cutting or construction. The force of circumstance is residential and occupational instability. The pioneering theatre company never overcame that, though it is possible that if, like Dance North, it had had based itself in just one place and fanned out to other centres it might have found a way to do so. It is worth recalling that the initiative came from Townsville; the model was developed in Townsville; the business case and the foundation funding came from there; when things got tough, the Company defaulted to Townsville; and the lasting legacy in La Luna remained for decades after in Townsville. But for good or ill, the personnel of New Moon were always tourists, never settlers.

The rapid turnover of board membership and thus leadership contributed to that unsettledness. The loss of two of the critical venue managers in John Lamb and Ian Satchwell so soon after the Company started operating robbed it of continuity in that as well. Both left for what then appeared greener pastures – Lamb to Darwin and Satchwell to Tasmania. In the event, neither proved as green as they had hoped. Lamb later returned to preside uneasily over the end of the company he had started. Meanwhile, the weight of local government representation on the New Moon Board almost ensured rapid changes, as noted earlier, short-term Directors and thereby chairpersons. Corporate memory was broken almost before it had begun. Along with a peripatetic management, there was no-one there continually to mind the farm. Until Ruth Bereson became General Manger in 1986, for the first five years of its existence there had been no full-time employee to represent the Company in Queensland year-round. Given the delicate political environment and Queensland's notoriously parochial sentiments, that was an extraordinary oversight. This, in turn, led to a revolving door of artistic leadership and thus problems in mid- and long-term planning and employment. There were, as well, accidents along the way. Of these the most appalling was the implausible recruitment and soon after death of Ian Tasker, virtually before he had taken over as Artistic Director and the disruption which that caused, along with the concomitant collapse of confidence and financial support.

On the political front, the absurdity of the 'Joh for PM' campaign highlighted his party's hubristic vision of itself and the State. While there was little chance that the leader of a breakaway branch of the junior coalition partner then in Opposition could succeed in taking on either the admittedly demoralised Liberal party or, more to the point, a highly successful Labor government, it could still have wreaked havoc at the next federal elections. But for Prime Minister Hawke's catching Bjelke-Petersen by surprise in calling an early poll, he might well have succeeded in that at least. In a similar manner some years later, had she been in any way intelligent, stuck to a few consistent messages and not got lost in the racial swamps, Pauline Hanson might have made a more than marginal national parliamentary breakthrough. But while cunning goes a long way in politics, it never quite replaces intelligence, as the resistible rise of Arturo Trump would demonstrate in time.

One giant step

But let us pause for a moment to consider the fair Verona in which our heroes laid their scene. To give some sense of the scale of the Company's reach, we should know that around 300,000 people lived in the New Moon catchment and from top to bottom it stretched 1000 kilometres. By contrast, according to the 1981 census, the population of the Newcastle statistical district, home of HVTC at that time, was a 195,000. If one added the rest of the Hunter region of some 36,000 souls, it amounted approximately to 241,000. At the same time, the population of statistical Wollongong was 113,000 with the rest of the Illawarra accounting for 35,000 or a regional total of 148,000. Both of these districts are a fraction of the size of North and Central Queensland. So the concept itself was already a huge bite out of the Australian landscape. No one had thought regionally about the arts on this scale since the launch of the Arts Council movement in the late 1940s and that, despite its breadth, was always city-based. In the old conundrum of 'Sydney or the Bush', New Moon unhesitatingly and loudly proclaimed for the bush – and what's more, a very large slice of it.

Yet its grander vision still was to serve the whole of a Northern Australia, to expand its circuit beyond the four founding cities and take it west to Mt Isa and into the Northern Territory and down to the outskirts of Brisbane. It was one of the many great, possibly grandiose goals that was never achieved but which might just have been achievable. Araluen Arts Centre in Alice Springs opened in 1984. The Darwin Centre, to which Lamb had gone, opened in 1985. Both could have been part of the touring network but already other wheels were turning. Only one production, 'Beach Blanket Tempest', ever got that far. Nevertheless, back in more optimistic times, on December 3, 1980 the Central and Northern Queensland Theatre Company Ltd was formally incorporated. On November 11, 1981 the Board resolved that it be called New Moon.[139] Regrettably there is no record of who championed that choice but it is not unreasonable to speculate that it was Paul Isles.

But earlier still, on May 22, 1980 the embryonic company had advertised nationally for both the Artistic Director and Administrator positions. We have noted that after John Milson had been appointed and withdrew for health reasons, the newly minted team of Peter Barclay and Terrence O'Connell were invited to submit a formal proposal as joint Artistic Directors for a first season in 1981/82 of a company to be based in Townsville.[140] They commenced formally on August 11, 1981.

After reviewing the applicants for Administrator, again as we saw earlier, Iles was invited to apply and he was quick to take advantage.[141] Not long after his appointment Iles wrote to the larger-than-life Minister for Local Government and Police and Racing, Hon Russell Hinze MLA, whose persona and traits were later to be notorious in Australian political annals and after whom one of Brisbane Greyhound racing stands is still named, advising him of his appointment. Somewhat slyly, he refers to the "superb new theatre in Rockhampton" but goes on, "I was talking to Brian Sweeney last week who tells me that you have taken an interest in the project. Brian recalled the day that Robyn Nevin, Pat Bishop and you went to the races. Theatre is just as big a gamble".[142]

It is a curious reminiscence at best, and one can't help wondering what those excellent actors (still actresses in those days) thought of their experience at the Turf. Iles went on to ask the Minister for suggestions for likely sponsors "from a charitable source". It is possible he imagined that Hinze might touch some of his racing mates for this purpose. If so, he knew not with whom he dealt. But overall, it was typical of Iles's tendency to leave nothing to chance as well as demonstrating his range of skills – and shortcomings. There is no suggestion that the Minister responded in kind. Better luck was forthcoming from Copper Refinery Pty Ltd (aka Mount Isa Mines Holdings) which wrote just five days later to offer $7,500 in sponsorship. On March 12 the following year, the Company received a letter from Shell confirming $7,500 originally for a production of 'Boy's Own Macbeth' which was to have been the opening production, though later shelved. Interestingly, Shell also advised that it was "setting aside" additional funds as a promotional budget to support the marketing campaign, indicating a level of sophistication and care which would not have been expected in a first time deal. Shell continued to be there for New Moon throughout, later sponsoring 'Cabaret' for $10,000 in 1984 and 'Guys and Dolls' in 1987. In all, private sector support for 1981/82 amounted to $17,000. For a start-up theatre company with no track record and little more than chutzpah to sustain it, this was remarkable. At a time when even major performing arts companies in capital cites struggled for the corporate dollar, tapping funds in the regions, especially from industrial sources, was largely unprecedented and was to grow slowly only over the next few decades. While Shell did have a record of arts support nationwide, New Moon's early success was still an impressive start.

But to return to our tangled web: Iles had by then already been involved in the selection of the initially appointed Artistic Director, John Milson. He had even provided a copy of Nimrod's contract for resident directors as a template for that position.[143] Yet, a later Board meeting stated that he was to be invited to be an "honorary consultant" to the Company.[144] That may just have been Iles playing for time while he extricated himself from the State Theatre. Jim Sharman was incoming with his historic Lighthouse model with Mary Vallentine as General Manager and Iles may not have wanted to rock the boat by leaving suddenly during that transition. Or he may simply have been hedging his bets, conceivably waiting for a better opportunity to emerge elsewhere. Any or all of these was well within the scope of his modus operandi.

Meanwhile, negotiations for Barclay and O'Connell were being handled by Hilary Furlong of M&L Casting. In a memo to the Steering Committee President, Sheila Keeffe cc Paul Iles, Lamb writes: "Paul Iles has agreed to handle the negotiations our behalf". Critically it goes on: "He will also give any assistance on interviews for the position of General Manager".[145] It is curious that Iles was not only helping out with the contracts for the Joint Artistic Directors, whose role was already announced – which was not unreasonable as a collegial act – but he was also assisting with interviews for a position to which he had been formally invited by the Board to apply. The term 'insider trading' springs to mind. What's more, and to add a further Byzantine touch to the proceedings, correspondence regarding Barclay and O'Connell was being addressed by M&L to Iles at the State Theatre Company where he was still employed and whose governance, one assumes, was not privy to these complex dealings.[146]

One of the sticking points in these negotiations was that both Artistic Directors insisted on being on the Board of the Company.[147] Also each wanted to be styled Artistic Director rather than *joint* Artistic Director. Although the Company's constitution did not allow them to become voting directors at that time, Iles went into bat with the Steering Committee for that to happen when the Articles could be suitably amended, pointing out that both HVTC and Nimrod had a similar provision. Iles was by then at least discreet enough to be conducting this correspondence as of his private PO Box and not from the State Theatre company's address. On May 28, 1981 Barclay and O'Connell, along with Iles, interviewed three Adelaide-based prospective General Managers who presumably little knew that their fate was already sealed.[148]

Either way, the new leadership of O'Connell, Barclay and Iles was plunged into a situation of which they were largely ignorant. The plan of operation was sketchy at best. None of the three knew Queensland, still less North Queensland. They were young, smart, talented and up for the challenge, but essentially they were flying blind.

With the hindsight of many decades, O'Connell reflected: "In retrospect, I probably should have spent more time in researching the possibilities and the character of the towns themselves before leaping in. But of course, the concept of the way the Company would operate had largely been worked out before I came on board. I think another 'issue' was that the four cities were, at least in my observation, radically different from each other, with totally different atmospheres and expectations at the time. I think this was a difficulty in 'branding' and establishing the Company and it would have been stronger had it established itself in one place first before undertaking the constant touring and attempting to please four theatres, four audiences and four sets of councils."[149]

Programming

Again, with the benefit of a long look back, the choice of works of that first season staged in the four cities in 1982 reveals much about the great leap forward and the uncertainty which attended it. Launching a new company in largely untried territory with a musical play about an Australian, semi-mythic figure like 'Ned Kelly' would have been brave at best. To do so with Reg Livermore's stage creation that had had one, largely unsuccessful, production was daring fate perhaps too far. To follow it with a less than conventional 'punk' production of 'Macbeth' would give little breathing space either for the Company or the audience, accustomed to their Shakespeare in more conventional terms. To finish off with a loopy rock musical, fantasy drama based upon The Who's album 'Tommy' about a "seemingly disabled" boy who becomes a pinball champion and religious leader was either a penetrating insight into a trend or just foolhardy. Ken Russell's film extravaganza on the subject was then just seven years old. The demands on the Company to match up to it and its star-studded cast, including the Who members themselves plus Ann-Margret, Oliver Reed, Eric Clapton, Tina Turner, Elton John, and Jack Nicholson, were enormous and yet ... and yet ... they pulled it all off!

In an odd way, those three works were all about the larger-than-life: heroes, heroes manqué, fallen heroes, anti-heroes, as you will. Yet strangely in the midst of all that came the choice of a minor black comedy from Glasgow about a kidnapping: 'No Orchids for Miss Blandish' which left all but some of the actors bemused and much of the public horrified by this violence and obscenity. Actor Bob Baines recalls: "I thought it was wonderfully powerful, aggressive piece of theatre."[150] Few of the critics or, it would seem, the public shared his enthusiasm. Even if they had, it was clear that right from the beginning the Company's trying to be too many things to different cities was already showing strains.

Even the working conditions were hazardous. As we've seen, set builder Kerry Saul had been brought in at short notice from New Zealand "I arrived in December and the first production was due to go up in January. There was just a set of working drawings. I had to go out, find the equipment and the materials and get it done". [151]

Designer Anthony Babicci who came in halfway through that first season saw the opposite end of the problem. "I was met at the [Rockhampton] airport and taken to the theatre to meet the company. It was in the afternoon before an evening performance. I was introduced as the new designer and had never seen a less enthusiastic group of people. I soon discovered why. They were on the road with 'Ned Kelly' The set was so heavy and so huge it wouldn't fit into most of the touring trucks. In fact, it didn't fit onto some of the stages. It was killing them". He soon realised that the designs for 'Macbeth' which came next were just as onerous. "It looked great but was totally impractical. I knew I couldn't make a show that would repeat that burden." His first production was 'No Orchids for Miss Blandish' The backdrop was a series of criminal faces painted on calico. "You could roll it up and carry it under your arm. The rest were light flats. The company loved me". [152]

Malcolm Calder, Administrator of the Pilbeam Theatre saw other issues: "the establishment of a theatre company serving all four could never work if it did precisely the same things in the same way in each of the four cities. To some extent this can still be observed today – although lurking beneath is a southern (i.e. certainly Sydney and to some extent even Brisbane) assumption that each of these areas is 'very similar'. This assumption may also have contributed to the ultimate funding issues of the Company. In the 1980s Rockhampton identified closely with its primary industry, and was often referred to as Australia's 'beef capital'. In turn, this affected and permeated most aspects of lifestyle, attitudes, culture and the economy through a social composite that was very different to Mackay, Townsville or Cairns. Mining had little impact in Rockie, nor did tourism but, by way of comparison, Cairns had far more exposure to inbound tourism from the south and social attitudes were markedly different." [153]

On the road

Somewhere along the line it had become part of the core plan that not only would New Moon service all four cities equally, but that at regular intervals the base of the Company's operations would also move from one to another. Hence, after effectively two years in Townsville (i.e. 1981/92), although only one of those actually had a performing season, they upped sticks and moved to Cairns. One senses that Cairns was viewed as being likely to be more "agreeable". Certainly, it was more obviously tropical; there was a great transient population; and there was the added allure of Ms Cilento and her establishment at nearby Karnak.

Founded in 1876 and named after the State Governor of the day, Cairns was formally declared a town in 1903 with a registered population of 3,500. Curiously, the initial white settlement in the region during the 1860s was driven by Bêche-de-mer fishing. However, it was the discovery of gold to the north (Palmer River field) and on the nearby Atherton Tableland (Hodgkinson River field) that saw the population begin to climb. Throughout the 1870s and early 1880s European and Chinese settlers opened up the region to agriculture, generating a large enough population base for the borough of Cairns to be declared a municipality in 1886. Railway connection was the next stimulus for the City's expansion attracting a large number of immigrants who went on to settle in the region and were responsible for establishing the sugar industry, predominantly in the lowlands, and extensive fruit orchards on the cooler inland plateau. By the early 1980s, the population of the city itself had reached about 40,000 boosted immensely by tourism to the Great Barrier Reef and the increasingly recognised and popular Daintree Rain Forest which would be declared a World Heritage site in 1988 but was then only slowly starting to be opened to visitors. There was, as well, the luxury resort developments at Port Douglas and on nearby islands.

Among the many complexities of this ambulant life style which had been adopted by New Moon was its sheer cost. As early as March 1983, Iles was reporting to his Board that consequent upon the move to Cairns the Company had secured rehearsal/wardrobe/office space at 30 Grafton Street, Cairns at a rent of $800 per month in addition to a workshop at $70 per week. It was clear that the Townsville trauma of establishing a base simultaneous to preproduction design and planning for the season could not be repeated.[154]

Notwithstanding, Iles made it very clear that his view was that the notional base of the Company should remain in Cairns now that New Moon had acquired relative security of premises. That, of course, made it necessary to budget for 52 weeks rent in the coming financial year rather than the six months of expenditure that had been in place for 1982. He hoped that it would be possible to recoup some of this by subletting it to other Cairns groups in New Moon's dark periods. It was typical of Iles's approach to public relations that he stressed that he would continue "to publicly emphasise that a New Moon is a 'resident' company to all four of its constituent cities... "I admit to a degree of 'window-dressing' by flirting the idea of moving the base to all centres over four years." He acknowledged that this was in fact now unrealistic and asked the Board to endorse Cairns (and 30 Grafton Street) as the primary rehearsal city henceforth. Perhaps unnecessarily in the circumstances he added coyly: "this needs no public statement".[155]

On the matter of window dressing, Robert Love recalls a day when visiting Iles in his office in Townsville he found Paul frantically signing cheques against a mountain of invoices and complaining how tight money was and how the company was always on the brink. On his way back to JCU Love turned on his car radio and heard Iles giving an interview in which he proclaimed New Moon was in the best of all possible financial and artistic health.[156] They call it 'spin' today and Iles was a master.

Given the extraordinary circumstances, the challenge of assembling a company, forging an identity, making four not inconsiderable productions *ab ovo* and touring each to four very different cities while rehearsing the next one the road, the first season must be accounted a resounding success. The demands on everyone both physical and emotional were immense but the locals were dazzled. However, the strains soon showed and after directing just two productions, Peter Barclay concluded it was not for him. "Let's attribute it to interpersonal difficulties" and he departed with some fireworks in mid-1982.[157] Others saw deeper conflict. This left O'Connell to continue as sole Artistic Director.

War of words

There were other tensions. The Company had hardly begun when a war of words broke out between Iles and the Theatre Board over funding. In the initial 'deal' which Lamb had forged between the new venture, the State government and the city councils it had been clear that the Australia Council's contribution was on an annually reducing basis.

Then in October 1982, with its first season not long completed, the news came that the funding agency would offer just $64,600 compared with the previous year's $87,000 or a cut of $22,400. Iles leapt to the Telex and fired off a Jeremiad to the Board's director, Michael FitzGerald: "News of your reduced grant is devastating and we are at a loss to understand what criteria this cruel turnabout stems from".[158] He accused the Federal Government of having "cynically ignored the potential of the arts in Northern Australia" and threatened to liquidate the Company on the grounds that it would otherwise be trading insolvent into 1983. This was followed three days later by a marginally more temperate letter appealing the decision but nevertheless referring to its "sledgehammer action" that would dictate the winding up of New Moon.[159]

Iles claimed that the Company was the "victim of an astonishingly different, artificial and repugnant policy of treating the so called "regions" as a subordinate priority".[160] He pointed that the State was already giving a 10% increase and therefore New Moon could not reasonably ask for more from that source. The LGAs were already contributing generously and the Company was making headway on corporate support. Co-incidentally, only a few days later the UTAH Foundation confirmed its sponsorship of 'A Midsummer Night's Dream' so that Iles's claim was not groundless in that respect. As well, he went into overdrive, firing off press statements including one which said: "we had no indication that our grant would not be the same as this year" and was quoted even by interstate journalists.[161] He had also sprayed letters of complaint to all and sundry, including the Federal Arts Minister.

Many of the apparent oddities of this behaviour can reasonably be attributed to the tension between Iles's theatrical sophistication and shrewdness on the one hand and on the other a personal immaturity which led him to flaunt his sexuality and in what was often a childish manner gratuitously offend those whom he undoubtedly regarded as stuffed shirts. In larger centres it might be and often was laughed off, in North Queensland it both proved to be fatal to him and to the Company.

A prime example of Iles and his tendency to fly into communication often extravagantly worded and not always reflective of known reality was the telex to FitzGerald. Iles knew very well that the Board's policy was a reducing sunset process, so the idea that it was a huge surprise to either him or Lamb is idle. Given the encouragement the Company had received from state and local government his claim that the arts in Northern Australia had, like so many other areas, been disregarded by the Federal Government, was arguable but unwise. New Moon had indeed received an establishment subsidy of $79,000 from the state in 1980 and was being offered $86,900 for 1983. The Australia Council drop from $87,000 to $64,600 was significant and in his words: "spells the closure of New Moon. A reduction of $22,400 cannot possible [sic] be found elsewhere". Given the 13% funding increase which the Australia Council had received from the government, New Moon had perhaps over excitedly anticipated a grant of $97,000. Accordingly and maybe cunningly, Iles went on to argue that it would be "imprudent for the Directors to proceed with 1983 season in the circumstances". Sir Albert Abbott CBE, Mayor of Mackay was among those who had written a "dear Tom" to the Minister to complain.

Somewhat mysteriously, Iles added: "invoking the letter of current regional theatre policy (we believe you have done worse than that) is a brutal move".[162] Presumably he is referring to the fact that the Australia Council policy had been to reduce by 20% annually over five years the forward commitment to regional companies, but since the base year grant in 1981 of $79,000 had risen to $87,000 in 1982 rather than declining the Theatre board was presumably trying to get back on track. In global terms, Iles's dismay is understandable, if somewhat deliberately disingenuous.

In any event, the Board had by then already started to move away from what Iles called: "this stillborn policy". "this scheme has not fulfilled the Theatre Board aims to generate broadly based funding of community/regional theatre".[163] Paradoxically in New Moon's case it had done exactly that, which made their determination to end it all the more ironic. At least one Theatre board staffer of the period remembers Iles virtually bursting unannounced and uninvited into a Board meeting held at Sydney University to protest his case. Other applicants sent satirical gifts from time to time to make their point, but only Iles chose to appear in person no doubt in his characteristic schoolboy garb.

Not long after, Iles is writing to Alan Edwards urging him not to "take anything personally in my letter to the Theatre Board" in which in referring to its "sledgehammer action" had been rather scathing about the state theatre companies (paradoxically one of which in Adelaide he had only recently run).[164] It is typical, too, that he adds perhaps only half tongue-in-cheek: "If we have to wind up, remember I'll be looking for work so if you are thinking of getting a general manager…!" It would have been hard to imagine a less likely to be successful pairing than those two personalities (the traditional, conservative, super-private British actor/director who was soon to rechristen QTC as Royal) and the tearaway young '70s remittance man who lived with his heart and his loves on his sleeve).

A newspaper article by Lucy Wagner noted that 'Paul finds regional theatre a disaster': "we had no indication that our grant would not be the same as last year".[165] Given the ample advice he had received from the Australia Council that was simply untrue. "The article in the *Sydney Morning Herald* plus letters you have written to Board members and I understand to the Minister for Home Affairs and Australia Council members as well as contacting CAPPA have put both your own credibility and that of your Company on the line", FitzGerald wrote in complaint.

FitzGerald was clearly agitated. In a letter to Iles he complains: "We feel that your actions have been irresponsible given the commitment by Elizabeth [Butcher] and myself to re-examine the amount of your 1983 grant.[166] But FitzGerald was in his own, much milder way as shrewd an operator as Iles. He advised Iles privately that he, FitzGerald, would have to write individually to each of the Theatre Board members to obtain their agreement to the change and then he would also write to each relevant local authority for confirmation of their direct grant to New Moon. That means, Iles observed in some exasperation to Carmel

Daveson one of the Directors and then Acting mayor of Mackay: "we will only get their money if we get your money!"[167] FitzGerald's brother was Australia's first Ambassador to the People's Republic of China. Clearly, an ability to manoeuvre around tricky objects ran in the family.

By October 27 New Moon's Chair, the more adept Bruce Shepherd, felt the need to write in conciliatory terms suggesting that there had perhaps been misunderstandings on both sides: "If we overreacted it was from a real sense of desperation. Maintaining the united support of seven local authorities spread over 1300 kilometres is not easy and there was no hope of our having a second chance if our 1983 season failed."[168]

In the letter to Daveson, Iles notes that FitzGerald had called him to advise of the back down: "he went on at some length about my lobbying over the last fortnight and said that it was getting his back up because we had already created such a fuss through writing to Tom McVeigh, the Federal Arts Minister, each member of the Theatre Board and the members of the Council".[169]

It was not the last time that Iles was to take this path. The Company also drew at various times on northern friends to lobby at state level. For instance, in late 1983 we find Charters Towers MLA, Bob Katter then Queensland Minister for Northern development and Aboriginal and Islander Affairs writing to his National Party colleague, Peter McKechnie, Minister for the Arts making "personal representations" regarding their $150,000 grant application for 1983/84".[170]

Not unnaturally, the Theatre Board took exception to the way Iles had handled the matter both in itself and in the extravagance of his language. Writing "on behalf of Elizabeth Butcher and myself", FitzGerald pointed out that they had been trying to resolve the matter, noting that both of them had given Iles assurances in various phone calls that if the calculation of the $64,600 announced under formula-funding was on the basis of incorrect figures, the Board would reconsider its decision if the Company could provide details of the actual amounts secured from other sources. Calling Iles's action "irresponsible" in the light of their commitment to re-examine the amount of the 1983 grant, he pointed out that the phase-out funding formula had been clearly stated and spelled out in discussion and correspondence between Theatre Board officers, John Lamb and Kevin Siddell and was contained in the letter of offer of grant on 21 January, 1981 acknowledged in acceptance of that on 7 March, 1981.

They were, he added, at a loss therefore to understand how Iles could have claimed to have "no indications" of this when the facts were long well known.[171] But from Iles's point of view all the brouhaha had the desired effect. On November 23, 1982 a letter arrived giving "conditional" approval of a grant of up to $98,000 for 1983. The conditions were that the Australia Council wanted written confirmation of the direct grants from each of the city councils concerned. That is to say, New Moon could not count the GALS or in-kind contributions; and the Board wanted written confirmation of guaranteed contributions of at least $10,000 from the corporate sector.[172] That precipitated a round of negotiations with the LGAs to convert their contributions from GALS and value-in-kind into hard cash so as to comply with the Theatre Board's demand.

In the event, Iles's campaign to embarrass the Board into backing down was successful. By December 13, 1982 Pat Galvin, Secretary of the Department of Home Affairs and the Environment was writing to him noting that: "the Theatre Board has reconsidered your applications for assistance and approved a grant of up to $98,000 for the Company's activity in 1983 together with an amount of $5061 towards interstate movement of artists".[173]

At the same time, the Board announced it would be abandoning its phase-out funding and would offer a choice to companies, such as New Moon, currently under the scheme. They would stay under the existing phase-out arrangement which offered guaranteed (albeit reducing) funding for five years or they could opt to go onto the open round for annual funding in competition with everyone else. That, of course, had no safety net. Thus there was a catch, but to a gambling man like Iles there was no doubt which way he would jump – and did.

Sideswipes

The fact is there were no limits to the new Company's ambition or perhaps, put more precisely, to Paul Iles's grand plan. But there was, as usual, an intensely practical side to this. New Moon could not subsist on grants alone or rely on the vagaries of box office. It needed to diversify its income. Almost from the beginning, Iles sought to find alternate or possibly parallel sources of revenue – something that would reduce the Company's overlarge dependence on government subvention. That, of course, is the pot of gold at the end of every arts company's rainbow. For New Moon it took a number of paths, as seen with the impressive start on corporate sponsorship. Another, and potentially greater step, lay in the chance to move into film.

A side deal which Iles tried to stitch up was New Moon Productions Pty Ltd. In essence, the aim was commercialise some of the theatre company's work in order to reach new markets and break the traditional straight-jacketing of a drama company by exploiting it in other media. He argued that an exciting opportunity had arisen for this purpose. Not surprisingly, it involved Cilento, herself an established actor with experience and connections in the film industry worldwide. [174]

One can't help feeling that the idea might have arisen over a three bottle meal at her licensed restaurant, The Nautilus at Port Douglas. But for all that it was a clever concept. After all, movies have been made in less promising territory. Iles had seen at first hand the early success of the South Australian Film Corporation in both feature films and Australian historical miniseries. At all events, the New Moon idea this was to be a money-making venture and an attempt both to develop a film-making enterprise in North Queensland and cross-benefit the theatre company. With an ensemble of actors employed for only half the year on live shows there could be abundant capacity. In Iles there was a budding producer with bags of get-up-and-go, always ready for a new adventure. In Ms Cilento they had an Oscar nominee with connections and, in Queensland at least, some clout. Her husband, Anthony Shaffer's 1970 play 'Sleuth' had been turned into a commercially successful 1972 film directed by Joseph L. Mankiewicz and starring Laurence Olivier and Michael Caine.

Thus, the idea was not without legs. But Townsville was not Hollywood or even Ealing. Funds were not easy to come by, though this *was* the height of the infamous Australian government 10BA 150% Tax write-off scheme which financed some 227 feature films in that decade, most of which never since saw the light of a silver screen. Producers still needed to raise the money up-front to avail themselves of that dubious tax dodge. New Moon Films began with more modest expectations and, undoubtedly, a legitimate cause. Cilento was prepared to start it up by directing a drama documentary about the making of 'Bush Tivoli' that new play to be written for the Company by Dorothy Hewitt. As things turned out, the play never materialised. But given that the proposed production was almost upon them at that stage, O'Connell, Cilento and Iles had held discussions with and submitted an application to the Queensland Film Corporation (QFC). Iles pointed out at the time that that New Moon's Memorandum of Association expressly stated its objects as 'theatre' and that the QFC did not invest in non-profit distributing companies which as a company limited New Moon was. Nor for that matter would it have complied under 10BA. Accordingly, a new Pty Ltd would need to be incorporated.[175]

They had applied to QFC for a $46,000 investment, the Queensland Travel and Tourist Corporation for a $22,500 donation and Shell Australia (which, as noted was already a sponsor of the Company) for $20,000. Even by the standards of the day, the sums are modest. The fourth party involved in this deal was Bruce Shepherd. To that stage, the four had signed a guarantee to repay New Moon in the event that the project did not proceed. It is not clear how much more widely Iles had consulted with the rest of the directors before landing this idea in their midst. There is no paper trail to suggest that he had, but he may have done so informally. However, some have suggested that it was his tactic to drop major reports on the board at little notice.[176] Whatever the case, on March 19, 1982 Iles asked that Board's permission for the management to act as producer for the film concurrent with obligations to New Moon itself.[177] Cilento claimed at that time that this was not an uncommon linkage and would not detract from the primacy of making the Company's theatre season work. In the event, QFC turned down their alluring offer. Iles, not to be deterred, tried lobbying the Executive Director of the QFC to reconsider and received for his trouble a curt letter from Allan Callaghan, Deputy Co-ordinator of the Department of the Arts, National Parks and Sport (which oversaw Cultural Affairs) telling him to pull his head in.[178] 'Deputy Coordinator' may seem an innocuous designation, but Callaghan, as well as being Chair of QFC, had been Joh's Press Secretary and, before a later, spectacular fall from grace which was to land both him and his free-spending wife alternately in jail for fraud, he had the Premier's ear and was known as something of a power in the land.

Nothing loathe, Ms Cilento then wrote to the Premier.[179] Somewhat oddly for a teetotaller, Joh had opened The Nautilus and might in other circumstances have been counted ideologically at least as a 'mate'. The medical Cilento family were notoriously conservative, even by Queensland standards. But this time her charm fell on deaf ears. One wonders if she had no idea who Dorothy Hewitt was in believing that her extreme left-wing politics would have proven attractive to the denizens of the Queensland National Party, or she naively thought it would not matter. In the event, both the play and the film concept sank without trace. On June 10, 1983. Iles advised that minor costs incurred in budgeting and planning the proposed documentary film of $1143.84 had been reimbursed by Cilento, Iles and O'Connell so that no loss was incurred by New Moon.[180]

Big claims

However, making theatre was always its core business and inveighing against the prime funding bodies to support the cause was a critical part of getting the Company on the yellow brick road and keeping it there. So, without greater aid, the budget approved for that first real year of operation had to provide for a deficit of ($25,611). The first return to the Corporate Affairs Office, which covered the period from incorporation in June 1981 to November 1982, showed a deficit position of ($35,239). Profit & Loss for 1981 revealed a minor shortfall of ($948). By the end of 1982, it had grown to ($34,291). Bear in mind, that overall this takes up two years of State government grants (1981 at $79,000 and 1982 at $72,000) rather than one. Added to that, was one year of Australia Council operating Grant of $79,000, plus a supplementary grant of $4,000 and a challenge grant of $4,000 for 1982 and approximately the same in cash or kind from the LGAs. In judging the result for 1981 one should also remember that while there were expenses in salaries and establishment costs there was no other income, so that the loss of just under $1,000 does not seem untoward. That the accumulated loss at the end of the first operating year had risen to effectively ($35,000) was, however, worrying. And the fact is that it only got worse year on year.

One aspect of this was the ongoing war of words with the Theatre Board. As we have seen, the diminishing annual funds from the starting level were always known, although Iles chose to behave as though he believed it to be a sudden and outrageous plot. Whatever one may think of the concept – and it is possible to argue the case rationally either way – the policy had been no secret. Clearly, Iles (strenuously backed by Queensland Cultural Activities which had gone out on a limb to underwrite the fledgling company) won the first round. He convinced the Theatre Board partly to restore the first diminished tranche with an ex gratia payment together with a Challenge Grant to be matched by contributions from the private sector. That scheme was back then very much the flavour of the day, having been borrowed from the US National Endowment for the Arts. In that country it made more sense than in 1982 Australia where the AETT was still one of the few conduits for personal income tax deductions to the performing arts.[181] But all knew such measures were just a temporary fix. The real battle needed to be on a wider front. Once the Australia Council had abandoned the sunset provision in its grants scheme, the door was open to contest funding for New Moon generally with all the rhetoric and not a little of the guile at Iles's disposal. And he went for it.

On the grounds of "in for a penny in for a pound" in the next grant round i.e. for 1984, he made an ambit claim for $150,000 – a quantum leap from the Theatre Board's previous years' annual subvention. He pulled out all stops to achieve it. Writing to FitzGerald, over the signature of New Moon's chair, Bruce Shepherd, Iles set out the case for such an immense hike.¹⁸² They were, he said, planning to extend their service to Ayr (in the recently opened Burdekin Theatre) and Gladstone (1981 which had seen the opening of the new City Theatre). The letter sought early discussion of their grant possibilities for the coming year. Since they were just half way through the second season of 'Cabaret' and 'A Midsummer Night's Dream' with 'Life on Mars' and 'Royal Show' still to come, he laid out like a magic carpet a third season of startling originality and more radical than anything that had gone before. Whereas all but one of the productions to date had been revivals, this was to be a menu of four "world premieres", starting with 'Bear Dinkum' a musical by Terry O'Connell; followed by 'The Girls from Cloudland' a new musical by actor and company member, David Sandford about Brisbane's emblematic, war-time dance hall; as well as an as a yet unnamed "musical thriller" set in a circus by Anthony Shaffer; and finally the Dorothy Hewitt silent screen tent show. The ensemble system would continue with actors (5 male, 5 female) all on $204.60 (award rate) plus touring allowance. Otherwise, it was to be an even braver, new world of New Moon.

In the course of this manifesto, Iles makes some telling and characteristically lurid observations. They appear under the heading of 'marketing' but really they go to the heart of his and the new Company's philosophy. He argued that the notions of widening the audience for subsided theatre were founded on mistaken assumptions. "The new breed of arts promoter in Australia has usually taken the view that cultural policy is quite distinct from political policy and social policy". As a result, he claimed only 2% of the population in the capital cities ever attended the subsided theatre: "the vast majority regard it as a boring, elite culture which they do not like. Usually with good reason". He later described this as "facile, passive porno-kitsch"! ¹⁸³ It is not clear to whom or what he is referring, but that not very collegial statement drew gasps from Theatre Board members when its Director was obliged to distribute it to them. It is worth reminding ourselves who constituted the audience for this diatribe. The Board was chaired by Elizabeth Butcher, long-serving and much loved administrator of NIDA, James McCaughey, Artistic Director of Geelong's Mill Theatre and a prime advocate of radical community theatre, Malcolm Moore, Director of Magpie Youth Theatre in Adelaide, Barry Moreland, Artistic Director of the WA Ballet Company, Carol Raye, actor and inventor of the 'Mavis Bramston Show', Andrew Ross, Artistic Director of Brisbane's La Boite and later founder of Perth's landmark Black Swan company, Gary Simpson, academic from Macquarie University and Cheryl Stock, then a freelance choreographer but later to establish and lead the groundbreaking Dance North. It was not exactly an establishment group and kitsch, whether pornographic or not, would have been far from their interest!

Iles went on to state that while the per capita proportion of attendance was only 6% in North Queensland, it was considerably better than in the metropolis but still not good enough. He also claimed that while the mix of audience New Moon was attracting was notably different in age and social class than what was to be found in, say, Brisbane, there was a long way to go. It is a specious argument of which Iles was no doubt aware. Almost any public event he might have chosen in any country town, from agricultural shows through race meetings to a church fete would have exhibited the same higher per capita proportion of attendance relative to those activities in the capital cities.

Programming was central to the change he advocated. Thus far "we combined 'pop' music with Shakespeare" or a new wave" look" with a twenty year old musical 'Cabaret'. "At no point do we separate 'artistic policy' from 'marketing'. We remain obsessed with solving the failures of 'establishment' programming whilst avoiding the 'ghetto' work of small venues". He went on to declare that "we want actions, body, knockabout – where the creativity of our performers is yoked to scenarios where images created by bodies, music and light are as important as the text". It is as close to the artistic vision as Iles ever expressed and one cannot help feeling that the sentiments are O'Connell's rather than his. As another example of double standards and despite New Moon's unsuccessfully trialling a subscription scheme in its first season, here he claimed that subscription is "built-in obsolescence."[184] He also lauded a cross-disciplinary approach, mentioning Chrissie Koltai who in addition to choreographing 'Cabaret' had run daily movement classes, illusionist Doug Triplett who taught everyone sleight-of-hand – no doubt a skill which was much in demand in tropical Queensland – and puppeteer Joe Gladwin. While worthy, this was not exactly revolutionary.

Potholes

But nor was it all beer and skittles. There were institutional and logistical problems as well for a company that spent its life on the road. In late 1983 the Northern Australian Performing Arts Centres Association (NARPACA) was formally complaining that New Moon had shifted it dates later in the year to times that were clashing with best periods for touring commercial product. Given their funding/guarantee relationship, New Moon could have been said to enjoy a preferred tenancy status with the four Council-owned venues in which it regularly played. But the Centres also had to be assured that they had prime dates for commercial hirers on whom their program balance, rent income, food-and-beverage sales and, above all, ticket levies heavily depended. In the face of this, Townsville Council's Community and Cultural Development Committee even went so far as to direct that, as a condition of grant, New Moon be required to schedule its first production in February that is to say in the Monsoon season.[185] Since moving one centre's dates effectively moved all, this brought the whole of the Company's annual program forward into less saleable dates the further north they went. It is not clear, but a nice thought, that this action influenced Bakaitis's choice of 'Key Largo' for his first season, (In the movie, Humphrey Bogart and Lauren Bacall are holed up in a crummy hotel with some gangsters while a Caribbean hurricane rages off South Florida). Mackay's old Theatre Royal had a tin roof under which it was impossible to be heard during torrential rain.

Not unaware that the venues had their own issues, New Moon tied up their dates and if a show failed to spark – and quite a few of them did – the presenters were down on three fronts. They were subsidising the Company, they were discounting staff and rents and, if sales were poor, they were reduced on box office or ticket charges, depending on the deal. Alternately, it needed only a couple of hits to make their fortunes for a season. 'Noises Off', 'Steaming' or 'The Rocky Horror Show' from commercial producers all fitted that bill. Those didn't come along every day or even every year, but when they did, if the venue was tied up with a New Moon booking it could be double trouble.

There were, however, other problems on the horizon. After just two seasons, O'Connell resigned not without some acrimony.[186] It was clear both from his going and the manner of it, that Iles had concluded that the talented young director no longer fitted his bill. The second year had been marginally less successful in some ways than the first. Oddly, despite its prestidigitation and generally favourable reviews, that most popular of Shakespeare's plays, 'A Midsummer Night's Dream' had not fired in Townsville and did poorly in Mackay and Rockhampton. The failure of 'Royal Show' everywhere seemed to be the last straw. "I recall it was said that the Board had decided I should go … I should say that, even with our differences, Paul was an extraordinary character. I'm not a grudge-holder and, a few years after recovering from this, I would meet him for a drink and to hear his hilarious stories …"[187] Nevertheless, it should be recorded to O'Connell's credit that overall there *was* growth. Seats sold went to a remarkable 19,338 in 1983, significantly buoyed by the Bowie show, 'Life on Mars' and to a lesser extent, 'Cabaret'.

Not long before, the long-running State coalition of the National and Liberal parties disintegrated with Premier Joh choosing to go it alone. Declaring that the government of Queensland was "in good hands" he dissolved parliament which had sat for just 15 days that year (exceeded in its infrequency only by Charles 1's legislature), called an election which he won on a notorious gerrymander attracting 38.9 % of the primary vote to give him exactly half of the parliament's 82 seats, just one short of a majority. Labor, on 44% of the vote, won just 32 seats. With the defection of two Liberal members, Ron Lane and Brian Austin (the latter afterwards to become Arts Minister), Bjelke-Petersen ruled as the only solo National Party government ever in Australia.[188]

When O'Connell was terminated there was a mild dispute over his entitlements. His contract had allowed for three months' severance from Sept 23 to 23 December, 1993. The Board resolved to pay that.[189] He also claimed payment to January 17, 1984 arguing that he had missed out on work elsewhere as a result of the late notice – a little later he became Artistic Director of the Marionette Theatre of Australia in Sydney although for a relatively short time. In the event, the Board did not agree he was due the difference and the matter lapsed. But given the time of year, irrespective of New Moon's liability, it was a less than sensitive parting with someone who had delivered the Company two years of hard foundation work and productions that had been widely acclaimed. With him, too, went the grand plan for 1984 with its slate of brand new plays of strong national and local resonance. But it was not the only unhappy severance. On January 10, 1984 a letter arrived from Poteri Woods & Co solicitors seeking compensation for designer, David Bell who had been a member of the company for the first two years and believed he had entered into a verbal agreement for work in Year Three. O'Connell's departure had put an end to that. Loose ends abounded. But however it is considered these moves marked the end of New Moon's the inaugural phase. Nothing would be quite the same again.

"Touring the Tropics"

6

The Tale Continued

Yet should we see on waking

Our tyrant's but a stone

We'll close the shutters, making

A moonlight of our own

Val Vallis – 'Song for a Moonlit Night'

Ducking and weaving

Clearly, given the timing and commitments already half entered into, the Company had to move fast to find a replacement Artistic Director. The Theatre Board was expressing concern about New Moon's having not advertised the top job and a letter to Michael FitzGerald.[190] Iles responded that they hoped to have a new person in place by mid-November. "After Terry O'Connell had decided [sic] to leave, the Board needed to consider the type of artistic director needed and opted not to advertise because we knew who we wanted to invite and didn't want to waste everyone's time with a window dressing. It would cost a lot." To that end, they drew up a list of over 90 (!!) names and tested them against their criteria. Perhaps in order to allay Queensland suspicions, they did however fly Bryan Nason up from Brisbane, though there is no indication that he was ever in serious contention.

In October 1983, Iles's funding gamble appeared to have paid off. Having chosen to enter into the general competitive round, the Company was advised it would receive $109,000 for 1984. There was however a catch. They had been placed in Category lll which meant that funding for 1985 could not be assumed. The letter of advice noted that New Moon was then without an Artistic Director and in the light of O'Connell's departure would be required to submit a revised program.[191] Iles was not so easily bought off. Further negotiations saw them elevated to Category ll which meant that there was *some* forward commitment. By early 1984, most City Councils, with the exception of Cairns, had converted their guarantees-against-loss into direct subsidy though the Shires of Thuringowa and Mulgrave continued to be guarantees. In mid-1984 Iles had written to all seven of the likely LGAs seeking an overall increase of 12.5% from $71,975 in 1984 to $91,130. He obtained a respectable $81,745, with Thuringowa still abstaining.[192]

More boldly still, in a 25 page letter of May 1 addressed to Kevin Siddell and Michael FitzGerald jointly Iles made a bid for a total of $385,000 between them or $215,000 from the State and $170,000 from Australia Council for 1985. In effect, this was 55/45 split and represented massive increases. On that basis the Federal grant increase (from $109,000) would be 58 % while the State increase would be 56%. It was a bridge too far and even Iles's unbounded optimism must have known it was unlikely to succeed. In the end, it was $123,824 from the Council and $150,000 from the State.

That said, this *was* the year of the notorious funding 'ceilings' when in truth anything might have happened.[193] The Budget had delivered a 14% increase to the Australia Council but, under the so-called Rotherwood Plan (known in some circles as the Robin Hood plan), the Theatre Board had embarked on a redistributive mechanism that aimed to clamp a ceiling of $300,000 on companies. Nevertheless, the Board's action represented a cut to its largest clients. It was the height, too, of the community theatre push and Iles aimed to position New Moon strategically as a regional company within that spectrum in the event that it should confer a financial benefit. Of course, New Moon was no more community theatre, in the sense that its practitioners like Sidetrack, Mill or Junction theatre understood it at that time, than was the Comédie-Française. New Moon was never other than serious mainstream theatre. Sexy, louche, fast and full of colour and movement it may have been, but it was never group-devised or made out of the concerns or consciousness of communities and aficionados of that world like James McCaughey, would have seen straight through such ploy.

Iles always had his ear to the ground. If there were funds to be redistributed he would hope to get some of the action and there is evidence that in this dispute he ran with the hares and hunted with the hounds. The plot is too labyrinthine to pursue here. Suffice it to say, that in the end it did not work out like that. New Moon did not gain from the imbroglio, though it is open to question if anyone did. Moreover, even if the plot had worked at Federal level there is no reason to believe that the State would have come to the party as: a) Joh's instinct would be to go against any Hawke government trend; and b) Queensland would have been busy shoring up those companies like QTC that would certainly lose out under the ceiling proposal.

Meanwhile back at the ranch, moves to replace O'Connell were well under way. A mere 23 days after his departure Helmut Bakaitis is described as "Artistic Director designate".[194] He commenced on November 21 at a salary of $425.76 per week after tax.[195] Thus, by a combination of active selection and sleight of hand, he became, in effect, New Moon's second Artistic Director. The choice was an interesting one. Bakaitis was a distinguished actor, notably at the Melbourne Theatre Company, and had been part of the landmark triumvirate that led the State Theatre of South Australia in the mid-1970s. There, among other achievements, he had pioneered youth theatre production in a State which was to become celebrated in that genre. At the time of the New Moon call he was Artistic Director of the well-regarded St Martin's Youth Theatre in Melbourne. He did not, however, have a significant record of directing adult theatre or of any experience in the regions. By his own account, the New Moon approach was a complete surprise. "I'd met Paul a few times and knew of his reputation, with Nimrod especially. Then one day he called and asked me if I knew anyone who might be suitable as Artistic Director. He filled me in on the Company". Bakaitis asked around his circle but they all had other commitments. "I thought about it and called him back had asked: would you be interested in me? And he said, yes." Then Bakaitis was off to check it out. "We flew to Cairns and then came right down the coast to Rockie". Bakaitis also did a lot of his own research among those who had been involved. "Valerie Bader and Gillian Hyde, had acted with the Company and were particularly helpful, including warning me about Paul and some of his aberrant behaviour. But I was ready for a change. The climate was a big factor. I'd had six years in damp Melbourne in a very demanding job with all the challenges of working with young people and I'd had a severe bout of hepatitis. It sounded like paradise".[196]

Yet, at his very first meeting with the Board, Bakaitis raised a crucial question, which in a way was never resolved as long as New Moon existed i.e. whether the Company was there: "to entertain the people of Central and North Queensland or to service its four civic centres?" "The kind of theatre wanted by audiences", he said "was not necessarily restricted to civic architecture".[197] It was the first overt questioning of whether the much-lauded and ground-breaking business model was necessarily fit for artistic purpose. It also suggested that he was to be a shrewder judge of circumstances than some of those who had come before him. He had, after all, lived through the highly politicised arts environment of Adelaide in the 1970s and gone on to do a Master's degree in the UK as well as run a theatre in Melbourne. Nevertheless: "Paul never really told me where he wanted the Company to go."[198]

But the on-again-off-again pattern of management also continued and again with occasional unhappy results. In 1984 Iles had retained the Rea Francis Company in Birchgrove, Sydney for the seemingly trifling sum of $1,000 to generate media coverage in the south to cover the forthcoming season.[199] It was one of a series of such shotgun moves which were to characterise his administration and generate unnecessary antagonism in the industry to no discernible benefit. A bare month later he had withdrawn the offer. The firm wrote in high dudgeon threatening legal action unless out-of-pocket expenses were met.

Happier for some, however, was the announcement that Her Majesty had seen fit early that year to create the Queensland Premier a Knight Commander of the Order of St Michael and St George (KCMG) for "services to parliamentary democracy". Some unkind folk suggested that Joh had made the nomination himself. Others searched in vain for instances of that democracy in George Street, Brisbane.[200]

Travelling south

Perhaps, in order to move closer to the glow of this anointing down south, or (as Bakaitis remembers it): "to get Paul further away from the fun on the Barrier Reef", in May 1984, after just two years residency in Cairns, New Moon declared they would be moving to Rockhampton that September. The announcement at the time declared: "We have greatly enjoyed living in Cairns, but the conditions in Rockhampton are as ideal; an energetic City Council which gives high priority to arts development; the modern and well-managed Pilbeam Theatre; and a new open-air theatre under construction". In addition, the City Council had offered New Moon "superb premises in the School of Arts building".[201] They aimed to spend no fewer than two years in Rockie.

Curiously, Iles chose to pull out even more stops about the move. In the local daily newspaper he was quoted as saying that provincial Queenslanders were the: "most cultured people in Australia". Even allowing for a degree of tongue-in-cheek, it was rather over the top. He based his claim on a recent Australia Council research publication *Australia's Attitudes to the Arts*. "It was consistently apparent", he said "that provincial Queensland has the highest proportion of people who attend or patronise all forms of the arts."[202] Ian Satchwell, the Pilbeam Theatre administrator, no doubt wary of linking sheer numbers with a value judgement such as the degree of being 'cultured' (whatever that might mean), more discreetly than Iles confined himself to pointing out that 70,000 patrons had attended his venue the previous year. Wisely, he chose not to argue for exceptionalism in that regard. Statistics, it has been said, can be used to prove everything or nothing and the Australia Council's periodic bulletins on these matters, beyond being obviously self-serving, have never proven particularly useful nor indeed always very reliable.

But not surprisingly this glorious relationship was destined soon to sour – for a number of reasons. The costs of using the Pilbeam Theatre for both production and performance weeks began to break the budget, though in fact *that* was becoming a problem everywhere in Australia. Despite the best endeavours of Satchwell's successor, Malcolm Calder who was also on the New Moon Board, to find ways to ameliorate the situation, it was a major contributor to the Company's ever-growing deficit. Moreover, Rockhampton audiences proved to be less enthusiastic and many fewer than had been anticipated and the City Council's largesse had hidden traps. Calder remembers it as being not as encouraging as New Moon's rhetoric had suggested. It was yet another example of where Iles's enthusiasm was not matched by Bakaitis's practicality. "I do recall [Helmut] being less than impressed with the rehearsal premises and 'base' provided by the Council. And, in truth, he was dead right – the old School of Arts was a pigeon-infested dump that current rules and regulations would prohibit from use. But I think the Council saw itself as assisting the Company by providing it to New Moon at no cost."[203]

But more than money, that first Bakaitis season also gave rise to some decidedly unpleasant public controversy. In fact, it was really *the* controversy of New Moon's career. Oddly, it occurred around what was in many ways the least likely of all the works chosen for that year and ostensibly for almost the least likely reason. Just as odd, it took place in Rockhampton, so recently extolled as a bastion of the cultured appreciation of high art.

David Williamson's play 'Don's Party' had been updated by New Moon from its original setting during the 1969 Federal Election in which a resurgent Labor Party, newly led by Gough Whitlam, had come close to defeating the Gorton Coalition government. The New Moon reference was, however, to the 1983 Queensland State election. The analogy was imperfect since no one seriously believed that the Bjelke-Petersen gerrymander was threatened at that time and the attempt at "relevance" was largely phoney. Nevertheless, the playwright had given it his seal of approval, a leading historian had worked on it and the production *qua* production had been well received.

Then the *l'affaire Doplo* erupted. This will be detailed in the next chapter. Suffice it to say here that a Rockhampton alderman took exception to what she regarded as obscene language. The front page publicity was invaluable and there were some who believed that Iles had deliberately stoked the flames. But in the end, it was a nine-day wonder. Or was it? To some extent Ms Doplo's concern had smothered a bigger issue and one that would soon emerge as a greater concern: the Company's tendency to bite the hand that was so generously feeding it. The political critique did not especially come to the surface then, but nerves were exposed and resentment was growing about Iles's tendency to rub the authorities' nose (whether at local or State level) in what he clearly saw as their antediluvian ways. Apart from four letter words, 'Don's Party' marked a turning point in the Company's fortunes. The Doplo effect had made waves nationally as a *cause célèbre*. With the following production, 'Beach Blanket Tempest' (BBT) New Moon aimed to make waves of a different sort as a flagship to sail across the country. But the tide had already turned.

However one interprets all this, by mid-1985 New Moon wanted out of Rockie. Cairns and Townsville had provided the better audience numbers though not always for the same productions, and unlike Rockhampton they were growth centres with significant tourism or at least transient populations. Actual events in the Capricornian 'capital' only intensified their disappointment. The next stop was planned to be Mackay, once its new theatre was built. That move was never to take place, despite some strenuous lobbying late in the Company's history by its then Director, the formidable John Young.

Moving sideways

At all events, 'BBT', the last production of that year and incidentally the last time New Moon undertook four productions in a year, had varied success. Generally well received critically at 'home', it had mixed fortunes elsewhere. For all that, it is perhaps the only New Moon production widely remembered by theatre-goers and the only one to tour extensively beyond the region. Later in the year, as noted, it was toured out of Queensland to southern capitals under a range of deals the making of which had always been one of Iles's strong suits. Today, he would be called transactional. Back then, he was just a wheeler dealer. The partners were, in turn, the Adelaide Festival Centre where obviously he had good connections, Canberra Theatre Centre and the newly rechristened Footbridge Theatre in Sydney. The last was the most interesting of all. Previously the Union Theatre at Sydney University on Parramatta Road, the licence had recently been granted to the novice Gordon Frost organisation, a partnership of Ashley Gordon and John Frost then starting out on what was to become one of the most successful commercial theatrical managements ever in Australia. The surviving partner, John Frost, remains one of a handful of home-grown producers (notably of musicals) who can genuinely be described as being of international stature. Then, they were just beginning and Iles offered them a slice of the action on his new wave musical adventure by Dennis Watkins and Chris Harriott. Those two already had a name in Sydney through such ragers as their satirical 'Dingo Girl' which had appeared at the Footbridge only two years before. In each case, Iles negotiated not a straight sell-off but a risk-sharing deal. He had endeavoured to lure the AETT as guarantor of last resort, but they had declined his offer. The plan was that the three-city tour should cost the parent company nothing, apply no Queensland grant money and ideally return a profit. The venture cost $136,912 and made $153,037 thereby rendering a net contribution to North Queensland activity of $16,125. It was useful but nowhere near what the Company had aimed for. All three seasons made a modest surplus: Adelaide $2,065, Canberra $2,387 and Sydney $11,082.[204]

The complex deal that Iles had entered into for 'Beach Blanket Tempest' thus made a small addition to the bottom line, but not nearly enough to stave off the impending storm. First-time tours with a new work by an unknown company have certainly fared much worse in Australia's theatrical history. An Australia Council Access and Participation grant enabled the production to tour also to Mt Isa and Alice Springs. The Isa stint recalled the grisly old days of Arts Council touring. There had not been a play visit there for four years. The caretaker/technician was on two weeks annual leave and Iles concluded in his board report that New Moon probably wouldn't return there in a hurry. By contrast, the Araluen Arts centre was the best managed and supportive presenting body in the country, he said. It was a dig no doubt, albeit a foolish one, at the Queensland theatres that were the Company's sustaining partners and typical of his lack of discretion in such matters.[205]

As a model for the future, the 'BBT' venture it must have been mildly heartening. The combination of government support to go to more remote communities plus commercial and co-presenting deals in the southern states seemed like a good mix and had resulted in the Company's most extensive tour to date. That, however, was never to be repeated. Had 'BBT' done better on home ground, it might have been accounted a triumph. Part of the problem was that the work itself just wasn't very good. It was not Shakespearean enough to pose a genuine spoof in the way that, for instance, 'Do Your Own Thing' had managed with 'Twelfth Night' in the 1960s or even 'Hair' with its clever bows to 'Hamlet'. In any event, the beach blanket movie phenomenon was a feature of American teenagery of the 1960s and peculiar to its hyper-naïve culture of the time. It had little reference to the beach experience of Australian youth. Like 'Stompin' at Maroubra, it was well and truly dead by 1968. True, there was a revival of cult interests in the film genre in the 1980s, but it is arguable if ironic camp was a prime aesthetic concern of Northern Queensland theatregoers in 1984; nor, as it turned out, with their allegedly more discerning peers in Sydney, Canberra and Adelaide. Melbourne and Brisbane were spared the experience. Meanwhile, back home in the *Daily Bulletin*, Jill Mathers asked: "Is New Moon more interested in Adelaide acclaim than servicing the North?"

By then, other matters had also gone sour. "The moment we opened 'Beach Blanket Tempest' it was as though I didn't exist," Bakaitis recalled. "Paul called company meetings to which I wasn't invited. By the end of that first year our relationship had entirely broken down and I felt increasingly pushed out".[206]

The 1985 season of just three works seemed ill-assorted and scarcely calculated to inject new energy into the Company's fortunes. The American musical 'Guys and Dolls' and the stage adaption of 'On Our Selection' seemed curiously mismatched with the Marxist Italian Dario Fo's 'Trumpets and Raspberries'. Bakaitis had seen the last in London on a lightning and unexpected trip there with Iles. "In my naivety I thought all those Italians in North Queensland would love it!"[207] One might argue that the line-up was no less coherent than the three previous years, but with one fewer production the imbalance had increased proportionately. The resultant numbers spoke for themselves: 'Guys and Dolls' sold 5,767 making it marginally better than 'Cabaret' two years earlier (5,368); 'On our Selection' as one might hope with an Australian classic, sold a more than a respectable 4,706; 'Trumpets and Raspberries' achieved a pitiful 1055 with a mere 172 in total attending in Rockhampton; 'Royal Show' in 1983, which until then had been the worst-attended New Moon production, managed over twice that at 2,310 including 538 in Rockhampton.

Various options

To get a sense of what this all meant, let us look at the broader financial picture during those first four years. The bottom line over the period is critical, but the detail, item by item, is also instructive. On the face of it, there are two foundation years of sharp growth in expenses followed by two years of relative stabilising.

EXPENDITURE	1982 $	1983	% inc	1984	% inc	1985	% inc
Wages	202,970	257,941	27%	302,031	17%	343,873	14%
Production/Theatre	132,486	155,126	17%	222,724	43%	193,703	(13%)
Sales/Promotions	31,652	92,455	192%	105,139	14%	82,000	(22%)
Administration	17,843	29,791	70%	34,766	17%	35,475	2%
	384,951	535,313	39%	664,660	24%	665,051	(1)
INCOME							
Box office	133,324	172,127	29%	201,709	22%	151,000	(28%)
Other earned	15,578	11,690	(24%)	30,521	161%	28,068	(8%)
Australia Council	87,000	102,691	18%	144,000	40%	123,824	(14%)
State Government	158,000	86,961	(45%)	136,250	56%	150,000	10%
Local Government	42,272	68,074	61%	72,476	6%	82,495	14%
Sponsorship	17,740	59,936	237%	54,432	(9%)	46,050	(15%)
	453,914	501,688	10%	648,388	29%	581,437	(10%)

While there is a similar pattern for the first three years in revenue, in the fourth year it alters abruptly. Certainly, one show failed dismally, but the real problem was the change in level of activity. Wages continued to rise although there were three plays not four. Production/Theatre costs sank 13%, but box office declined by 28%. In other words, just at the point where deficits, while increasing were still containable at ($59,665) for 1984/85, the Company took the decision to cut the season, thereby exposing themselves to greater not less risk, The deficit skyrocketed. It is a common paradox and indicative of an absence of proper financial modelling.

The data above are too summarised to demonstrate entirely clear conclusions as to why there was a widening gap between the costs of operation and income. However, Bakaitis has one (albeit minor) explanation: "We flew everywhere on tour. I wondered why and suggested we could do just as well by hiring some cars or even a bus. Later I understand that somehow Paul benefitted from the Ansett discount deal".[208] Whatever the case, the figures clearly show that 1985 was the crucial year. The vulnerability of the Company to box office shortfall was well known to the Board. Iles stated at the time "I have warned with monotonous regularity how one box-office failure would ruin the company as we have no capital base."²⁰⁹ Indeed, analysis created at that time by Australia Council's senior financial officer, Bob Taylor agreed.²¹⁰ The problem with comparing one year to another was slightly distorted by special events and these must be taken into account in calculating and interpreting the percentages rise and fall. In short those factors were:

> 1982: Conversion of two years' State Government subsidy into one year (the Company started a year later than planned so $79,000 was carried forward into 1982 even though there was some expenditure in 1981).
>
> 1983: Local government box office guarantees were converted to direct grants resulting in extra grant income of $25,802.
>
> 1984: New Moon obtained supplementary Australia Council 'Access and Participation' funds of $35,000 towards a two week tour of 'Beach Blanket Tempest' to Mount Isa and Alice Springs with net costs of only $20,000 yielding a 'bonus' of $15,000.
>
> 1985: New Moon made a surplus of $16,125 as noted above on the interstate tour of 'Beach Blanket Tempest' which fed into the 1985 budget.

In retrospect, the scale of New Moon's financial worries pales beside other money dealings in Queensland at that time. Later investigations would reveal that by 1985 the Police Commissioner, Sir Terrence Lewis, was estimated to be receiving some $114,996 in bribes and other kickbacks for which he was subsequently to be de-knighted and jailed. A struggling theatre company was small beer by comparison.²¹¹

Nevertheless, by August 1985 before the last production it was clear that things had reached a crisis point for New Moon. Despite its overall success 'Guys and Dolls' had failed in all but Cairns to sell to the level needed. The Board was divided on just about every issue. At its August meeting in Mackay that year, it considered the 'Future Options' paper prepared by Iles but allegedly with input from company members and a Board committee.²¹² The meeting was attended by Kevin Radbourne, Acting Director of Queensland Department of Cultural Activities and Bob Taylor and David Thompson from the Australia Council. While the paper made no recommendations as such, among the options canvassed were that the Company might close down or that it should change leadership – a rather daring suggestion considering its source!

There is almost a note of exasperation in the document. While Iles is at pains to point out that the management was not recommending any particular "exclusive option", some suggestions are more loaded than others and for obvious reasons all were not mutually exclusive. He did, however, rank the 13 wildly disparate preferences as: postpone next season from February to July 1986, tour to cities beyond the core four; move back to Townsville; replace the current management; cease to be a subsidised company; change to being a Theatre-in-Education company; liquidate; reduce activities to small cast plays; merge with Brisbane-based Queensland companies; merge with NQ ballet; increase ticket prices, reduce expenditure, continue operating at present level of activity. It was a hodgepodge.

The first four were taken up. La Luna, though not TIE as such, did evolve from the wreckage. While the idea of merging with the Royal Queensland Theatre Company, Lyric Opera and even TN was palpably loopy, the notion of an amalgamation, perhaps through a shared management, with what was to become Dance North might well have proved useful. Increasing ticket prices and reducing expenditure were motherhood devices which who has not tried at some time? Attention at the meeting fractured over a variety of issues. Ms Cilento in the Chair, perhaps naturally considering her background, attributed the box office reversals to lack of 'personality' in the acting company, although she acknowledged that the production values were the "best she had seen at New Moon".[213] She quibbled, too, about poor attendances on opening nights in all cities. Fred Thompson, director from Townsville, perceptively took the view that the Company had simply "run of out goodwill". Audiences could not relate to it because they did not get to know the actors. He himself was hard-pressed to put a single face to a name. But his greatest criticism was that: "for four years its philosophical outlook to each city ... had been contemptuous from the outset". All this was a not-so-veiled attack on Iles and, in particular, his "failing to appreciate the environment in which the Company worked and his ignorance of the disciplines imposed by those circumstances." As well', Thompson argued: "management's failure to recognise those factors would undo any good work achieved and bring the Company to a crashing halt through Mr Iles' [sic] propensity for casual, facetious remarks".[214] Even the 'Future Options' paper he said "contained sideswipes at Local Government". Some directors also considered that its subtext was that Iles wanted the Company to fold. Bakaitis had no doubt of that: "At a meeting in Brisbane with Bruce Shepherd he said: "Every theatre company has a logical life"" with the implication that New Moon had reached it. "I didn't agree. By then, the Board hated Paul and he treated them with contempt. His method was to inundate them with figures. He would table a 35 page report that they could never have got round to reading. That was his method."[215]

Councillor Dawson and Alderman Moore, who had worked in local government for many years, argued to the contrary. They did not find those references offensive, though they had other reservations. Townsville's Alderman Valentine was more concerned with whether the LGAs were getting value for their money. Long-term Company advocate businessman and Associate Director, Brian Sweeney, tried to come to the rescue. He declared himself at a loss to reconcile all the supposed public alienation and talk of failure with the overall box office trend. He noted that attendance had averaged 234 in 1982, 302 in 1983 and 316 in 1984 and thus far in 1985 it was 343, (though that was to change markedly with the downturn of Dario Fo's 'Trumpets and Raspberries' from which, as we have seen, the public abstained in droves.) The time in Queensland was not quite right for revolutionary fervour. The sound of the political tumbrels was still some way off. They would not begin to roll in earnest for another two years sounding the knell of the ancient "Joh" regime. But in 1985 the regime, antique or otherwise, was still riding high and the Jacobins of New Moon challenged it at their peril.

At the meeting, even Kevin Radbourne's legendary calming presence and overt support expressed for the Company by the State Government, could not entirely conceal his reservations about Iles's cavalier behaviour. He "cautioned the Company not to offend the Queensland Government in its choice of plays" (a reference presumably to 'Don's Party') or in its public statements. Iles, he said, had "occasionally made disrespectful comments about the Queensland Government". That said, Radbourne, ever the compleat public servant, stressed that the Department "had a

Treasury commitment to forward funding" provided New Moon didn't go off the financial rails.[216] In other words, he warned them not to bite the hand that fed them, which was sage advice in any place, but especially in a state of, shall we say, 'guided democracy'. Perhaps, more tellingly of all, even while strenuously defending the range of the Company's outreach through such workshops and collaborations as it was able to undertake, Bakaitis acknowledged that the Company had indeed "run out of goodwill". He instanced as proof of this the reduction in media sponsorships and discounts".[217] These were the very things Iles was supposed to secure and to be a master at securing. Bakaitis meanwhile continued to feel sidelined: "I was interested in the administrative side, but Paul was very possessive of all that aspect".[218]

Is there a further subtext in all of this rising negativity? Hardly spoken above a whisper and even now studiously avoided in most of the conversations which the author has had, is the question of sexuality in all of this. That is to say, what significance was there in the fact, verging at times on the notorious, that a number of the key players in New Moon were gay? Joh and his government were famously homophobic.[219] Beyond doubt, it was an attitude shared across state and local government on both sides of politics and in much if not most of the general public. Equally, it was held in society, accurately or not, that the arts harboured a higher proportion of gay people than other occupations. The author has not conducted a survey to establish whether this might have been true in New Moon's case. Nor is it factually relevant. Certainly, the Company exhibited a flamboyance often mistaken as a determinant for being 'gay'. (Not so long ago an Afghan refugee claiming gay persecution in his homeland was denied asylum in Austria because he appeared insufficiently flamboyant in manner and dress).[220] How much of the sudden turn-off to New Moon might have been so attributed?

It is perhaps indicative of the dilemma at this point that, on the one hand, the Board resolved at the meeting that it wanted the Company to continue and even expand. Item 6 in the 'Future Options' paper was to grow activities with the aim of touring state-wide, or in other words, to become *the* touring company of regional Queensland. On the other, it believed that undertaking four productions in 1986 to even the four base centres could lift the deficit to an unsustainable ($120,000). Accordingly, Directors voted to again undertake just three in that year. This was further unravelling of the grand adventure and, as we have seen earlier, probably and paradoxically contributed to worsening rather than improving the bottom line. It was also the writing on the wall for Iles. Clearly, Bakaitis had lost confidence in the chief executive. The Board was increasingly, though not unanimously, stacked against him. Iles had simply offended too many people along the way. While the city-based funders could accept that with a pinch of snuff, a wink and a nod in view of his many other skills and talents, the good burghers of Capricornia had had enough. By the end of the year he was gone, leaving Bakaitis to try to put the pieces back together. But try as he might, like Humpty Dumpty they never quite fitted again.

While New Moon seemed to be, temporarily at least, heading down hill, other aspects of public life were looking up. Lest we provide only a negative view of the Bjelke-Petersen government, it is important to record that 1985 saw the opening of the splendacious Queensland Performing Centre on Brisbane's Southbank which provided the venue-starved capital with a new Concert Hall, Lyric Theatre and studio space, added to the complex of cultural institutions growing on the former Expo site and completed the circuit of performing arts complexes in Canberra, Adelaide, Sydney and Melbourne. Joh was at the same time extolling the potential of a Space Port on Cape York, arguably one of his better ideas. On a more terrestrial level along with the many other major projects to his credit, may be counted the electrification of the entire North-South railway line up the Queensland Coast to Cairns which joined the four cities in New Moon's domain, and incidentally created the most extensive such non-diesel track in the country. It was, of course, all about coal-burning furnaces driving cheap electricity production, but let that pass.

Paul has left the building

Iles left New Moon in October 1985: It is typical that his departure was as tortured in the telling as was his arrival. Directors noted at the proximate Board meeting that he was inclined to give different versions to different listeners.[221] To some, he claimed to have been sacked but it was clear that after his return from a flying trip to Sydney, he had his letter of resignation already written. To others that he had resigned though it is Bakaitis's clear recollection that Iles was in fact let go.[222] Whatever the truth of the matter, there was a measure of relief all round. The final straw had been his absence during the premiere of 'Trumpets and Raspberries'. Much of the negativity surrounding the Company had focussed on him and his often, to North Queensland eyes, outlandish behaviour. Bakaitis was respected as a talented, professional, hard-working director liked even by those who did not always see eye to eye with his artistic decisions. Love it or hate it, the public could see and understand his value and the hugely talented company of actors, directors and designers he assembled and was bringing to audiences in the North. Outsiders (and even some insiders) found it harder to understand what Iles was by then really contributing. While to this day Bakaitis has only esteem for the energy and flair that Iles brought to the enterprise, some frustration is apparent in documents at the time.

Above all, the criticism which Rodney Fisher would make the following year in a further commissioned analysis of the downturn in publicity and in particular the lack of promotion of the acting company is telling.[223] Especially given his long professional and personal association with Bakaitis, it is likely that to some degree his opinions echoed the Artistic Director's own views. But the greater reality is probably that by 1985 Iles had lost interest. His rapid succession of tenures in England, at Nimrod and the State Theatre SA suggests a short attention span in any job. He was still a very restless young man whose temper operated on a short wick and by then he thought New Moon had run its race.

Iles did play a classic impresario role. As the song in 'Chicago' goes he always tried to "razzle-dazzle 'em". Most of the time he was doing a rather elaborate tap routine and then someone just took the dance floor away. But for as long as he was there tapping, it seemed believable. Bakaitis's verdict is appropriately mixed: "He was enlivening; he was extraordinary; he was a live wire; and yes he cared about theatre. He mainly knew about how to work the system and by that I mean how to get the most out of every dollar for the benefit of whoever."[224]

However, despite his private claim to some of being sacked, Iles stated publicly that he was to take up a position of Artistic associate of the Toneelgroep Theatre in Amsterdam, commencing the following May.[225] The implication of that announcement was that this had been something in negotiation for some time and scarcely fits either with being fired or a sudden wilful act of resignation. In fact, he went to Perth for a brief stint at the Hole in the Wall theatre which was then also sliding downhill. Thence, he returned to the UK to undertake stellar work first with the Grand Theatre Blackpool. thereafter moving to the Theatre Royal in Edinburgh in 1996 and, finally, as a respected teacher of arts management at the Liverpool Institute of the Arts until his untimely death from a rare cancer in 2011.[226]

A new beginning

Iles was quickly succeeded by the very novice administrator, Ruth Bereson. Like Bakaitis before her Bereson was yanked out of Melbourne and out of the blue to serve the New Moon cause. Unlike Bakaitis however she was a complete tyro: "I think the only reason I was chosen was because I knew so little and they thought they could mould me".[227] A graduate of Melbourne University, she had briefly worked at the Victorian Arts Ministry before moving to study in Paris then returning to her home city where she was employed at the Griffin Gallery. "My work there and background was if anything in community arts. I knew nothing about theatre management". Dona Greaves, by then Director of Cultural Activities in Brisbane, had been an Assistant Director at the Victorian Ministry before going to Queensland and used her contacts to locate a likely suspect. "One day I had a call from Michael Mitchener at the Ministry whom I'd known at University. He told me to expect a call from Helmut Bakaitis. I knew Helmut by reputation, especially his great work at St Martin's, but had never met him." Again, it was typical of the off-the-cuff New Moon method that the Company would veer from having one of the most well-known and experienced CEOs to selecting a completely unknown and untried recruit. Panic? Urgency? Complacency? Needs must? No doubt all of these, but there is no hard evidence to suggest which. Indeed, there is no evidence, least of all from the appointee, to suggest that there was process of any kind. Bereson leapt at the chance. "I was 26. It seemed like a fabulous opportunity to be part of something extraordinary and ground-breaking". Today, she describes is as "the audacity of ignorance. Literally one day I was in Melbourne. The next in Sydney meeting Helmut at the Regent Hotel, then Brisbane to meet Greaves and Radbourne and then Townsville".[228]

Certainly, the Job description for the" manager" circulated at the time was more optimistic than realistic. They sought a "theatre promoter, fund raiser, cost controller, theatre manager and funding bureaucrat". While Bereson had some experience in the last and proved adept at cost control, she had little or no experience in the rest. Curiously, too, the JD stated that "the artistic policy for 1986/87 will most likely shift towards "community theatre" activities, as opposed to mainstream-musical theatre."[229] Quite how Diane Cilento starring in a Broadway play about a crazed nun, an Australian showbiz mother and son in a two person autobiographical musical, and a homage to John Lennon with a rock star stage personality could be said to fulfil the community theatre brief is hard to fathom. There were a few feints in that direction with the tangential involvement in a community theatre project in Rockhampton, but realistically little had changed. At all events, Bereson was appointed as "Administrator" which later became "General Manager". For two years she endeavoured to keep the sinking ship afloat . One of those years was with Bakaitis, the other effectively on her own. It was by anyone's standards trial by fire.

By 31 December, 1985 the accumulated deficit had soared to ($158,040). The paradox of that is that, when the decision was taken to reduce from four to three productions, the forecast had been for a net operating deficit for the year of ($82,242) or an accumulated deficit of ($97,828).[230] The reduced season resulted in an accumulated deficit one third greater again. Another blow was registered in private sector support for 1986 that fell to $22,700. It is scarcely surprising given a) less activity, b) negative commentary and c) news of the dire financial position that had spread far and wide. Notwithstanding, that aspect of the Company's revenue had been impressive for its first few years. Total private sector support to that point was $198,200. Shell had been a consistent sponsor together with local media. But other notables were UTAH, MIM, Ian Potter Foundation, Ansett, Avis, Wolf Blass, BHP and Castlemaine Perkins.

Nevertheless, leading into 1986 it had become clear to all that, as Giuseppe di Lampedusa observed: if we seek to have everything stay as it is, some things need to change. At the previous Board meeting several amendments were made to the company structure and management. Alderman Valentine was elected chair of the Board.[231] The immediate task facing the Company in February 1986 was to rebuild its credibility, particularly within the home base. This was attempted on a various levels: public meetings were called in all four centres.[232] Groups interested in theatre and drama were invited to bring their needs to New Moon's attention. As a consequence, a series of community projects was developed for each of the cities. It was the first time that a serious and concerted attempt was made to think along these lines and was, perhaps, a measure of the change that the partnership of Bakaitis and Bereson – who had come from a very different background and understanding from that which Paul Iles had bought to the mix. Bakaitis, of course, had a long and distinguished record in youth theatre and in and through that in community outreach, though he was not himself someone who focussed particularly on grassroots activity. Whatever and whoever was driving the change, the difference was notable.

Curiously, Bakaitis recounts that: "it was only after the board sacked him [that Paul remarked] 'so now you are going to do all the stuff I wanted you to do in the first place'. 'What are you talking about?' [I asked and] he said: 'the community stuff'. 'But you never mentioned that, Paul. That was never part of the plan'."[233]

Suddenly, everyone was on the road making contacts, spreading the word and offering counsel. Bereson met with amateur associations in Rockhampton and assisted them with submissions for funding at state level. Bakaitis had given a week-long workshop on the development of writing skills for aspiring authors and it was hoped that some of the individuals who had participated in the workshop would submit scripts to the Northern Queensland playwrights conference later in that year. Bakaitis also spent a week in Glendon. a mining town approximately 1½ hours drive out of Mackay where he worked with teachers and students of that town on drama workshops focusing on mime and skills development. The response to these initiatives had been "overwhelming". Ruth Bereson was able to report to her Board that "New Moon confidently looked forward to seeing busloads of town dwellers at its productions in the near future."[234]

Guest experts were also part of the new wave. Jeremy Wright from Ogilvie and Mather in Sydney, who went on to play a significant role in marketing and fundraising for many Australian arts organisations, had been sponsored by the Australia Council and the DCA to undertake workshops on marketing the arts. New Moon was eager to use him. He gave sessions in Mackay and which benefitted the Company and its reputation with the many community groups that participated. A working relationship had also been forged between the Company and the regional music coordinator based in Mackay whose knowledge and daily contact with groups in that city had facilitated easy contacts for New Moon. As a consequence, Bereson was able to meet with some fifteen community groups with diverse interests and help them to formulate their ideas and needs for state government submissions.

Meanwhile, during the whole year Joh had been pushing a scheme to build the world tallest skyscraper in Brisbane. Many thought it odd that the analogy of Babel should have escaped the notice of such a man of faith as he.

One of the items eagerly taken up from Iles's earlier 'Options Paper' was that of extending the Company's touring reach. This was all part of a yet bigger picture. Dona Greaves had seen the Company's playing to more regional centres as a critical trade-off for its increased funding; as was the concept she had urged on it to become a re-granting agency for the state government of small arts grant recipients north of the Tropic of Capricorn; and from 1986/87 taking on a role as, in effect, an auspicing body for that purpose. But the function went further into more active advocacy aimed at advising such applicants not only about how they might access support from DCA but also how to apply to the Australia Council and under what categories.

Saving the furniture

Greaves made all that very clear in a letter to the Company congratulating it on its work. The process, she claimed, had led to more success for Queensland in Australia Council grant rounds and thus represented a net increase in Federal money coming into the State.[235] It was an argument not dissimilar to that which Brian Sweeney had made two years before when local government was being restive about their contributions, asking if they genuinely wanted to forego the matching state and federal money their funding attracted into their districts. This was also at a time when the Premier had virtually forbidden his public servants to have any dealings with their Federal counterparts. Thus, for Ms Greaves and her colleagues in DCA such moves had to be subtle and multifaceted, even if they felt more like cloak and dagger at the time. Nevertheless, this approach was also not without its concerns and internal critics. Some feared too close an alignment with the Government might be a conflict of interest. Malcolm Calder wrote to the Chairman: "I wish to record my concern at the direction the Company is taking with respect to the processing of Queensland Government grant applications. While the community benefits which accrue from this are self-evident, it should also be pointed out the dangers potentially exist when a subsidised company is fulfilling a quasi-governmental (albeit advisory) function ... It might also be pointed out that this role is out of step with the relationship of most other subsidised companies in this State."[236]

That New Moon was to be based in Townsville from 1986 had meant that for the first time it could also develop a year-round series of drama classes. The Company had begun to work with Jocelyn McKinnon, a trained drama teacher who had recently relocated from Melbourne. She started Saturday morning classes at just $2 a session for children aged 7 to 13. The response was high and consistent. Within a very short time there was a waiting list. Until that time the better-off schools in Townsville had offered in-house drama teaching, but there was little for the less well-resourced sectors of society. Accordingly, New Moon was tapping into real demand and presumably at a price parents could afford. It was the birth of what was to become the estimable La Luna and despite some counter claims and some comings and goings, it is McKinnon must be considered that company's prime mover. There was as yet no distinct subsidy for this activity which began simply as an outreach of New Moon itself.[237] Bakaitis also encouraged a recent NIDA graduate Jeremy Johnson into this arrangement, with mixed and finally fractious results.

At the same time, the door was slowing opening to liaison with James Cook University. Both Bereson and Bakaitis had been invited to take places on its drama course advisory committee and as well as the Townsville Youth Theatre committee. Both visited Cairns on a number of occasions and assisted amateur theatrical groups on administrative and artistic matters. Members of the Cairns community were invited to contribute backstage crew on 'Agnes of God' and as a consequence a member of the Cairns Little theatre was employed by the Company. New Moon actors, including Cilento, gave workshops on the Laban technique to over 50 participants and more were planned. These were all important developments and represented activities in which the Company was only now belatedly becoming involved – perhaps too belatedly.

Above all, and arguably for the first time, the Company was taking seriously the need to have a coherent marketing plan rather than a series of ad hoc approaches which until then had not been well developed. This was mostly because of the curiosities of their business model in which so much promotion was in the hands of the four principal presenters. That is not a new dilemma. Many touring organisations in Australia and elsewhere whose sales are handled by third party gatekeepers, such as performing arts centres, festivals and the like, find themselves with limited capacity to develop their own identity in those different markets separate from that of the presenters themselves. Now, for the first time, New Moon recognised the need to engage a full-time marketing officer in an attempt to control more of its branding and sales.

But looming overall was one very large problem. It has become clear that the artistic policy of the previous four years combined with the financial strain of employing between 20 and 25 company members touring for six months each year had resulted in an unsustainable deficit. The folly of maintaining a policy demonstrably ineffective for too long had now to be regretfully acknowledged. It had also become clear that there were three possible brands of "theatre product" of which the New Moon Theatre Company ("pleasure tested" or otherwise) was by then in desperate need.

Rodney Fisher recognised this in his 1986 analysis: He argued that those brands were first: "a small cast play that is easy and inexpensive to mount featuring well-known players" whose personalities and expertise would help boost the image of the Company and whose presence considerably aid box office appeal. A "solid gold hit could obviously have a dramatic impact on the fortunes of New Moon". The second, (again small cast) was to find an outstanding New Moon production which emanated from the North and which "having succeeded locally is of sufficiently high calibre to tour elsewhere" thus making money while New Moon maintained its community interaction. And third would be the eventual major achievement of a play 'written in the North about the North, performed by New Moon, creating both controversy and admiration" and putting the Company on the map once and for all. There was little reason, he felt, why all three shouldn't be attained over the next three years.[238]

In addition, New Moon was also anticipating that support would continue from the five local funding authorities, as well as a considerable injection of funds by DCA and the Australia Council. That meant that by mid-year 1986 the Company was projecting a $50,000 surplus on that year's operations which would defray the accumulated deficit by about one third and thereby be able to trade out of its difficulties by 1988. Nevertheless, it had to take quite serious steps to achieve that end.

The most significant of these was that the Company would no longer be an ensemble but rather have to employ actors and crew on short term contracts. This was a marked departure from the founding concept. It was also a final recognition of the reality of the way in which the previous practice had locked in costs and virtually compelled it to make every production a large cast one. Even theatre companies resident in one place, presenting an annual season of plays on a regular basis would reserve the right to balance three-handers, two-handers etc with a larger scale production of, say, Shakespeare. New Moon's previous model had constrained it to an average 10 actors per show. While the aesthetic and artistic impact of that was not negligible, it had come at enormous price in wages, accommodation, support mechanisms and above all economic inflexibility. In a sense, the change was probably inevitable. It must however have been disheartening at the time and almost certainly contributed to the progressive loss of interest which Bakaitis seemed to exhibit during his last season with the Company.

The second step aimed at defraying costs was an effort to use regional resources wherever possible such as engaging amateur theatre groups as crew. The third approach was to develop a greater emphasis on marketing, or rather more coherent marketing, aimed at increased attendances by raising the profile of the Company in the cities which it served even among those who did not attend. Fourth and finally, there would be a greater degree of financial supervision exercised by

DCA in Brisbane. It was, after all, the agency with the greatest stake in New Moon's success and the greatest political exposure to its potential failure.

A prime example of the greater flexibility offered by the abandonment of the ensemble was in the first production planned for that year: the American play 'Agnes of God'. Unlike anything New Moon had done before, it was every inch a star vehicle, having cast actors like Ann Pitroniak, Geraldine Page, Mercedes McCambridge and Honor Blackman variously in New York and London and Anne Bancroft in the film version. It was natural for Diane Cilento to be cast as the lead in this intense, claustrophobic three-hander set in a convent. In the same way, the production which followed, 'Return Engagement' (originally entitled 'Madonna and Child') fulfilled a similar function in the changed strategy. It was a two-hander featuring veteran musical star Toni Lamond and her son Tony Sheldon, himself a seasoned performer whose career was subsequently to become stellar in the musical 'Priscilla'. As might be expected, the semi-biographical production devised by him and Ron Creagar contained elements of humour, family history and conflict punctuated with numbers by Irving Berlin, Hayley Carmichael, Cole Porter and many, many others. Again, the flexibility of being able to program a two-person show enabled New Moon to continue its trajectory in intimate music theatre – which had been one of the foundation principles – but now in a cost-effective way while featuring at least one personality well known from national television.

Imagine that

As if all that weren't enough star power, the third production for the year was intended to be something that could genuinely pull the Company out of its immediate slough and arguably even provide it with a longer term financial benefit. It was to be 'Imagine', originally entitled 'A Day in the Death of John Lennon', a work devised by Rodney Fisher around the music and words of the former Beatle a mere six years after his assassination. Fisher had recently co-devised and directed Robyn Archer's landmark 'A Star is Torn' which was similarly a compilation around the work and lives of great singing artists, in that case of women. The combination then seemed a propitious one for the re-invigorated company. The addition of singer/actor John Waters was a further measure both of the changes which had overtaken New Moon and the new model rapidly being rolled out. In this case, the new way was further highlighted by the fact that Fisher and Waters rehearsed mostly in Sydney because of the actor's television commitments there, so far had the Company by then departed from any idea of its mainstream productions being part or arising out of a local artistic community. Nevertheless, the fact that Waters, with his collaborator Stewart D'Arrieta, were later to adopt the concept, convert it into 'Through a Glass Onion' and tour it far and wide until this day, suggests that conceptually New Moon was on the right track. It could well have been an ongoing profit-centre for them and continue to deliver benefit well after its life in Central and North Queensland had passed. Alas, it was not to be.

During 1986 various kinds of outside advice had been sought. Marketing manager, Andrew Porter had been flown in from Melbourne to better promote the Company but the relationship soon soured as others of this type had before it. On this occasion however, Iles was scarcely to blame. Jeremy Wright was brought back from Sydney to advise on branding (before the term was hardly heard in the arts) and fundraising at which the Company had been successful but was now sinking. With Iles's departure there was no one skilled in either area. His success was a result of his flair and tended to burn brightly but burn out. It was time for a more considered and strategic approach. Wright was even brought on the Board as another Associate Director. Unfortunately, just as these moves were being made, direct local government involvement was receding. That had been a key element in the pitch to the private sector all of which relied to some extent on local government goodwill. Absent that factor, and the way in which New Moon had burnt its bridges so often, that even its loyalest sponsors withdrew or just failed to renew quoting "other priorities".

A third to be brought in was Barbara Tiernan who had worked with Bakaitis in Melbourne as General Manager of St Martin's. An experienced, take-no-prisoners administrator, her brief at New Moon was imprecise. Though called Marketing Coordinator, it left open the way for her to intervene in many areas in a manner that was not always conducive to maintaining a happy staff already groaning under financial and political pressure. For instance, she had a propensity to fire off missives to the media and others which were not best calculated to win friends at the very moment when the Company needed all the friends it could get. But at the end of 1986, she was reporting that expressions of interest to stage 'Imagine' had been received from every State and New Zealand. Quite how this was to be achieved is unclear since by then it must have been apparent that the performing rights to the Lennon material were so contested as to render those outcomes close to a pipe dream.[239] Nonetheless, given her experience, a role she might usefully have performed was to produce that show which, if properly handled, could have been the Company's saviour. But that rug was pulled summarily from under their feet by a combination of naivety and sleight of others' hand.

By then, Bakaitis was clearly worn out. He had led the Company for three tumultuous years through ten productions most of which he directed, all of which had toured to the four integral cities and one much further afield. On December 4, 1986 he advised the Board he would be moving on, effective the end of December. Diane Cilento stood down from the Board at the same time, though there is no suggestion that the two events were directly related.[240] If Bakaitis's departure was received with genuine regret, Bereson's announcement that she too wished to leave was met with panic. Three years was a respectable term for an Artistic Director and could be argued as such with the financial underwriters. But losing the General Manager at the same time after only one year could seriously erode confidence, so that in the event she was persuaded to stay for another year.

Notwithstanding the many ups and downs that had led to this pass, some progress at recovery had been made. Overall, it could be claimed reasonably that the year had been successful. The productions were well received and the deficit had been reduced by 44% to ($87,642), albeit by some deft bringing forward of part of a State Government grant-in-advance. However, by the end of 1986 it was clear that only Townsville and Mackay/Pioneer would continue to directly fund the Company into the future. The business model which had been launched with such fanfare was dissolving. In mid-1986 Malcolm Calder had reported that retaining support from his Rockhampton Council had been an annual fight.[241] It now proved unwinnable for 1987. Henceforth, New Moon's touring commitment would cover only Townsville and Mackay. This did not, of course, mean that other towns would be abandoned, rather that they would be negotiated on a case-by-case basis and, in particular, on a "favoured nation" rate with Rockhampton and Cairns as having been members of the founding cohort. Dona Greaves who attended the fateful meeting at which this was resolved, was quick to reassure the Company that the Government was committed to the continued development of professional theatre in the region and "saw no impediment to the continuance of funding without local government support", but recognised that the Australia Council might take a different view.[242]

One of the pluses of losing the Cairns and Rockhampton funding was that New Moon was no longer tied to an elaborate system of municipal Board nominees. In 1987 The Board was restructured to include only two local government representatives, one being the joint appointment of Mackay and Pioneer Shire, the other designated by Townsville. Financial support would come from these Councils only, totalling around $50,000 of which Townsville provided $20,000. This change of governance allowed the recruitment of a more skills-based board with members from business, law, media, public administration and academe elected, though it is not clear how these new faces were arrived at. As with many not-for-profit arts companies, there was no real body of membership from which new directors could be drawn. One is left with the impression, as so often these cases, that "dob in a mate" was the preferred method of recruitment rather than any hotly-contested community plebiscite. Nevertheless, for the time being, things boded well. Private sector support still trickled in with $5000 coming from Shell together with an Ansett contra of $5000. The Queensland Government would contribute $100,000 for 1987 with a similar amount from the Australia Council but in its case with the Company on "notice", down from 1986's $130,000 and a third less than the $156,000 New Moon had sought.

Interim arrangements

Bakaitis's departure confronted the Board with a much greater challenge than the previous change of artistic leadership. Then, the Company's reputation had been riding high, the funding agencies were onside, finances were positive, local governments were supportive if not always enthusiastic and the theatre-going public was generally engaged. Now, the opposite applied in almost every department and the word was out in the industry that this was, if not a poisoned chalice, certainly a dangerous deal. The job was advertised and drew a thin field of what could best be described as "apprentices". Not one had a serious track record of directing in the professional theatre and none had run a theatre company of any scale. In the end, the choice fell on Ian Tasker, notable as a former senior stage manager with the Old Tote Theatre Company, who had "directed" Barry Humphries (whatever that may mean!) in 'An Evening's Intercourse' and had put together a few independent pub shows in Sydney since the Tote's demise. He was knowledgeable in theatre, experienced in production and touring and well-connected in the business, but it is improbable that in happier circumstances he would have made the short list for such a position. It was a sign of New Moon's times.

All that, however, might have turned out fine. Many unlikely appointees in all sorts of roles have risen to the occasion. Some surprisingly. Just as "ideal" candidates have failed. New Moon needed strong clear leadership and a sense of renewed purpose. Talented directors for individual plays could have been found. Bereson had proven she could keep the ship steady. Tasker's first moves suggested that he was prepared to scour the scene for existing product to bridge the short-term gap while he settled in. His buy-in of the Ensemble Theatre's 'Intimate Exchanges' which he turned into an Alan Ayckbourn Festival failed to sell, but was a good try. However, a crucial detail had not been disclosed in his résumé at the time of recruitment. Tasker was HIV positive, a condition which rapidly converted to full-blown AIDS. It was early in the Australian epidemic that peaked in the mid-to-late 1980s. Few understood the condition. Many were alarmed or prejudiced. Concealment was understandable, albeit in this instance close to disastrous. He died in Townsville in April that year having hardly begun his job.

Meanwhile, the political background was hotting up. The Fitzgerald Inquiry had been called. It was to turn the politics of Queensland on its ear and reveal buried but long-suspected corruption at the highest levels. It would begin its formal hearings on 27 July 1987. Yet not everything was negative. Bob Katter, Minister for Aboriginal and Islander Affairs and then, as later, a loud voice in the land, was arguing for (and secured) the payment of award wages to Indigenous workers in the State. It was a peculiarly Queensland paradox and suited to Katter's oddly moralistic world view of the greater good that he doggedly pursued this goal knowing that once achieved it would almost certainly reduce employment for Aboriginal rural workers.

In a report to the Board and in the wake of the Tasker crisis and much else, Bereson went out on a limb to promote another unfashionable "greater good".[243] She argued that financial considerations had largely determined Company policy for the preceding 18 months. They had governed artistic plans with monetary issues clouding the philosophical basis of the Company. For example, concessions such as budgetary allocations for community works had denied New Moon the funds and time necessary to work towards an artistically viable future. In short, the Company had tried to buy goodwill rather than earning it. Coherent artistic policy reflected in the choice of an Artistic Director was the only way forward and that person had to have "cognisance of the market" as well as artistic leadership skills.

In the meantime, the Board had commissioned her to pull the rest of the 1987 season together until a replacement Artistic Director could be found. She hired versatile actor/director Gary Down and together they chose two Australian plays: 'Away' and 'Are You Lonesome Tonight?' and sold them to the various presenters. While there were obviously only half the number of productions of past years, the touring pattern would be extended beyond the original four cities. Thus, the Company would be seen further afield. This was partly due to the growing awareness of what had become the NARPACA circuit of presenting theatres and partly to justify the increased reliance on State as against Federal funding. For instance, Bereson was able to sell both shows to Gladstone in order to make up in part for the reduced number of nights in Rockhampton.[244] But for all that, two plays did not a company make and even with the increasingly energetic contribution of La Luna's youth program (albeit confined to Townsville), it was looking less and less like the Valhalla that had been enunciated six years before.

Gary Down was another real chance at renewal after Ian Tasker's unfortunate death but as it happened it proved a false dawn. Nevertheless, his production of Gow's play showed that the Company could still assemble an excellent cast with the likes of Monica Maughan and Liddy Clark in a first rate production. If Down, who was a fine artist and a negotiator in every way, had stayed New Moon might well have survived. As Robert Spencer noted: "He really knew how to bring people together and he worked well with Ruth. But it wasn't to be." [245]

The productions were critically well-received but the public failed to respond in adequate numbers and by October 1987 the Company was again in crisis.[246] The Australia Council had put it on notice in 1987. At a round-table in July that year attended by both the Council's General Manager, Max Bourke and Chris Mangin, Director of the Performing Arts Board, it had been made clear that future funding would depend on the success of the two remaining productions.[247] New Moon had sought and obtained guarantees for forward funding from the State Government but by then there was doubt they would be honoured.

Bjelke-Petersen was about to be voted out of the leadership of his party. By December 1 he would be gone from Parliament. He was succeeded as 32nd Premier by the arts-friendly Mike Ahern who in turn lasted fewer than two years. But instability in government means uncertainty in funding in any field. With most of the local government money gone there was little to rely on.[248] That uncertainty was exacerbated by New Moon's chair, Val Valentine resigning at the end of October citing family ill health.[249] Board member, Ray Dickson, from the Townsville *Daily Bulletin* stepped up in an acting capacity. While Valentine had been at times sceptical of the Company's modus operandi, she had provided continuity and was, at least in part, responsible for the Townsville Council's ongoing support in the face of criticism. Her departure further weakened New Moon's public presence.

Gary Down's brief sojourn with the Company had been much appreciated. He was in many ways an ideal choice to lead it forward: he had the talent, was personally engaging and possessed a light touch with the decision-makers. But, in the event, he elected not to apply for the Artistic Directorship citing that he had just relocated from Sydney to Melbourne and wanted to re-establish himself there. He left at the end of the season. For whatever reason, he subsequently changed his mind. Two years later he took up the similar position with another regional company, the New England Theatre Company based in Armidale. Perhaps he had been bitten by the regional bug. Speaking with the author he considered that it was just because "it came along" and there was no link between the two.[250] NETC was itself a different kind of challenge but equally daunting in its way since its Executive Director was the formidable Anna Glover with whom like many before and after he had a less than perfect relationship. Armidale was another university town, much smaller than Townsville. While touring was also basic to NETC's survival, Glover saw other towns not as partners in a grand collaborative venture as New Moon at its best had done, but rather as series of villages needing to be inducted into the benefits of higher civilisation, as she saw it. That was not Down's way nor was it the way of most Australian theatre artists, however little they might have cared for the rigours of country touring.

A last throw

Ruth Bereson finally threw in the towel at end of 1987. It was a double blow to New Moon's chances of building on its third incarnation that at this point it lost its General Manager. We have seen that she tried to resign back in 1986 when Bakaitis left, but had been persuaded by the Board to stay on. She had made an effective if, given their widely divergent backgrounds, unequal partnership with him. She had also overseen many changes and had negotiated the Company into a sounder financial position with the prospect of steadily reducing the debt. At the end of the 1985 financial year the Company was facing a deficit of ($158,000). By the end of 1986 this had reduced to $86,694. Her ways, much less erratic than Iles's, had in part restored the funding agencies' confidence that New Moon was in steady if less experienced hands. Most of all, she had survived the trauma of having an Artistic Director die in her presence of a medical condition little understood at the time and which still terrified many.[251] But it had been two years of hell and she was determined to leave and did so at the end of January 1988. John Lamb having returned from Darwin held the fort in a part-time consulting capacity with chairman Ray Dickson until local actor and arts worker, Kirsty Veron became secretary/administrator.[252]

However, during 1987 earned income including box office had crashed from almost $200,000 in 1986 to $86,521 in 1987. Operating costs had gone up marginally, production costs had halved but the bottom line saw the accumulated deficit rise to a staggering ($213,663). Of course, funding had declined but the essential problem was simple: New Moon was simply not selling enough tickets.[253]

In many ways, what happened next was the most remarkable occurrence in New Moon's remarkable history. On the face of it, the Company was finished. Not surprisingly, the Australia Council pulled its plug. But almost as surprising the Queensland Arts Division, which it had then become, agreed to permit New Moon to use its entire 1988 grant of $200,000 to settle with its creditors. Similarly, the three remaining LGAs: Townsville, Mackay and Pioneer permitted the same – all in the face of nil adult activity. That manoeuvre left the Company $2,000 in the black![254] It was an extraordinary act of faith and one that probably no other government in Australia would have contemplated at that time. Of course, it reflects the peculiar demographics of the State, not to say its fast and loose politics, as well as Dona Greaves's influence with the new Premier. But it must to some degree also be taken as a measure of the impact which the Company and its work had had on the public in the preceding seven years and the government's wish not to abandon that achievement.

Nevertheless, in 1988 when virtually every other arts body was going overboard in pursuit of government largesse to commemorate 200 hundred years of European settlement, there would be no main-stage New Moon productions. The Company was effectively broke with no Australia Council grant and relying on life support from the Queensland government. Nevertheless, there was still La Luna activity. It at least was bolstered by projects associated with the Bicentenary which for the first and only time in New Moon's history involved Indigenous participants. Some measure of the depression all this engendered may be found in Ray Dickson's understated reflection the following year when he surrendered the leadership to John Lamb: "to be the chair of a theatre company board that has no actors, no productions and therefore no performances is rather perturbing".[255]

Once again, New Moon was faced with the question of how to get things back on track. In May 1988 the Board decided to seek yet more expert advice. This time, it called for tenders and hired Arts Action, aka Rob Adams, by then a consultant but back when New Moon had been first mooted, the Director of the Australia Council's Theatre Board. He consulted widely on the matter and concluded that the Company should continue, provided it restructured and could be properly resourced to pursue more limited goals. Adams went back to the idea of an ensemble company though now of just six actors. He recommended a base in Townsville in a close association with JCU though the University would not present its work on their campus. He urged that New Moon should retain its name; that for part of the year it should convert itself into a TIE team; and, while keeping Townsville and Mackay/Pioneer as it twin focuses, tour more widely on a fee-for-services arrangement. He also canvassed the concept of a mobile stage which would enable the Company to visit smaller centres without managed venues or any venues at all.[256]

Clearly, there were many benefits in the proposed University association. These ranged from tax exemption, administrative back-up and fundraising expertise through to offering a source of young, enthusiastic actors and production staff newly minted from JCU's courses. The last of these had been canvassed at the very inception of the Company. Accordingly, in August that year the Vice-Chancellor, Professor Golding wrote advising that, subject to the continuation of external funding, the University was willing to accept responsibility for hosting New Moon for an initial period of three years in accordance with the model Adams had put forth. It was New Moon's last real hope of revival and they bungled. The Company, perhaps not unnaturally, wanted a joint venture. The University just as understandably wanted a marriage, but not without a dowry. Its position was further complicated by the ambitions of one Jean-Pierre Voos who had joined the Department of Creative and Expressive Studies as Senior Lecturer in Performing Arts. For the previous fifteen years he had been Artistic Director of the International Theatre Research Group KISS which between 1980 and 1982 had toured Australia and developed something of a cult following, including among students at JCU. Clearly, Voos had not wanted to take on most of the heavy lifting involved in running a touring company such as New Moon had been and needed to continue to be and he had no interest whatever in the hard yakka of TIE. However, he did want to position himself to be able to influence and, in effect, call that part of the avant-garde artistic shots which interested him. Wissler observed more mildly: "my take on Jean-Pierre's work at the time was that it was very idiosyncratic and unlikely to be able to be scaled up or engineered in such a way as to fit what I could see as a potential artistic program as represented in that [New Moon] 1990 program."[257]

There followed, through the balance of 1988 and into 1989, an exchange of correspondence in which on the Vice-Chancellor's side became increasingly terse. In the end, the Company opted to go it alone. It is debatable if the Adams model could have worked anyway. While an ability to find actors capable of undertaking the grind of schools touring as well as the equally rigorous but different demands of adult productions is not unknown, there was little evidence that New Moon had the resources to accomplish that. The intimate association which Voos sought, operating below the radar, might well have crippled its capacity to engage in more popular even commercial ventures which Adams had also advocated. But there is little doubt that the negotiations were poorly handled. Ray Dickson today attributes some of that to John Lamb's overenthusiastic attempt to network simultaneously at too many levels within the University hierarchy. That had ended only in alienating some of its senior staff.[258]

Return of the Jedi

Despite its long slow decline, there was a real burst of energy in what was to be the final year of the New Moon decade. John Lamb's relentless determination to get the Company back up and running, and presumably to forge a new role for himself within it, is undoubted. In the last period, he was variously a board member, secretary and for a while chair. His moves were not always well-considered. Perhaps they were born of desperation or perhaps his experience in Darwin had made him lose the touch he had so amply exhibited in getting the Company originally off the ground. As often happens when things have come to an unhappy pass, he turned to someone who had been there at the beginning: Rod Wissler by then a Senior Lecturer in Drama at Kelvin Grove CAE in Brisbane, a person with sound theatre credentials and respected by the profession and the Arts Division.[259] "I had finished with the TN Theatre Company at the beginning of '88 and I went to Kelvin Grove. I had continued on the Board of TN and I'd also done some performing. I had been involved in a TN production of 'Who's Afraid of Virginia Woolf?' in 1989 which then toured with the Arts

Council up to North Queensland. So I suspect it was somewhere during 1989 John must have thought about contacting me to talk about what was going on with New Moon. And my interest was piqued and I agreed to undertake what I guess everyone thought of as some kind of artistic consultancy."[260] The New Moon board was happy to lure him back part-time as much to give credence to their cause as to obtain some much-needed quality advice and focus. The main game was to retain or regain (depending on how one looked at it) State Government annual funding; to rescue what they could of the local government relationships by then shrunken to Townsville and Mackay; and to hope that they could present a plausible body of activity to the Australia Council for, at the very least, some project funding.

That meant assembling a "package" of programs that offered profile to the opinion-makers as well as to the public. Wissler had a full-time job at his College so the most he could accept was yet again a fi/fo role. But to satisfy the Articles of Association and thereby the stakeholders, he needed to be seen to occupy a position that appeared more substantial and ongoing. Thus, to some he was termed Artistic Advisor while to others he was Artistic Director. It was a balancing act which might have worked in a more stable organisation and financial environment. But by then New Moon was neither. No doubt part of the hope was that, given Wissler's academic credentials, he might also be able to revive the fractured relationship with James Cook University. Certainly, influential board member, Associate Professor Elizabeth Perkins, who did not always see eye-to-eye with Lamb, had not given up on that. Nevertheless, it was by then fairly clear that the University had other irons in the fire with Voos. More urgent was to assemble the scattered elements of New Moon into something that could be offered as a coherent whole to whoever or whatever might provide support. Wissler also brought other connections. "By that time I had people who'd been around TN or had been around the College in Brisbane – the likes of David Fenton, Stephen Clark, Andrew Buchanan, and others who I thought understood the mix of things needed to be brought together under a new New Moon, including the youth theatre component, including the theatre productions."[261] Each of these was to play a role in the Company's final days.

While their ambitions to return after an absence of two years to a regular touring season of main stage plays was by no means abandoned, it was clear that youth and community programs offered the best bet to create presence, obtain subsidy and generate earned income. Since 1987 La Luna had been steadily growing. From Saturday morning classes for children and teenagers it had expanded into a youth theatre program with classes and productions that not only provided a shopfront for the Company as a whole, but also more or less paid its way from fees-for-services. By then, it had almost take on a life and certainly a personality of its own and the relationship to the parent company was already somewhat frayed. However, it *was* still a New Moon project, and could with some energetic management have remained a jewel in its crown.

In May 1989, plans to relaunch the main company in September were revised. For both funding and marketing reasons the Board decided to postpone until February 1990 so as to do so with a full year's program in view. That would also involve strengthening La Luna, organising another playwrights' conference similar to that held in 1987 and hold readings of new works. Intriguingly, they would include 'The Dreaming of Christie Palmerston' by Ric Nelson now living in Adelaide and who, like Wissler, had also in an odd way come full circle from the Company's original days.

Partial funding had been reinstated in December, 1988 with a grant of $12,000 from Townsville City Council and $30,000 from the Queensland government to fund activities of the Company such as planning the relaunch and re-establishing the La Luna program up to 30 June, 1989. Australia Council funding was also restarted in April 1989 with a project grant of $25,000 towards the staging of 'The Summer of the Seventeenth Doll', originally in late 1989 but later rescheduled for early 1990. These were pitiful numbers compared with where New Moon had been and are probably the best measure of how far it had fallen. Meanwhile, the Company had still not entirely given up on negotiations with JCU. They proceeded fitfully throughout the year.

Otherwise, all that was on offer would be a pilot tour of 'Grumblegrunt: a North Queensland Fairy Tale' offered with workshops in October to some isolated schools such as Greenvale, Mt Surprise, Georgetown and Croydon. From July to December La Luna ran three youth productions: 'Jeremiah's Trip' for 10-13 year olds: the ever-popular 'Hating Alison Ashley' (14-17 years) and 'Let Me In' (18-25 years). It was far from where the New Moon had started, but it kept the flag flying if somewhat limply. But the postponement of an adult season meant that there were now two years in which it produced no touring work in that category and was thus not seen in any meaningful way outside of Townsville. That lull made all the more remarkable the sensational success of what was to follow. Because in almost every way 'The Summer of the Seventeenth Doll' was a hit and a hit far and wide; farther and wider, in fact, than any previous New Moon production had ever been seen in Queensland.

As well, some good news came to hand. On October 5 the Company was advised by the Arts Division that it would receive $90,000 of the $230,000 it had sought. That left a $140,000 gap in the plan which Lamb from the chair proposed to bridge pro tem in the following ways: to budget for a reduced surplus $27,000; cut the existing budget by $7,000; secure a Remote Area grant of $25,000; obtain fees from the NARPACA theatres of $36,000; and negotiate a review by the State Government in February thereby gaining an extra. $45,000.[262]

Now, after a lapse of years, the first two of these strike one as being what Prime Minister Paul Keating was fond of calling "voodoo" economics. To claim as a saving the reduction of a surplus not already earned is, put mildly, a dodgy proposition. The Remote Areas grant seemed to be on firmer ground. NARPACA theatres had indeed indicated that they would support the Company on a show-by-show basis. The funds provided were to be for the engagement of northern talent and the running of workshops. In the event, they received $3000-4000 per centre for 'The Doll'. Nonetheless, one cannot avoid the suspicion of some double dipping in this arrangement since the same Centres were also buying in the shows.

The review by the State Government had been promised for February 1990 by the Minister and the Departmental head, Brian Stewart. Subsequently, Dona Greaves, ever a dab hand at moving the deckchairs on a sinking ship, had proposed a forward commitment in 1990/91 of $115,000 to be applied to calendar year 1990 (i.e. used up six months early) and that the Company could apply for $230,000 in April to be used in calendar year 1991. Cairns and Mackay had also been approached for support. But meanwhile an election would fall and few doubted the outcome. Chinese whispers from the ALP suggested that leader Wayne Goss would commit $140,000 "on election". Yet It was a house of cards and such was the conflict in understanding, even within the Board of New Moon, that when the Tropic winds blew it all came tumbling down.

Coda

In December 1989 a Labor government was elected in Queensland for the first time since 1957 and just one month later Premier and Minister for the Arts, Goss duly announced that additional financial support of $115,000 had been provisionally set aside to undertake: "an exciting and diverse program of arts activities."[263] The statement went on to declare that overall the Government would be contributing $230,000 to support New Moon in 1990 in line with the level of funding which the Company had requested. That total included the $25,000 Touring and Remote Areas Access Scheme (as Lamb had foreshadowed) which would enable the second production, 'We Can't Pay, We Won't Pay' to visit a string of smaller centres like Ayr, Ingham, Charters Towers, Hughenden and Mt Isa. But note the word "provisionally". What the statement did not say was that to release the rest, certain conditions needed to be met. That was contained in the letter of offer which followed. In the end, those conditions were never met.

As a result, the much touted relaunch was crippled from the outset. The Government would not provide a guarantee to enable the Company to obtain an overdraft nor would it release the promised funds. A crisis meeting was held on March 25 joined by Dona Greaves and other Arts Division staff. Lamb advised that in the absence of a firm guarantee they would have to close at the end of the Townsville season of ironically 'We Can't pay...'. Greaves urged them to hang on, but to no avail. Contingency plans were made to struggle through to the end of the year with a skeleton staff including a newly ordained Artistic Director in David Fenton and the La Luna co-ordinator based on known funding, and that was that. Yet even then, New Moon refused to die.[264]

Part of the problem was differing interpretations of what had been promised. Lamb believed (possibly on the basis of Greaves's earlier undertaking before the election) that the sum of money that could be used in calendar year 1990 meant that it could be released before July 1 of that year.[265] The Government took the view that the grant was always for the financial year as set out in the conditions and then only if various budgetary undertakings were met. Elizabeth Perkins, who by then had been on the New Moon board for a year, disputed Lamb's interpretation claiming that the real problem was due to an "over-enthusiastic and visionary budget proposal" which predated the current problems. That, in lay terms, might be read as "spending money you don't have".[266] She urged that the promised remote areas tour of 'We Can't Pay...' should still go ahead.

Kevin Radbourne, long-term functionary of the Queensland government arts scene and an acute observer of it has an interesting take on the background to these events: "the Department had a Cultural Advisory Council but [under the previous government] it was made up of business people. The incoming Government appointed an Arts Advisory Committee made up of artistic people, totally different. Some of those members had a particular agenda that they wanted to push."[267] One may choose to interpret this as meaning that their agenda did not push in New Moon's direction.

After this debacle, Wissler resigned his consultancy and David Fenton was appointed Artistic Director in May 1990.[268] "There was an amalgamation between BCAE and Queensland Institute of Technology in train (to create the Queensland University of Technology). In the lead up to it, I became Acting Head of the Drama Program in Kelvin Grove ... at some point in this I must have thought I can manage all of this. I [then] came to the conclusion in early 1990 I just couldn't do it in a way that would actually resonate with my beliefs about what the Company needed to be in terms of an embedded company in the region. It had become clear to me that I could not relocate to north Queensland, as I had done in 1980, and I felt you couldn't have a kind of part-time Artistic Director operating from Brisbane long term."[269]

Fenton had been with the Company since January 1990 as director-in-residence and effectively holding the fort on a variety of fronts. During the year that followed, so great was the confidence that resurrection was still possible under Fenton's leadership, a four year plan for an essentially Townsville-based company was drawn up. The State grant of $115,000 was finally released but too late to save the projected 1990 touring season. As well, Voos's new company Tropic Line was now snapping at their heels.

The history of New Moon is replete with what we might call "deep end" training, that is to say the inexperienced cast into the depths to sink or swim. Ruth Bereson was one and David Fenton another. In 1988 he had just finished a Drama & History diploma at the Brisbane CAE and was "on the market". Because of a freeze on teaching positions he'd gone into a mix of acting and teaching drama classes with the Theatre Company TN2 with which Rod Wissler, was still associated, doing a bit of everything as recent graduates do at that age. Towards the end of '89, Wissler invited him to go up to Townsville to be Resident Director at New Moon. At the time he didn't understand that Wissler was a consultant. "It was always made clear to me that he was the Artistic Director and I was a Resident Director and that the big artistic decisions, kind of global perspective on the Company was his gig but that I was just there to direct on behalf of the Company and maintain that conduit back to Brisbane." [270] Even then, he felt the arrangement was extremely odd: "It always struck me it as immensely colonial... it was ill-conceived but yet I came to understand that the only way they would get the money was if someone who had Rod's gravitas was involved and I understood that... So, I went in lieu of Rod going up himself. That was very interesting because he was working with TN but also as a lecturer or running the Drama Department at the time..."[271]

When Fenton first went up to Townsville he took charge of the youth theatre arm and did an education tour that went through the QAC system and circuits. Meanwhile, Stephen Clark was directing the first part of what was to be five-show season marketed as "The Road Girl". Today Fenton recalls just 'Summer of the Seventeenth Doll' and Dario Fo's 'We Can't Pay, We Won't Pay' and "the rest of it falls into oblivion pretty much like myself at the end of 1990". While they were doing that, he was producing and directing the TIE production and then it became his turn at the "main stage" and he went into production for Fo's work. "I remember it being very difficult because all of a sudden we were rehearsing in summer... It was basically my first professional production other than that TIE. We got it on. It was at the Civic Theatre; it was well received and it did, I think, around about three shows and by the time we got to the Saturday matinee we were told that it was it. The Company was wrapping up, all, everything, you know, is closing up. There is no money left so take your box and dice and go home."[272] The blow when it fell was brutal. No one in the production had any inkling and Fenton himself had not been involved in any of the decision-making leading up to it. "it was heartbreaking ... we did three and a half weeks of rehearsal to close after four performances and it was all over Red Rover."[273]

Nevertheless, after the event it was clear to all that basically the money had simply dried up and the whole enterprise came to a crashing halt. Yet, mystifyingly, in that condition, Fenton was asked out of the blue to take on the role of Artistic Director. By his own admission, he had little idea of what that would entail or how they were to go about it. "I think it might have been some kind of 'here's a consolation prize. You've re-located here and are you willing to hang around for a little bit longer and see if we can sift out of the emperor's ashes'. And I stayed until early 1991." In the event, the Company limped along with some money for another TIE production. Fenton secured the licence for Theatresports in Townsville. He had been heavily involved in that at La Boite in Brisbane so undertook it there as a kind of outreach activity. La Luna also survived the blitz. "That didn't want to fold and kept going and it was also at that time, when we talk about legacy, that Susan Prince, Katherine Ash and Sue-Ellen Maunder [who the very next year founded Jute Theatre] came down [from Cairns] with a group of very bright, very wide-eyed and chipper practitioners – that weren't practitioners at the time, they were amateurs – and had come down for a series of workshops that I was running around Theatresports, and around acting ... And little did I know that close to twenty years' time I would be working with them as a Director and doing a lot of their educational stuff and so that's been a long-term relationship. Indeed, Sue-Ellen followed me and did her first secondment as Artistic Director when I was Artistic Director of Riverina. But the key thing was, I remember, being let go [from New Moon] and how unceremonious it was." [274]

Fenton has gone on to have an extensive theatre career in many parts of Australia, but perhaps most notably in Queensland, as director and teacher but remains among those who were, in part at least, understandably scarred by the New Moon experience and perhaps made forever wary of claims that are overly ambitious or dubious in their profferings. But at that moment the first and most important option for him was the maintenance and growth of La Luna. Allied to this was a newer development: that of Theatre-in-Education which had earlier been floated by the Adams report. New Moon, like many companies before and at the time, saw outreach to kids captive in the classroom as the best way to create continuous employment for performers, grow new audiences among the young and above all snare some much needed subsidy.

As it happened, the Queensland Arts Council had the largest and most effective schools touring network in the country. What's more, it was effectively the sole gatekeeper to gaining approval to do so by the Queensland Education Department and was likewise trusted by the Catholic and independent schools. The Council was a natural partner for any artists seeking entry to that arcane world. As well, its practice was often to buy in productions from outside producers and pick up all the costs of touring them. Northern Queensland was an important catchment and but often harder to supply in this way than the southern parts of the State. QAC had long been well disposed to New Moon.[275] The Company's acquiring a TIE dimension raised the all-important community outreach flag with funding authorities. Nor was there any shortage of newly-minted drama graduates to be fodder for schools touring. In time, and not all that long after this, the tide would start to turn on the TIE concept. But in 1990 there was still enough energy to make it work. So driven by Wissler and managed first by Andrew Buchanan who had been running La Luna and later David Fenton, a TIE team was born.

A second tour of 'Grumble Grunt' set out in March/April 1990 and played to over 50 primary schools up and down the coast and inland, some in single school premises others to bussed-in multi-school audiences, all seemingly to considerable success. It was a piece of the ongoing New Moon puzzle that could well have continued to provide life to the stumbling enterprise. But along with everything else, it would die within the year. These two prongs of Youth Theatre and TIE were a logical if belated development and whatever one thinks of their potential to lay the foundations for future audiences – for which generally speaking there is little evidence – from the point of view of rebuilding a tarnished image, they had much to commend them.

The third element of earning revenue from a more commercial source was offered by New Moon's acquisition of the North Queensland licence to operate Theatre Sports. This they did finally in mid-1990.[276] although they had been earlier operating under a personal agreement. For those not in the know, this is essentially a competition in theatrical improvisation not unlike TV's 'Who's line is It Anyway'. Today it is commonplace; in 1990 it was still relatively new. As of 1985 Belvoir Theatre in Sydney had held the Australian licence from the International Theatre Sports Institute from which it grew a substantial mostly youthful audience but also derived a significant stream of income. Townsville took to it with glee.[277]

Not long after these plans were launched, a New Moon Open Forum was convened among performing arts interests and practitioners in the area. This aimed to form some consensus about a way forward. Yet again, the idea of a liaison between the University and the Company raised its head, but by then JCU had other plans. Those culminated in the establishment of Tropic Line is its theatre company with Voos as Artistic Director. At the forum, its administrator declared that it was now "the professional theatre company for North Queensland".[278] The Tropic Line Research Theatre Company Limited (to give it is full pedigree) achieved genuine company status in 1992. As one of its university-funded activities in that year it presented 'Twelfth Night' in the garden setting of the Vincent Centre for Creative Arts which had become its new home and where it maintained a core group of six professional actors with the addition of ten community actors and two technicians. In other words, it "lifted" many of the proposals which Rob Adams had laid out for New Moon. For those who choose to contemplate it, virtually everything about the denouement of New Moon in 1990 has aspects of irony. The personnel, the new/old beginning and even the titles of the plays chosen for that concluding season seem to almost mock the grand aspirations and the long, sad goodbye.

Terrence O'Connell noted in his recollections: "maybe we should have started with 'The Doll'". Whether or not that might have been an auspicious opener, it provided a fitting conclusion.[279] Chosen by Rod Wissler who been there when the idea of the company was born, presided over by John Lamb who had put the complex pieces together and directed by Stephen Clark who had been an actor in the original company, all these provided a certain nostalgic symmetry to the choice of 'The Doll'. That Lawler's play deals with love and loss out of time and its kewpie symbolism of fantasy which has faded into disillusion and regret, only adds to the pain of New Moon's waning. That its tour in March of that year to Mackay, Ayr, Cairns, Townsville, Rockhampton recalling the "good old days" should also have been a resounding success, saluted by favourable press, featuring local actors and seeming to herald a brand new day, only redoubled the paradox.

At all events, by further irony the next and, as it turned out, final production, directed by David Fenton, should have been Dario Fo's 'We Can't Pay, We Won't Pay'. The metaphor is almost too acute. It survived just one week in Townsville and just, as it began, so it ended in the city that had seen New Moon rise, now saw its setting almost exactly a decade later. A full year's season had originally been planned. The titles of the rest of the works which were never to see the light of day seem calculated to add to the sense of hope and despair: 'Emerald City', 'Zen and Now' and 'The Floating World'.

Through the balance of 1990 there followed a series of unsatisfactory negotiations with the Arts Division about forward funding for the following year. Greaves had now gone and with her went the continuity of understanding and advocacy for New Moon (arguably, to an unwise degree at times). A discussion paper with suggestions of collaborations with local groups in Townsville and Cairns as a survival mode failed to persuade.[280] Finally, on November 2, a take-it-or-leave-it fax arrived from the Division's new Director making what the Board decided to be an inadequate offer. Moreover, its purpose was to be limited to TIE and youth activities. Meeting four days later, the Board resolved to reject the offer.[281] Further exchanges followed but to little avail. On November 19, the Board revolved to restate its rejection and to wind up.[282]

Thus, despite all the rear-guard effort, the money really had run out or could not be assured (depending on one's point of view). A further touch of paradox might be added in that the arrival of a Labor government – so longed for in the arts community and across the community – should have seemed so little sympathetic to New Moon. Perhaps Goss and his colleagues saw it as too much a creature of the Nationals or too tainted by a chequered history to bother trying to save. Perhaps the government was just too new and its arts administrative arrangements still too uncertain after thirty-two years of uninterrupted Conservative rule.[283]

So David Fenton, the fifth and final Artistic Director, finished up at the end of that year (not without some controversy regarding the payment of his fees) and the Company folded soon afterwards on a sombre note. The last document in the record is set of minutes hand-written by Elizabeth Perkins in January 1991. By then, no one had either the time or the energy left to type them up.

A Midsummer Night's Dream
Photo: Ponch Hawkes
Gina Riley

Helmut Bakaitis

7

What did it do ?

When the flush of a new-born sun fell first on Eden's green and gold,

Our father Adam sat under the Tree and scratched with a stick in the mould;

And the first rude sketch that the world had seen was joy to his mighty heart,

Till the Devil whispered behind the leaves, "It's pretty, but is it Art?"

Rudyard Kipling – 'The Conundrum of the Workshops'

Views and reviews

This aspect of New Moon's story draws heavily on reporting and other commentary found in the major regional newspapers. They reflect both the scope and nature of response to the Company's work in each city and also offer a sense of scale since that response, not unnaturally, varied greatly from play to play, from city to city and year-to-year. References to and quotes from letters to the editor in these publications also give a feel – though scarcely comprehensive – for wider public sentiment toward the work and about the Company. They are also illuminating in other ways. They demonstrate up to a point that audiences *were* interested, engaged and sometimes provoked into joining open debate about the productions, their subject matter, public funding of the arts and indeed the purpose of theatre itself. The content of reviews, likewise, sometimes strays beyond evaluation of a particular show into broader questions of the role and significance of having such a company in their midst. There is also often a depth of observation and subtlety of insight by critics to a degree which might well have surprised their metropolitan peers.

That, too, serves to underline the fact that New Moon did not enter into a redneck wilderness as it was frequently portrayed. Its media and audiences were as capable of sustaining a serious and informed dialogue about the performing arts, both as to their value and at times their shortcomings, as their capital city brethren. No doubt there were proportionately as many people of conservative inclination as may be found in the suburbs of major cities and sometimes their views might seem a little archaic even for the times. But let us also not forget that Queensland, over time, has had its more adventurous side. In the 1890s it elected the world's first Labor government, albeit one that lasted only five days. It produced in Andrew Fisher one of Australia's early reforming prime ministers. It is the only State to have abandoned the tiresome bi-cameral parliamentary system (in 1922). It abolished capital punishment fifty years before any other State. It was alone in the Commonwealth in having a free public hospital system; it has twice radically redrawn and reformed local government to a degree far in advance of anything elsewhere in Australia; and from the 1920s adopted state funded grammar schools in the major provincial cities. Spectacularly, it is the only State ever to elect a member of the Communist Party to its parliament – Fred Patterson MLA for Bowen 1945-1950 – also incidentally an Alderman of the Townsville City Council and first to be so elected anywhere in Australia. Other mavericks also abound.

The Company

The New Moon company that assembled in Townsville in early 1982 was a multitalented, multi-skilled band many of whom afterwards went on to significant careers. They are recorded here in full as a tribute to their extraordinary achievement in this valiant, pioneering endeavour. They were actors: Robert Arthur, Valerie Bader, Gillian

Hyde, Bob Baines, Peter Barclay (also director), Stephen Clark, Debra May, Margaret Moore, Terry O'Connell (also director), Wayne Pigram, Kris Ralph, John Rush, Joe Spano and David Sandford. The designers were Anthony Babicci and David Bell; sound design and operator was Ross Brewer and lighting design and operator, Michael Elliott with choreographer, Aku Kadogo. Stage managers were Jimmy Mann and Nicole Mitchell; costume maker and designer assistant, Eleanor Donald and construction manager, Kerry Saul.

There were thus ten actors plus the two Artistic Directors who also acted. Of those, four were Queensland-based: Robert Arthur, Margaret Moore, John Rush and David Sandford. Moore was the sole Northern-based member. Robert Arthur was originally from Innisfail though largely working in Brisbane often with Bryan Nason on his Shakespeare projects. Thus one might, at a stretch, claim there were two (token?) North Queenslanders.

Stephen Clark recalls: "It was a bit of a mixed mob. Terry and Peter did bring a cohort of people that they had worked with in Wagga so there was a core of people who'd come out of the Wagga experience and then they picked up me from Melbourne and Robert Arthur and others from Brisbane, I think, and a few others from Sydney and other places... they'd done at least an eastern seaboard call-out...some people knew each other pretty well and the rest of us were all new... [of course] there's a difference between the remembered and reflected self and as I kind of remember it, there was a group of people who...had bonds and were connected and that's always useful when you are on tour in Australia. You've got to establish relationships and some knew Terry and Peter very well and knew and understood how they worked, so that probably made some difference, but I don't remember it being a marked difference."[284]

On the subject of talent, Peter Barclay echoes the sentiments: "we had a very talented young band. ... Johnny Rush was musical director and played keyboards. We had David Sandford who played saxophone beautifully and handled several other instruments quite well. I think Joe

Spano learnt bass guitar. We said okay you are playing bass and he said: whaddya mean? I said you are playing bass, you have got two or three months in your spare time to pick it up. We had Wayne Pigram who was a great drummer. I first met Wayne when he was a drummer."[285]

In that first season, O'Connell's production of 'Ned Kelly' played a very tight schedule of Cairns Civic Centre, January 27-30, Townsville Civic Theatre, February 4-9, Mackay Theatre Royal, February 12-13 and Rockhampton's Pilbeam Theatre, February 17-20. Bear in mind that throughout, the Company was rehearsing Peter Barclay's production of 'Macbeth' which followed hard on its heels. That was the pattern for the first three productions of each season through to 1985.

Finding their feet

Clark was a jobbing actor in Melbourne and had had what he now calls "a reasonably fair career there". He'd worked with J C Williamson and Harry M Miller and a done a lot of TV and a variety in drama but, as an actor, he was still searching for adventure. "When I saw the advertisement that they were looking for actors to join this Company in North Queensland it tripped my adventurous spirit immediately, and I really worked hard – harder than ever, I think – on my audition pieces. I remember auditioning with Terry [O'Connell] and Peter Barclay and was lucky enough to get the job. I didn't know what to expect – it was just very exciting. I'd never previously worked with either Terry or Peter or even heard of them before. I was very much established and based in Melbourne... As I understand it – at least directly prior to New Moon experience – they had come out of the theatre company in Wagga." [286]

What he does remember vividly was that the entire experience was: "pretty full on. But that was what we were there to do. The day would begin with an exercise session or a tai chi session or something and you would rehearse all day and learn your lines at night ... and then we hit the road." After a week of being on the road, by the time they got to Rockhampton, they would start rehearsing the next piece. So, they'd be rehearsing during the day and playing at night. "I think the only saving grace was Mackay which was the third leg of each tour; we didn't have to rehearse during the day; so we had the days off and played at night". It was a brief respite in the midst of an otherwise intense cycle of getting the next show up while performing the current one. Then, by the time they got to Rockie, it was rehearse and play again. "I don't remember ever resenting that. It was just the way it was. It was full on and over time you came to be living in this bubble, really. You didn't intersect or interact much with the community around us, if I recall". [287]

Clark opted to stay for a second year in 1983 and acknowledges that familiarity and the experience of a number of those who returned having worked together under such intense circumstances made the situation both more relaxed and at the same time individually and, he suspects collectively, more creative. But at the end, he felt that the acting part of his life had come to a close and he was anxious to explore other pathways. Nevertheless, his association with New Moon had a certain symmetry in that he returned in 1990 to direct the Company's last real success and last tour with 'The Summer of the Seventeenth Doll'. But theatrically for him, that was it. "Little did I know that it was to be the beginning of the rest of my life as an adventurer and traveller and especially my love for Queensland". [288]

What is intriguing is that Clark is yet another key person in New Moon's history for whom the experience "turned [me] on to Queensland and its possibilities in culture, community and the arts". He went on to acquire a diploma in Leisure Studies at the Brisbane College of Advanced Education and later a Master's degree in International Tourism Management from the University of Queensland. From there he went into various roles at Tourism Queensland first for five years as a Destination Marketing Manager and later as Manager, Strategic Planning. Thence he moved into more specifically arts management areas first as Managing Producer at the Queensland Music Festival which has a strong regional remit and later as Executive Officer of

Flying Arts Alliance.

Today, Clark is Director of Aha!goodthinking and an experienced, independent planning and management consultant with specialist expertise in the fields of arts, culture, tourism and special events. He works extensively around Queensland with a range of local government and not-for-profit sector clients, delivering high-calibre services in policy, planning, management, research and marketing and management advisory and consulting services for the arts, cultural development, tourism and special event sectors, specialising in research and development for local government, the small-to- medium arts sector and regional and remote communities. He undertakes customised training programs in arts business and management, special event/project planning and management, cultural and creative tourism and association governance. In the midst of all that he has found time to work with Volunteers International assisting with economic empowerment in developing nations most recently acting as Tourism Development Officer in Budhanilkantha, Nepal. In some ways it has been a long journey from the rough-and-tumble touring in the ensemble of Australia's first, pioneering, regional, touring theatre company. But perhaps in another way, it is not so very far...

The Kelly gang

One initiative that New Moon attempted right at the beginning was to create a subscription scheme for the dates in all four cities. A "subs" advertisement appeared in newspapers across the region offering a season package based on the issue of vouchers redeemable at the box office. The main deal was 4 plays for only $30, which, even back then, seems extraordinarily cheap. However, the campaign failed to take off and was quickly abandoned. While the leadership considered that it had been a worthwhile effort to launch the season and thus the Company as a whole in each market, audiences were not used to booking ahead even for single tickets let alone a season ticket, and the management concluded that money could be saved by not going to the expense of such advance promotion again.

'Ned Kelly, the Electric Music Show' – to give it its full title – was the first to take to the road and designed to display the acting and musical versatility of the ensemble and the in-your-face New Moon production style. In that respect, it might be regarded as an ideal opener to brand the Company and its aesthetic. Undertaken without a Production Manager, there were, as Kerry Saul observed, worrying overruns which forced the projected deficit up and thereby budgets down for the other three shows that year. In order to offset some of those accumulating losses, Iles was compelled to propose to the participating Councils that they retrospectively convert their guarantees into box office sharing arrangements.[289]

While 'Ned Kelly' had had mixed success when originally produced down South, its creators were a winning combination. Reg Livermore was still widely remembered for his ground-breaking, mega-success, high camp and high energy 'Betty Blokkbuster Follies' followed by 'Wonder Woman'. Today, they would almost certainly be picketed or worse for demeaning women (though a much watered-down Spiegeltent version of 'Betty Blokkbuster' was presented at the 2020 Sydney Festival – to mild applause), but in the '70s and '80s they were packed out and acclaimed as sensational. Music for 'Ned Kelly' was by Patrick Flynn who had shot to prominence over a decade earlier as music director of 'Hair' and was at that time a resident conductor with American Ballet Theatre in New York City. Their names were joined in the publicity by Bob Ellis who had contributed "additional lyrics". One would not have thought his star shone then or later so brightly as to warrant that billing. Perhaps he had a pushy agent, since he himself was always shy and retiring. Director, Terry O'Connell's name is absent. That began a trend of barely acknowledging resident artists in the Company's advertising of which Helmut Bakaitis was later to complain[290] and Rodney Fisher to place blame on Iles as being a factor in the Queensland public's not taking them to its heart.

Nevertheless, *Cairns Post* declared "Ned Kelly – an electrifying performance", singling out Stephen Clark's Ned and performances of Bob Baines, Joe Spano and "the two Kelly women, Margaret Moore and Kris Ralph".[291] Not everyone was as impressed. Julia Guthrie noted that for residents used to "a diet of amateur stage productions and traditional ballet and concert performances, the rock opera was probably strange and overwhelming".[292] She was unhappy with the sound level and the clutter of leads and mikes on stage and felt it was the wrong choice to start with. Members of the public chimed in about the music volume, some even turned on the reviewers for what they perceived as fawning praise instead of having the guts to give honest appraisal. The *Cairns Advertiser* however, felt Ned himself would have been "proud" and claimed that the production: "took Cairns by storm".[293]

With such a disparate group of performers of such diverse backgrounds, there was inevitably a period of adjustment. Stephen Clark recalls: "I do remember [that] in the first rehearsal process for 'Ned Kelly'. I'd come out of a mainstream background. I'd worked for Melbourne Theatre Company and Playbox and [such] places so I'd had that pretty solid background and I guess I was used to working in a certain kind of way, and it took a while to get used to finding the best way to work in this new environment, given my background and that some others knew each other pretty well".[294]

Fiona Perry in the Townsville *Daily Bulletin* urged: "Go to 'Ned Kelly' – it rocks, it grips. It explodes. It unmasks things about the legend, about Australia that have been asleep too long. . . From the first impact of a black umbrella rising a like a bird of prey to the final image of the noose it's an impressive first production. It has to be seen to be believed. North Queensland has culturally come of age. We've waited too long".[295] By contrast, Cameron Thompson in the *Gladstone Observer* was underwhelmed, considering that Ned himself lacked: "... magnetism" and that the production was somewhat "muddied" Nevertheless, it was "certainly a great night to remember. Marking an excellent Queensland debut for Northern Queensland's own professional theatre company".[296] Meanwhile, Mackay's JS noted with commendable insight, that it was: "as much about the tragedy of Ireland as it is about the Kelly myth."[297]

Rockhampton's Judith Anderson wrote: "it's an impressive production and certainly has the impact needed for a "first" by a new company. They have those vital theatrical qualities of energy and commitment." There was, however, a side swipe at the provenance of the acting company which made it a little difficult "to avoid the impression of "jobs for the boys" with at least nine of the 24 members having been associated at one time or another with the Riverina Trucking Company where New Moon's joint artistic directors, Peter Barclay and Terry O'Connell established their reputation for adventurous frontier theatre". (Though she failed to point out, not at the same time.)[298]

Iles leapt to riposte. But rather than merely setting the record straight, chose to attack – an unwise tactic one would have thought for a new company seeking to grow goodwill. His remarks set the tone for much of the Company's future PR – or lack thereof: "The parochialism of Miss Anderson's comment about our giving 'jobs for the boys' is divisive rubbish", he wrote next day to the paper. The Artistic Directors, he claimed, had auditioned in Brisbane, Sydney, Melbourne and Adelaide and "few Queenslanders applied" implying that perhaps there just wasn't enough talent in the State. "What director would be stupid enough to employ "friends" if they did not have excitement, vibrancy, glamour, warmth and intelligence?".[299]

Anderson responded mildly two days later, and with rather more grace than Iles's remarks might have warranted. She noted that his explanation of why so few Queenslanders were selected was "both plausible and reasonable. However, I am not totally convinced of the need for "excitement, glamour vibrancy and warmth" in the lighting designer, assistant stage manager, sound designer and wardrobe mistress".[300] Touché.

The Scottish play

Next came 'Macbeth' This time Barclay directed. Fiona Perry pronounced it "an intensely dramatic spectacle ... brooding and potent..." David Bell's design, tattered cloaks and shaggy silhouettes, has the monotone impact of a nightmare."³⁰¹ SOH at the Mackay *Daily Mercury* declared 'Macbeth' to be: "different" and "scored a remarkable success" ³⁰² but shed little further light, while the 'Central Queensland Express' opined: "Last week's theatre audience could be excused for surmising they had been teleported into 'Blake [sic] Seven' or 'The Rocky Horror Show' rather than Shakespeare's 'Macbeth'. However, once they had become accustomed... they settled down to enjoy a spectacular, quite brilliant performance". ³⁰³

Down in Rockie, Judith Anderson noted that for those who were normally subject to badly directed touring productions performed by faded actors in false beards "New Moon's 'Macbeth' comes as both a relief and a pleasant surprise" concentrating "on the underlying themes of ambition, pride and lust for power".³⁰⁴ Lesley Boaden lamented that his town could not yet "enjoy the pleasure and privilege of our own professional theatre company" by including Gladstone in their circuit and added: "to Peter Barclay, I say – an awe-inspiring direction".³⁰⁵

QTC's Alan Edwards, visiting Rockhampton from Brisbane "to check out the competition", described 'Macbeth' as "terrific".³⁰⁶ Well, in that situation he would, wouldn't he? Far off in Sydney *The Australian* reported: "New Moon is Australia's only fully touring company, performing nightly and rehearsing daily as they convoy in rented cars. That requires discipline."³⁰⁷ The literary journal *Westerly* commended New Moon: "as a company creating its own style as APG, Nimrod and Popular Theatre Troupe have done" contrasting them with more traditional companies like STC and MTC.³⁰⁸

But let us walk away for a moment from professional evaluation to a starker anecdote related by designer Anthony Babicci about a much blunter and at the same time enlightening response. He had undertaken to do some teaching in the art program at the Technical College in Townsville. During a workshop, the students had asked what he was doing at the moment and he replied that he was designing 'Tommy' which of course appealed to them but, he added, the Company was about to present 'Macbeth' – which is Shakespeare, he explained: "In the group of all these youths – they were 18 – 22/23 – there was one guy in his early 30s: he was a milkman who was married with children but was doing art school part-time. He was like: everybody knows Shakespeare is shit and it is boring and what do you want to do shit like that for?" Babicci asked if they'd ever seen Shakespeare. The milkman said no, but that everyone knew it was crap. The designer made the point to them that they could go through life having opinions like that about things they'd never seen, or they could try them out. Subsequently, he went first to Barclay and then to Iles asking if he could bring them to a performance for free, perhaps a matinee or a dress rehearsal since most of the students couldn't afford to buy tickets. Both agreed. There was a Wednesday matinee and he arranged their free admission. "So they all came and they entered and first up we've got this huge stage set-up in the theatre with a giant sound system and rock 'n' roll [expletive deleted] spotlights, scraggly feather costumes and the witches are tromping around on this massive steel grid and [there were] wild sword fights. And they came out at interval and said: 'wow!' I asked: 'are you getting it and understanding it?' They replied: 'I think so.' But they were just completely blown away and this milkman who was the most cynical of them said: nobody told us it was like this ... [and] nobody left".[309] That last is perhaps the ultimate endorsement that every theatre practitioner craves.

Controversy

The third production in that inaugural year – 'No Orchids for Miss Blandish' – was a quirky choice by any measure. James Hadley Chase wrote this thriller-shocker in 1939 and it became at once a best seller, later made into two successful films. The actor-playwright, Robert David MacDonald, who wrote for the Glasgow Citizens Theatre, made the stage version which was a European fantasy of how the world saw the gangster situation in America in the 1940s. Peter Barclay recalls that it had an odd provenance at New Moon.

Although Iles never interfered in the programming as such, even before they were appointed, back at Nimrod Barclay recalls his lending him a book with superb black-and-white photos of the Scottish production. He was entranced. Generally, however, the response in North Queensland was not as enthusiastic as clearly it had been in Glasgow. Leonard Marriott in the *Cairns Post* thought the result: "a bad play very well acted".[310] Paul Mitchell, purportedly a 19 year old from Cairns, was: "utterly disgusted. It was a high class pornographic exhibition".[311] There were some who surmised that that letter to the editor was not all it claimed to be, possibly emanating in fact from a source close to the Company. However that might have been, 46 year old John Clarke replied, asking where Paul Mitchell had been if he found the production so offensive: "The only serious note in the 'pornographic exhibition' is the high calibre of acting displayed". G E Richards also took exception to the teenager's lament, wondering if the young man realised that he had done the Company a service in generating adverse publicity. "People would flock to this questionable play to find out if their education is sexually complete". [312]

Post critic, Leonard Marriott returned to the argument quoting from 'Trousered Apes' that literature (and plays) should inspire men with vision of higher possibility rather than merely reflecting ugly modern reality". Sartre, he suggested, had urged the opposite and clearly New Moon in 'No Orchids...' inclined to that view. However, for those seeking a more cheery theatre the local audiences could, he said, look forward to the Cairns Little Theatre's forthcoming production of the Ben Travers farce, 'The Bed Before Yesterday'.[313] Nothing grubby to be seen there.

Post reader, Bruce Whereat, no doubt with a touch of irony, suggested that as the production featured an explicit rape scene involving a corn cob, perhaps the Cairns Civic Centre should adopt a "giant corn cob in their gardens to represent the state of the arts in North Queensland." [314] An emotionally fragile Raymond Everard declared that "this is the kind of play to give pornography a bad name ... It has left a scar which will remain with me for the rest of my life ... If the play is a success it will be the end of theatre as we know it." He also reported having seen two nuns in the audience though not whether they remained after interval.[315] G Welch, Secretary of the Cairns Branch of the Australian Family Association wrote to the Mayor of Cairns: "the current season's plays could not be described as suitable for family entertainment and. after all, families also contribute to the finances for the New Moon Theatre through their taxes and rates."[316]

Post columnist, Heather Harvey replied suggesting that perhaps many of those agitated by the content had missed the point. "Rather than stimulating sexual excitement, the much discussed rape episode in the play engendered only sexual revulsion…Thank you, New Moon, for stirring up us apathetic Northerners. You held up the mirror to a sick society, and we didn't like what we saw".[317] Iles then joined the fray in thanking one and all for their "lively debate" and in the process asked how different a reaction to the sex and violence in 'No Orchids…' there might have been if found in a Jacobean tragedy such as 'The Duchess of Malfi' where murder and grotesquerie were rife.[318] That is rather like saying we might approve of incest because it appears in Genesis, though mostly people of the Book do not.

Fiona Perry in the Townsville *Daily Bulletin* took a more nuanced view, observing that the Company had: "fingered the script lightly" and describing it as "a cool trot for New Moon" through which it demonstrated yet again its flexibility.[319] However, Rockhampton's Judith Anderson found the production "disappointing" not so much the fault of the performers or of the direction but of an "inherently poor script which wavers uncertainly between high comedy and realistic drama and from clever literate jokes and some good one-liners to gratuitous, heavy-handed obscenity".[320] R. G. Jorgensen (Mrs) chose to complain direct to Ian Satchwell, Administrator of the Pilbeam Theatre: "we were not offended out of a sense of morality or prudishness but because we felt assaulted by this gutter language."[321] An interesting view from inside is offered by actor, Margaret Bornhorst who played the title role: "I loathed 'Miss Blandish. I thought it had no value at all".[322]

On the other hand, in the *Morning Bulletin* correspondent, Bob Martin considered that "the show was good entertainment and was value for money".³²³ While Graeme Robertson agreed, having found it a: "delightful, larger than life romp through a fantasy world of comedy and drama, again showing the versatility of those professional players".³²⁴ Though given the bleak and violent nature of the piece one wonders if he was entirely awake throughout. But *de gustibus*, as we poncy schoolboys used to say.

Rock 'n' roll

Then along came 'Tommy', an Australian stage premiere (remarkable in itself for an infant company) and as different from its predecessors as one could imagine. It was Barclay's second and, as things turned out, last production for New Moon or rather last half, since in reality he directed only part of it (Stephen Clark reports that after Barclay's somewhat abrupt departure the actors improvised the rest.)³²⁵ This put an end – albeit unhappily – to what had been an interesting if tension-filled diarchy with O'Connell. He had announced that he wished to "freelance"³²⁶ but, in fact, it resulted from a series of confrontations culminating in that decision. "Peter was devastated, absolutely devastated and the sense of betrayal was massive", Babicci noted.³²⁷

Despite these issues Peter Symes wrote of 'Tommy': "A nearly full house with many new faces was held spellbound by both the excellent theatre and clean crisp rock music". ³²⁸ Fiona Perry, was more tongue-in-cheek: "If 'Ned Kelly', 'Miss Blandish' and 'Macbeth' disturbed your sense of equilibrium, then 'Tommy' ... will send you tripping back to the psychedelic 60s"... If you're inclined to like Salvador Dali and the op-pop art of the '60s, comics and the full-on music of The Who (taken liberties with) then pump your jugulars full of 'Tommy'".³²⁹ Stephen Clark pronounced it "a blast to do!"³³⁰ But at least one audience member, R E Sutton was unhappy, not so much with the show itself but rather with the attitude of the company: "Tonight for the first time I can recall, a cast was not prepared to accept the standing ovation the audience clearly wanted to give it ... My support for one, in 1983, will hinge on a change of attitude in the company to one which is not patronising but rather accepting of social mores in the North" [331] Iles replied: "We are not unfriendly or withdrawn" and invited Mr Sutton to join the Company's Friends association. At this distance it's hard to know whether sheer exhaustion by then had sapped the performers' energy or the departure of Barclay, for all his eccentric behaviour, had left a hole in their spirits. The point is that the audience took note and had reservations thereafter.

During the run of 'Tommy', as if its world were not weird enough in itself, greater surrealism still was added when Britain went to war with Argentina over a rock in the south Atlantic few had heard of and whose inhabitants to this day do not have a vote in UK elections. But in the process it turned British Prime Minister, Margaret Thatcher into a sort of latter day Boudica, though it achieved little else. It was not to be the last time in New Moon's history that life would eclipse art.

A split in the ranks

Nothing loath, Rockhampton's Mayor, Ald. Webber (ALP) sweepingly declared New Moon's productions "garbage" prior to a meeting with his fellow mayors of Mackay, Cairns and Townville to discuss the Company's joint funding arrangement with them. He, and some of his municipal colleagues, suggested that a rating scheme should be introduced for shows at the Pilbeam. At base, the issue was, of course, 'No Orchids...' which, almost needlessly to recount, he hadn't seen. In the event, the mayors continued their funding, but resolved that they wanted to see scripts in advance. [332] New Moon (aka Paul Iles) fiercely rejected that notion[333] and for the moment the proposal went nowhere but like many such apparently minor incidents it continued to fester quietly. The newspaper itself tried to have a bob each way, pointing out that as the four Councils funded the Company Iles couldn't just dismiss what they had to say. But equally, it declared that censorship as such could not be condoned. "In the case of 'No Orchids...' the public stayed away in droves and many who did opt to see the play walked out in disgust. And that's the way it should be. In the long run, the people should decide that they should or should not see."³³⁴ And, as if to revert to things that really mattered, the same Editorial hailed the birth of a son to Prince Charles and Lady Diana!

Almost, as though to cast a dissenting voice on all this attempt at restriction, the Mulgrave Shire, which had previously rejected New Moon's application for financial support, approved a GAL of $13,530] though not it must be said, without dissent. Cr. Shirley Harwood who voted against the measure said she was opposed to local government guarantees for cultural pursuits. "Culture means different things to different people", she penetratingly observed. However, New Moon Chairman, Bruce Shepherd was at pains to point out that it wasn't costing them all that much anyway. The first season had charged Pioneer Shire and the Mackay Council a mere $650 each rather that the GAL which had been budgeted at $9,614. Regrettably New Moon's finances would never look as good again.³³⁵

Some citizens of those towns hailed the results: "If the sum of $4,900 rent is all that the ratepayers of Cairns have outlaid for New Moon, then we have got off lightly." Peter Davies declared.³³⁶ Rosemary Nason added her voice to a chorus wanting to guarantee the city's funding and decrying mayoral philistinism: "I came away from all performances feeling exhilarated ... We laughed in some shows and were moved to tears during some moments in 'Macbeth' truly brought to life by talented vigorous young Australians".³³⁷

At the same time, John Clarke in the *Gladstone Observer* found 'Tommy': "not just another rock show, it is a rock event",³³⁸ while in the Mackay *Daily Mercury*, "SS" pronounced 'Tommy' a "sensation" and added that it would "have to be the most exciting piece of theatre Mackay has seen in years". On the technical side, he could only resort to superlatives.³³⁹ Letter writer, T Cartmel who had been twice noted that the production was: "extremely well received by Mackay audiences, readily displayed by the reception at the conclusion of the show".³⁴⁰

However, Anna Bock in the *Townsville Advertiser* was less impressed. Finding its ideas clichéd and the production doing: "little to overcome the weakness of the play", she felt that the New Moon "wave of rocking and blinking theatre (see also 'Macbeth') comes about 15 years late and accordingly much diluted".[341] Not only the Company but the configuration of the venues also came in for criticism. Peter Davies: "watching [New Moon's] productions I often felt there was an aesthetic apartheid whereby my response was dictated by the [Cairns Civic] centre. I did not feel I was participating in a collaborative event".[342] It was a sentiment with which covertly at least the Company agreed.

So far, so good

Judith Anderson, looking back on the inaugural season observed: "From the first production 'Ned Kelly', New Moon has shown that music theatre is its forte but now after six months together the group has developed a cohesiveness and laid-back confidence ... The result ['Tommy'] is top-quality music theatre, enhanced by Anthony Babicci's vibrant comic-strip pinball parlour set and Michael Elliott's extravaganza of flashing lights".[343]

The first New Moon season had secured 17,000 paying customers and made an operating surplus of $34,291. That was achieved on top of a deficit of ($948) in 1981. It is interesting to note that HVTC, with the advantage of nearly a decade of operation and resident in just one city and in its own theatre year-round, peaked at 17,041 attendances only in 1985 and thereafter declined to 12,681 by 1992.[344]

Also reviewing that first year, Heather Harvey in the *Cairns Post* remarked:. "I can recall no other artistic event in Cairns which has created the interest and controversy aroused by the New Moon Theatre Company". After the initial predictable outcry about one production, expressions of personal opinion, both for and against, still continued through 'Letters to the Editor'. She considered that to be a healthy sign and a "measure of the impact the Company has had in the first six months of its existence". Her comprehensive coverage of the various confrontations with local government was impressive, noting lack of physical resources, absence of a permanent home and the pitiful remuneration of the actors ("would [the critics] be prepared to work 75 hours per week for six months with no overtime or penalty rates, for $204.60 for half the season and $187.10 for the other?", she asked). As well those remarks demonstrate an understanding of the funding environment and show that at least some in the local media were just as aware of the economics of the arts at that time as any of the commentariat in capital cities.[345]

Reflecting on all of this with Ms Harvey, it is possible to consider that New Moon had well and truly arrived in the North. The following year there were some changes to the line-up but, given the rigours of the touring and production schedule, not as many as might have been expected. Six actors returned: David Sandford, Gillian Hyde, Valerie Bader, Bob Baines, Stephen Clark and Wayne Pigram, seven if you count O'Connell, thought he didn't perform that year. Five departed and four joined: Nicholas Flanaghan, Penny McCue, Gina Riley and Deirdre Chambers. Chambers, a graduate of the JCU drama course, was the first genuinely local actor to be engaged. Guests included illusionist Doug Tremblatt, puppeteer Joe Gladwin, choreographer, Chrissie Koltai and visual artist, Ponch Hawkes. Yet nothing that came after could quite recapture the excitement or controversy of that first year. Certainly, the response of the critics and as far as one can judge the public, was muted by comparison.

Inside looking out

But what had the experience offered the actors in this extraordinary ensemble? Unlike Clark or Margaret Bornhorst whose stories we have related, Bob Baines was one of those whom some observers regarded as being in Terrence O'Connell's 'inner circle'. He'd met O'Connell through the Riverina Trucking Company. "I was blown away by the quality of the work. I was coming from Adelaide and Flinders to Sydney – the big lights – and you think: this is what I am going to be and then a friend invites you down to Wagga and you see the best the theatre you've ever seen".[346] Baines was a graduate of the Flinders University Drama Centre where both the training and aesthetic environment had been somewhat more austere than what he found at RTC. As a result O'Connell's work came as quite a shock: "He did a black and white 'Romeo & Juliet' and the 'Strangler of Rillington Place' a little one-hander about Christie the murderer. That was done in a playpen filled with paper. A one man show and he stood up out of the paper and started. That was radical then."[347]

Baines expressed his enthusiasm to O'Connell and was invited to join RTC for the next play in their season. "And there was me and the Stage Manager. [We] shared one salary because that's all there was and we lived hand-to-mouth and it was great and we had so much fun." All that lasted for about six months and "Peter Barclay was on the edge of that as well. He was in love with Berkoff. So we did a couple of Berkoff plays there as well and Terrence did some shows in Sydney including a thing called 'Depression Darlings' at the Seymour Centre."[348]

But when Baines got to North Queensland it was all a great deal harder: "We used to do an advanced Jane Fonda work-out as a warm up; that's how fit we were. We used to do that to get ready. But we [also] had advice from the Israeli Army about how to hydrate, because they had to keep their soldiers being able to function in the desert. So we have all these rules about drinking and when we were doing these stretches and stuff and we were sweating so much that our nostrils would fill up. It was such a vile climate," Baines remembers. The experience play-by-play was a wild ride, "but for me the biggest thing was "Life on Mars" which was a devised piece. It was fifteen songs of David Bowie in the first act and fifteen in the second. No band – we had a few people who could play [instruments] But I think Gillian Hyde learnt fifteen songs on the bass guitar in four weeks."[349]

Unlike some of our other cast of characters Baines has had a lifelong career as an actor appearing on the stages of all the State Theatre

Companies and Bell Shakespeare, most of the then regional theatre companies playing everything from Shakespeare through musicals to contemporary drama. His list of appearances on television is like a roll call of series over the last 30 years from the early 'Sons and Daughters', 'Country Practice', 'Water Rats' or 'Coroner' to the more recent 'Blue Heelers', 'Home and Away', 'Rake' and 'Redfern Now'. "New Moon is where I lost the fear because I am standing there ... the curtain is going to go up in a second and you know intellectually that with your Flinders training, this is impossible, this is ridiculous, but you still had to do it. In a minute I am going to have to do it and that's when [the fear] just left me." There were other kinds of learning too: "'Ned Kelly' was fun. The only drag role I have ever played – Mrs Jones the publican".[350]

Baines would not attribute this long and continuous career solely to that early New Moon experience but he does believe that much of the resilience necessary and the endurance learnt was formed in the hard yakka of those two years: "It was my coming of age. They were a great bunch. Very brave. I wouldn't be the actor I became without New Moon. It was our version of "Rep". You had to be fairly tough internally and "I've always thought of it as my postgraduate studies in acting. Because there was no room for excuses, no room for dilatoriness, no room for vapours." [351]

Second time around

Starting the second year with Kander and Ebb's musical 'Cabaret' probably didn't help to move things forward from what had been a very successful beginning. Most audience members knew it only from the somewhat cheery and cheesy Liza Minelli movie. The original stage show had been both darker and less glitzy. Judi Dench had played the role of Sally Bowles in the West End. No glamour puss she. Moreover, the great era of the Broadway filmed musical was long over. So when 'Cabaret' movie came along in 1972, it had perhaps a disproportionate impact. Either way, the New Moon choice seemed less than the adventurousness that had come to be expected of them. Critics, in general were reserved, pronouncing it "enjoyable" and "entertaining" and praised the cast: Gina Riley as Sally Bowles, Valerie Bader as Fraulein Schneider and Bob Baines as Herr Schultz in particular. But one feels a tinge of restraint. Maybe it was also a little anti-climatic after first year's flash and dazzle. As if to underscore this, the *Townsville Magazine* observed: "New Moon's 'Cabaret' may not have Liza and Joel, but this is still good entertainment".[352] Nevertheless, Martin Hirsch in *Cairns Focus* reported that reported that thunderous applause throughout credited a talented and well-co-ordinated cast. "G" in Rockhampton's *Morning Bulletin* called it the: "first dazzling production of the season ... Definitely not to be missed".[353]

Leonard Marriott. in the *Cairns Post* wrote: "The impact of this production... relied heavily on the raw energy of the performers, in the clarity of diction, well drilled movements and musical backing".[354] "Cabaret is not a light and frothy musical but, music aside, a rather austere play," said the *Daily Bulletin*[355] and Linda Turnley in the Gladstone *Observer* felt that: "the New Moon Theatre Company has come up with a production that compares to the best works of other companies". [356]

This was followed by their second Shakespeare, 'A Midsummer Night's Dream' ever popular but often a place to pull out stops and add arabesques. Leonard Marriott: felt it was all rather over the top and that Shakespeare got lost somewhere along the way, but agreed that the real wonder of the show was the magic conjuring and the puppetry supplied by Tremblatt and Gladwin. "The stage effects obtained as much applause as the players... This updated version was a dream of a show". It was also O'Connell at his most prodigious.[357]

Peter Cresswell in the *Cairns Focus* considered that: "the bard of Avon would never, in his wildest dreams have imagined the type of treatment which the... company gave to his comedy... New Moon gave it a pop "Hollywood" style. Thick accents from the New York Bronx ...Has Hermia ever been called Hoymia before by Lysander, I wonder?".[358] 'A

Midsummer Night's Dream' as produced by New Moon was simply magic wrote Andrew Miller. 'G' in the Rockhampton *Morning Bulletin* enthused: "The casting is superb. The music is exciting. Skilful puppetry and breathtaking illusion have the audience of the edge of their seats".[359]

Around this time a selection of the general public was also commending New Moon. One happy punter from Townsville was overjoyed with 'A Midsummer Night's Dream'. Despite some initial "trepidation" she wrote to: "compliment the New Moon Theatre group on their originality... The actors were superb..." The production she felt "will be a long remembered event in the minds of many citizens of Townsville.[360] And it got a very big tick from 15 year old Toni Groves of Heatley High School initially wary, like many who are forced to slog through Shakespeare. She wrote: "to my amazement I thoroughly enjoyed their performances".[361]

Baines's favourite, 'Life on Mars' came next and somewhat revived the Company's monetary fortunes. A musical production knitted together by O'Connell and the company, it featured some 30 Bowie songs centred loosely around the general theme of the alienation of the human spirit and tenuously linked by Chrissie Koltai's imaginative choreography and an impressive slide show.

Terry Carroll in the Townville hailed it as the: "Best sustained performance yet and [New Moon has] come up with two hours of near-perfect rock opera".[362] "G" thought it: "A stunning and exciting rock revue that explodes on stage in a rhythm of light, colour and sound".[363] Although, in the Gladstone *Observer's* John Clarke felt that it was ok, but questioned: "where was the theatrical inventiveness for which the New Moon has become renowned? He considered that the lack of any dialogue to connect the songs into a plot or even framework meant the production was rather directionless: "there was no developing story to absorb the audience". He contrasted it with 'Tommy' where the strength lay not simply in its great rock music but in the "absorbingly bizarre storyline and in the strength of its central character."[364]

Meanwhile, Iles could boast that with over 8000 attendances it was the most successful New Moon production to date.[365] Two years later, O'Connell revived it with some of the original cast at the Sailors Home Theatre in Sydney. Writing in *The Sydney Morning Herald*, Prue Charlton declared it (posthumously) as: "another success for The New Moon Theatre Company" although she herself did not care much for it.[366]

Outside looking in

Lucinda Shaw, a young North Queenslander, was one who did, however, care very much. She would say today that her life was completely turned around by her encounter with New Moon. In her case, it was the impact of seeing extraordinary performances which the Company produced in these early years that led her to make a performing career out of what she had witnessed there.

It was the early eighties and Lucinda found herself in Townsville in mid-to-late teens trying to create some sense of self out of high school musicals and part-time jobs in sales, window dressing and fashion parades. She quotes Lou Reed on Andy Warhol: "There's one good thing about a small town, you hate it and you want to leave". Yet she sensed there was more to be found if she stayed open to it and reasoned that theatre could be where the meaning of her life could be revealed. There was some rough but disciplined training to be had at JCU, some rock musicals and Shakespeare to be attended here and there and, wonder of wonders, Marcia Hines and Khamal popping through Townsville occasionally on the commercial touring circuit.

Then New Moon appeared on the scene: "Suddenly there were powerful young actor/vocalists with a sense of beauty and grit and sass creating these fierce alternative shows in our town. A young Gina Riley with an attitude and a Broadway belt took the stage [in 'Cabaret']. I was mesmerised." She recalls that one of New Moon's early works was a "show" of Bowie's songs." She was around seventeen and hungry. Sitting in the audience of Townsville Civic Theatre where she'd already done several rock operas and musicals she wondered what more there was to be had and where any of this might take her. "My New Moon memory is visceral, even thirty-seven years on. Time stood still as a section of my brain opened up in the way others describe LSD trips (corny I know but I swear!). Stephen Clark with angular red hair and a white jump suit and Valerie Bader with a red mouth and white hair stood still on a black stage in two individual spotlights and out of the void brought 'Space Oddity' into being. I had never before seen and heard such powerful stillness, beholding the moments that define 'Major Tom' as everyman floating in existence. Stephen had a tender resonant tenor cut to his voice that moved me through and through. Later he sang 'Wild is the Wind', and hearing it for the first time I fell in love. I was awake".[367]

Not many performers have experienced such an apotheosis in seeing just one artist, Lucinda had the luck to experience it in three and she was hooked: "Valerie Bader had an intensity and assurance to her that I craved and wanted to embrace within myself. This show not only made me shudder to the core but was also a master class in performance. 'I'm doing that!' I thought, 'I must do this'. I took from that generous show the permission to be a performer, and training on how to bring commanding performances, celebrate gender nonconformity, relish music and poetry, and to interpret work with raw honesty and focus".[368] Later when she moved to Brisbane and got to know Clark personally and professionally she expressed her gratitude for opening that possibility in her.

As Shaw has developed her own work as a vocalist, actor, writer and theatre maker she's carried this moment with her. She's done several iterations of a show of the music of Ziggy Stardust and the Spiders from Mars under the direction of her long-time soul friend and musical collaborator, James Lees of Electric Moon. "When we were struck by the news that Bowie had passed, the work became a celebration and requiem and a privilege to share. These are the threads of theatre that bring beings to life".[369]

Act one finale

The final production of the second year and, as it happened, the last production by O'Connell was 'Royal Show' by Louis Nowra. It replaced the originally programmed and announced 'Bush Tivoli' and in some ways sought to occupy the same territory of reflection of a much larger community experience in country towns. However, 'nostalgia' and 'too long' were pretty well the twin responses. All critics agreed that the cast playing a vast number of vignette roles was impressive and once more demonstrated their versatility but even with lashings of *le temps perdu*, it was not enough to satisfy nor as it turned out to draw a crowd.

Judith Anderson in the *Morning Bulletin* characterised this by remarking that it was: "Warmly affectionate and unashamedly nostalgic ... A thoroughly satisfying evening's theatre and a reminder, 40 years on that (as Mr Fox, the show official says) 'we'll never be as innocent again'."[370] Leonard Marriott echoed her sentiments: "The audience is left not only with the memories of a very fine evening's entertainment but had also been carried in time to when the first post war "Royal" of 1946 opened on an era of hope and euphoria."[371] Terry Carroll in the Townsville *Daily Bulletin*, by contrast, thought the Company should have: "torn the script of 'Royal Show' in two and used only the first half".[372]

Certainly, the public voted with its feet. 'Royal Show' had the worst public response of the year, in fact of the two years thus far, while 'Life on Mars' had been the best. With O'Connell's departure and Bakaitis's arrival there was inevitably a change of pace, of personnel and of aesthetic. 1984 was also the year "Pleasure tested for the Tropics" came into vogue as what in those days was still called a slogan. Malcolm Calder recalls: "[Paul was] an in-your-face marketer. There is a logo on their programs and posters and stuff that that said 'pleasure-tested for the Tropics'. I can vividly recall Paul telling me that idea came off the sign on a mattress in a used furniture shop in Mackay – you know, one of the old junk shops – and he took a photograph of it and [then] graphically did it – a flea-bitten mildewed mattress".[373]

By November 1983 freshly arrived, Bakaitis had been already publicly stating that he was looking for a different kind of performing space. He even considered that the 1984 season would be preferable in different theatres from those they had. That set the scene for a confrontation with the managements which had been the essential driving force and *raison d'etre* for the Company in the first place. To that end, in a letter to British director, Richard Cottrell earlier in the year, he laid out his concept of a touring installation that would streamline the whole process.[374] This was, in effect, a thrust with a ceiling piece to be erected in front of the existing stages which were more conventionally proscenium format, so that the actors would be surrounded by the audience. It would also simplify design, bump-in and bump-out and to some extent standardise the four touring venues which unlike the circuit in South Australia, had each been built to a different design and scale, supposedly to reflect what had been deemed to be local needs. The basic idea of the touring structure was that it would jut out into the auditorium losing about 80 existing seats, on average. "Composed of three elements – a forestage, a ceiling piece and three lighting bridges. [It] solves the huge problem of inadequate FOH lighting in all the venues. Also [makes it] possible to mike the acting area", he explained. [375]

In reflecting on what his predecessor achieved and, indeed, on what he stood for, Bakaitis was perhaps less than gracious at the time. Admitting he hadn't seen any of the previous New Moon productions and basing his assessment largely on productions in the cabaret mode which O'Connell had directed in Melbourne, he was prepared to damn them with faint praise as being in effect full of colour and movement but low on (serious) content.[376] Yet with a long look back, one might argue to the contrary: that O'Connell's two year tenure was overall the only consistently successful period that New Moon enjoyed. That it came to a sticky end with 'Royal Show' and led to O'Connell's termination was unfortunate, to put it mildly. His balance of showbiz and Shakespeare with a bit of rock'n'roll and Australian humour probably hit the mark more than most of what followed. The downturn with the Nowra play, which had also had a shaky life when it premiered at Jim Sharman's Lighthouse Company in Adelaide, could well have been overcome by his plans for the following year.

But this all turns on speculation. What in fact happened was the Iles was determined to go in a markedly different direction. It wasn't that musicals were abandoned or at least shows with a strong musical content. 'Gentlemen Prefer Blondes', 'Guys and Dolls', 'Beach Blanket Tempest' and 'Imagine' all fitted that slot. And if Bakaitis caused a show on John Lennon to be invented, well O'Connell had done likewise with the music of David Bowie. 'Key Largo' is no more aberrant a choice than 'No Orchids for Miss Blandish' though probably rather more intelligible to the average punter. But whatever the case may be, the box office failed to fire. Seasons 1 and 2 had shown consistent growth (29% and 22% respectively). Season 3 stalled (just 5% audience growth) and Season 4 sagged. Reduced to three productions with the unpromising combination of 'Guys and Dolls', 'On Our Selection' and, mystifyingly, Dario Fo's 'Trumpets and Raspberries' that is perhaps not entirely surprising.

Second act opening

But to go back to the beginning of the new regime: the season announced for 1984 was an adaption of 'Gentlemen Prefer Blondes' originally the novel by American, Anita Loos; an adaptation of 'Key Largo" (chosen Bakaitis said, not entirely tongue-in-cheek, on first seeing Mackay's ageing, tropical Theatre Royal); then followed a strenuously updated version of 'The Tempest' marking in theory at least New Moon's third Shakespeare; and 'Don's Party' by David Williamson. That choice of works did not go down well in all quarters. Writing to the daily paper, Graeme Griffin asked: "are other Rockhampton theatregoers as disappointed as I am at the 1984 New Moon Theatre programme?"...'Don's Party' had already been done and the film widely screened. "Next, we are to be subjected to a couple of faddish indulgences in cultish nostalgia – 'Gentlemen Prefer Blondes' and 'Key Largo'. Why two attempts? Surely one snippet of stylised camp is enough for even the trendiest aficionado?" And finally 'The Tempest'.[377] There our correspondent little knew what campery awaited him. Bakaitis replied endeavouring to rebut the arguments and noting: "the public will *pleasure test* the season on the night".[378] Be careful, they say, what you wish for.

Overtly or not, there is a curious theme running through the first three of these four plays. All are in some way linked to the sea. 'Key Largo' in a hurricane on the edge of the Caribbean – the cruel sea, if you will. "Gentlemen Prefer Blondes" is set, in part at least, on an ocean liner – the benign sea and the reference of 'Beach Blanket Tempest' is plainly to the most fictive of oceans in California as well, of course, as to the sea of uncertainty in which metaphorically Shakespeare has marooned his characters in the original play – again a cruel sea. All three are also, in one way or another, linked to Hollywood film culture. It needed only the Titanic to complete a marine quadrella. But with unerring oddity, the other choice fell on Williamson's quintessentially suburban Australia where the only water apparent at 'Don's Party' was mixed with the whisky. Even that play had been made into a film which fact, as we've seen, was already among the many local criticisms of its choice.

Conscious of the tremendous wear and tear of rehearsing and performing with a constant team in the first two seasons, Bakaitis opted to modify the original fixed ensemble scheme to one of a rolling company of actors engaged for only two of the four productions. He would direct three of the works with the fourth having a guest director. "Rather than have a tired company of ten, we use a small nucleus company of three who stay for the whole season with additional actors on a two or three show basis. The only show that will have extra performers is the last one ('Beach Blanket Tempest') which needs a rock band of sorts"[379] The four-show actors were: John Paramor, Mark Daly and Julie Haseler, three-show actors: Vanessa Downing, Deborah Kennedy and John Turnbull; while the two-show actors were: Todd Boyce, Dennis Watkins, Liddy Clark and Julie McGregor. In short, there were no survivors from the previous ensemble. All were new faces and all faced anew the perils of travelling North. However some at least of the previous group were considered. Stephen Clark was one: "I remember running into Helmut in Cairns and he said come back for a third season. You can direct a show. We want you back in the third season and I just said no, sorry, not interested." [380]

Bakaitis in that same letter to Cottrell further noted: "The company has an accepted (and promoted) a popular poofter/mountebank image carefully exploited in marketing terms by Paul [Iles]. The actors had, to a large extent, been sold in the past on the basis of their sex appeal – swinging hedonists from decadent Sydney fucking their way through the tropics. This really only applies to the men of the company, since their sexual freedom is unaffected by touring. The women have fared less well. How can city women cope with the sexist attitudes of ten years ago that exist in North Queensland, simply for a one night stand?"[381]

Into the fray

'Gentlemen Prefer Blondes' which was a new version by John Paramour and Bakaitis, used all the musical numbers from the (Marilyn Monroe/Jane Russell) film, restoring sequences from the original book so that the show became a musical celebration of sex appeal. Leonard Marriott declared it was: "difficult to make a preference between the blonde heroine, Vanessa Downing and brunette soubrette, Deborah Kennedy. ...[but whichever] the audience was aware of a touch of class".[382] John Gagliardi in the Townsville *Daily Bulletin* pronounced: "Blondes – a New Moon success ...Take a bow New Moon – you succeeded admirably. If this is a taste of what is to come in the future, we've really got a team to be proud of"[383] while SOH in the Mackay *Daily Mercury* was full of praise for all aspects and declared it: "A happy choice".[384]

The second of Bakaitis's productions, 'Key Largo' was basically the film script (of the Bogart/Bacall version) by John Huston and Richard Brooks, but adding in scenes from the original play by Maxwell Anderson and reworked overall by Rodney Fisher. It was to be a film noir on stage – all black and white and highly erotic. Once more, Leonard Marriott was right behind it as: Another winner for New Moon "... credit must go to the tastefully and often brilliant direction of Helmut Bakaitis" along with the hurricane effects which were "a magnificent if terrifying piece of realism".[385] Given that this was a town no stranger to cyclonic weather, that is high praise indeed. Terry Carroll in the *Daily Bulletin* thought: "The innovative New Moon Theatre Company ... may make the gangster story line trendy again with its excellent presentation."[386] SO'H considered it: "Good theatre, well presented by a talented group of players ... another splendid play from the NMTC ... Director Helmut Bakaitis is to be commended." [387] Judith Anderson, on the contrary, found it all a bit "rusty". She noted that the predominantly young audience in the Pilbeam Theatre failed to be engrossed by the 1940 cinematic values: "a black and white view of the world where God and democracy are right and Franco and fascism are wrong is too far removed from today's grey values".[388]

'Don's Party' was equally no stranger to the North. Notwithstanding, historian Henry Reynolds had provided the political commentary for the play which was remade to a setting in the North Queensland political landscape, it is rather hard to imagine why one would choose a Williamson work – that had already been made into a successful film and recently performed by a number of local amateur groups – about a national election night more than ten years previous, relocate it to Queensland, then engage an English director, however talented, who was still resident in the UK and who had never directed an Australian play. Did they think that theatregoers in North Queensland could not grasp that they lived in a country called Australia and that there was a national political scene? Or that their memories could not stretch back a decade to the close shave, Gorton election victory around which the play was originally based? More likely, it was yet another example of that distrust of the public's intelligence which still infects much Australian theatre seemingly convinced that no one can grasp Arthur Miller unless it is set in Moonee Ponds or that Garcia Lorca is intelligible only if it is relocated to a Western Australian wheat farm.

Nevertheless, some were convinced. Terry Carroll commented that: "Associate Professor Henry Reynolds of James Cook University, who injected the local content has breathed new life into the play, with Williamson's blessing. Set in Townsville, it has found new relevance especially because, in the North, parties and political argument are like Lyle and Mal – there's not one without the other ... New Moon keeps on getting better and better. Their new guest director, Richard Cottrell, as taken this peculiarly Australian play and given it extra oomph. If you're a prude, still go along. It could change your mind about realism in the theatre". Prophetically, he also observed: "The language, to say the least, is colourful but it's oh so necessary to the plot and the development of the characters that it would lose all impact without the four-letter words".[389] In Cairns, Leonard Marriott wrote: "Extremely well directed and very professionally performed." Interestingly, for what was to come, he also noted that: "when David Williamson wrote 'Don's Party' Ocker, and Anglo-Saxon words were less usual on stage and had some 'shock' effect missing today".[390]

In Mackay, similarly, both play and production went down well "Don's Party seems to have struck a chord in audience response" wrote critic RW, "that points the way to a new direction for theatre – make it contemporary and relevant, and live theatre will not die". While noting the electoral setting, he perceptively added that: "the play, however, is not about politics, but rather is a sociological study of a band of professional or semi-professional people who make up the guests. The main focus is on the wide gulf between the sexes that is apparent in the Australian way of life."[391] All seemed to be smooth sailing until the production reached the city of "sin, sweat and sorrow" where the *Morning Bulletin* considered that "guest director Richard Cottrell ... has taken his first Australian play and brought it to the Queensland stage with inspired realism and total clarity."[392] However, Alderman Teresa Doplo was a first-nighter and took exception to the "obscenity" she heard. If anything, one might have expected this conservative lady to be more troubled by the political comment, so obviously anti-Joh. Not so, it would seem. Curiously too, she acknowledged that such raw usages were not uncommon: "I personally don't find the bad languages offensive – it's just not nice and its shows a lack of vocabulary. Sure, this sort of language goes on – you hear it every day," she was reported as saying. Quirkily, she was quick to point out that it was the actors playing Labor supporters in the show who used it. "I've been to stacks of Liberal-National Party election parties and nothing like what went on in the play has ever happened". Her obviously sheltered life aside, the good Alderman proceeded to call for a "censorship committee" to vet the scripts of all future City Council-sponsored productions at the Pilbeam Theatre.[393]

To its credit, the local newspaper once more leapt into the fray. Its editorial that day thundered: "Well intentioned though she may be, Rockhampton's Ald. Doplo needs to accept the fact that it is 1984 when she talks about censorship. This newspaper will be the first to oppose any City Council censorship committee which tries to vet the scripts of productions at the city's theatre ... Censorship in the form being suggested by Ald. Doplo may have been considered the norm in the 1930s, but not today." And, as if to add salt to the wound, the editor went on: "Ald. Doplo should direct her energies into seeing that the New Moon company not only survives, but gets more money and delivers Central Queenslanders ever better shows".[394] RD Lanyon congratulated the Editorial saying: "the last thing this town needs is another Rev Fred Nile".[395] The "scandal" even went national. Ever hot on the trail of a juicy story, *The Australian*'s Maria Prerauer in her gossip column 'Marietta' declared: "It really is the Deep North!".[396] It wasn't, of course, but Ms Prerauer never let her slender grasp of geography get in the way of a good line. She went on to quote Iles as suggesting that if Doplo really believed that the language had been obscene, she could always report it to the police.

Ald. Doplo then declared she would enlist the help of the Premier in "setting the standards" for New Moon productions. However, there is no evidence that she did or if she did that that he responded. Curiously, the mayor, Ald. Webber who had been so agitated over 'No Orchids...' two years earlier now promptly told Ald. Doplo that there would be no censorship and no censoring committee. However, that did not stop him – who had never seen a New Moon production – declaring it all "disgraceful"[397] Ah Queensland...

Over the next weeks claim and counter claim flew through Letters to the Editor. Some adopted a high moral stance: "Whether in 1984 or 2034, society must follow a code of behaviour and not transgress it, so to suggest because this is 1984 we should throw our heritage of common decency to the winds is ludicrous in the extreme," wrote T W Hinchliffe, 'Glen Alva'm Dululu.[398] RG Mackay of Rhoda Street North Rockhampton was more pragmatic: "I do not favour strict censorship, but that does not have to be the whole story. Paul Iles of the New Moon group claims artistic freedom. What humbug. He should remember where his pay comes from". This was the town that only a few months earlier Iles was extolling: "I am not being patronising when I say Rockhampton has changed radically over the last few years".[399] But not everyone, and perhaps not enough.

RG Hay of Alton Downs considered that these attacks missed the play's meaning altogether: "While Mrs Doplo is entitled to her taste in entertainment, Alderman Doplo has no right whatever to impose her personal preferences on the people of Central Queensland." The writer, presumably female, went on to provide an exegesis: "In 'Don's Party', as in many of his plays. Williamson brings to our attention two things; the absurdity of urban men's attempts to affirm their masculine identity by reproducing on social occasions a pathetic parody of a backblock's shearer on a spree and the consequent need these men have to constantly undermine the self-respect of their womenfolk. This assault on the women takes three forms: the conscious one of language that the backblock's shearer would never have used in mixed company, crude sexual advances, and swinish drunkenness. Much of the comedy comes, as comedy usually does, from the great gap between verbal self-presentation and actual performance."[400]

Another, speaking from the heart while pointing out the mixed standards at play was LAL Lanyon of The Gallery Uptop in Rockhampton: "As a promoter of fine arts in Central Queensland for the past twenty years, and a believer in the integration of the arts, I wish to point out that never at any time have I received adverse criticism of work hung in my galleries, despite the fact that some of it could have been considered, if viewed without knowledge of art, erotic".[401]

Various prominent citizens were canvassed. Graham Bloxom, local manager of the Confederation of Industry affirmed: "I enjoyed it. It was an utterly good performance. Everyone that I know who went enjoyed the show". Rockhampton High School Principal, Ross Lever took the view that: "I wouldn't be prepared to say it [swearing] is a good thing on stage ... [but] if you take offence there is one easy answer ... Don't go". Wisely the Chief Superintendent of police avoided conflict: "I better not buy into it." However, State Opposition leader and local member, former Baptist preacher, Keith Wright, later jailed for child rape, while arguing free speech piously said: 'the four letter words were uncalled for and did not enhance the dialogue in any way". National party Senator Mal Collard was a little more benign: "I am one who does not like an over-abundance of bad language in plays as is it often not called for. But then again, theatre does not set community standards, it just reflects them". HR and David French of North Rockhampton had in many ways the final word: "in my opinion, one viewing of 'Don's Party' is more valuable than ten visits to 'The Sound of Music'.[402]

Calmer waters

After those storms, 'Beach Blanket Tempest' (BBT) must have seemed like very light relief all round, and so it was: a soft rock show based on the films of Annette Funicello and Frankie Avalon – sixties high camp with some marginal Shakespearean references by Dennis Watkins who was also an actor in the Company, appearing in 'Don's Party' and in his own work. Talking to Delphine Zwar who wrote for the *Gourmet Traveller* he mused that it was: "a cross between Shakespeare's 'The Tempest', Walt Disney's 'Fantasia' and 'Countdown' [referencing the ABC's highly successful weekly popular music TV show of the day]. Most simply it is Countdown with a story".[403] That was something of a stretch, but by then the show had opened and Watkins was relaxing on Green Island. However one looks at it, 'BBT' took off, was mostly applauded, went national and was for five minutes, arguably, New Moon's claim for a Top 40 slot.

Gary Schofield in the *Cairns Post* raved: "New Moon's actors jump into 'Beach Blanket Tempest' with the same dynamic, pulsating enthusiasm the musical's original score belts out. Shakespeare's work merely gave the musical its framework. The rest is original, exciting, different and downright entertaining".[404] Terry Carroll likewise approved calling it: "Brilliantly conceived and brilliantly executed. The show stopper was a big production number called 'Temptation' and with choreography by the new artistic director of the North Queensland Ballet [soon to be renamed Dance North] Cheryl Stock. It's magnificent".[405] *Gladstone Observer* Tom Lewis found: "'Beach Blanket Tempest' ... a colourful, comic assault on the senses".[406]

Judith Anderson was, as we have become accustomed to note, a little more restrained: "If you go to the theatre to be prompted to deep thought or to have your complacency jolted, then 'Beach Blanket Tempest' is not for you. But if sheer fun, colour and energy appeal, you'll thoroughly enjoy this show...This is an original and a Far North Queensland product of which we can be proud".[407] That was just as well, because it was headed on the road, further than any New Moon show was ever to travel. First, with a special grant from the Australia Council, it went to Mt Isa and Alice Springs and thence on to Sydney, Canberra and Adelaide where for the most part it was also well, if not deliriously, received.

Susan Bedow in *The Australian* noted that: "New Moon has certainly added a bright light to our horizon. Roll over Shakespeare"[408] and Pru Charlton in *The Sydney Morning Herald* regarded it as: "fresh, new, vital and it's all the proof you need that regional companies have it in them to flog the socks off the big city companies, if given a little encouragement."[409]

Michael Morley in *The National Times* considered that "the production's real strength lies in the energy and enthusiasm of the performers and the way they sell the songs."[410] However, his colleague in the same publication, James Waites damned it with faint praise noting: "it is at least lively".[411] And Colin Menzies in Sydney wrote: "it's a high-energy, wild and wacky rock spectacular loosely based on Shakespeare's 'The

Tempest' ... a kind of down under version of Rocky Horror meets Gilligan's Island"[412] while in the national capital, Ken Healey enthused: "this show is a delight ... I was rapt." [413] Leo Schofield in the gay magazine *Campaign* observed: "BBT is not teeming with charm or entertainment value" adding that it was: "totally unorganised and rather hackneyed". Perhaps camp had become passé.

But for some it was life-changing: In 1984 and 1985 Karen Jacobsen was a pupil at Mackay North State High School. They had a brand new theatre department and the timing could not have been better for the arrival of the new regional theatre company on the scene and regularly visiting Mackay with ground-breaking productions. As theatre students she and her fellow pupils attended performances, wrote reviews of the shows for class assignments, on one occasion even met cast members and had the opportunity to ask questions. Today, she regards the impact that this had on her own creative future was "immeasurable". It represented a world, a wider world beyond the small town where she was born. There were professional actors making a living from the arts, and she had met and spoken with them! The new work that left the most lasting impression was 'Beach Blanket Tempest'. "I can sing you songs from that show to this day, more than three decades later: 'beach blanket tempest', dance up a summer storm", and "'To the ends of the earth, I will follow you ... master, I come answering your call, faster, than a shooting star could fall.' I LOVED this show so much in the way only at 15 year old creative spirit could".[414]

At the time of her writing this Jacobsen was living in New York City, where she is a songwriter, singer, voice-over artist and motivational speaker. Her speaking voice unexpectedly found its way into over a billion GPS and smartphone devices worldwide, and she created an empowerment brand 'The GPS Girl'. Recording and releasing nine albums on her own record label, making the trip to move to NYC on her own, having many memorable musical and creative experiences along the way were all influenced by that sense of possibility New Moon brought to her town where there were no full time professional musicians or actors in sight. She now lives in Airlie Beach and hers is the first face you see when arriving at Mackay airport advertising the Whitsundays.

But not everyone was quite so keen. On October 30, that year Iles was telling the *Cairns Post* that BBT had: "taken Sydney by storm" which was repeated in the *Daily Bulletin* the same day. But Adelaide declined to join the chorus of approval. Diane Beer in *The News* put it down as a: "Boring storm in a teacup".[415] Tim Lloyd in *The Advertiser* wrote: "The nicest way of putting it would be to say that it has been so relaxed and flavoured by the tropics, where New Moon Theatre Company comes from, that its goes all out for balminess, rather than sparkliness". While the ever acerbic, Peter Ward in *The Bulletin* added: "Pleasure Tested? Certainly not in any theatre laboratory south of Capricorn" in all of which one cannot help but detect a note of ad hominem sour grapes towards Mr Iles (perhaps for earlier having abandoned them for less chilly climes?)

Breakers ahead

Iles was meanwhile pointing out to the *Courier-Mail* that despite all this success, New Moon had not been able to find a "backer" in the Queensland capital to present BBT there,[416] though at that stage it's hard to think who that could have been, or even where. Brisbane was perilously short of venues at that time. The Queensland Performing Arts Centre (QPAC) would not open until April the following year. The SGIO Theatre was fully occupied by the QTC and, by Iles's own admission, the Twelfth Night Theatre was too small for the show. Again he chose to tilt unnecessarily at windmills.

Yet once more during this tour Iles misjudged the region from afar, touching a raw nerve up North with his throwaway lines down South. Jill Mather in the *Daily Bulletin* noted that his remarks in Sydney that the Company was: "shocking the Deep North into the 20th century" were a smack in the eye for those cities which had loyally supported New Moon. Reports, too, that he had said that the money received from the combined Queensland coastal towns was a: "mere drop in the ocean" to what was required. At this rate, she said, New Moon might soon be regarded as "a holiday camp for out of work Southerners".[417]

Even so, the Company was moving ahead on other financial fronts. With the Australia Council subsidy for 1985 announced at $123,824 Iles could loudly proclaim it as the largest drama recipient outside a capital city. Given all those successes, board member and Townsville mayor, Mike Reynolds had no hesitation in labelling shire councillors in neighbouring Thuringowa as a: "bunch of hillbillies" who did not appreciate the arts when for a second year in a row that LGA declined to fund New Moon.[418]

By the fourth Season in 1985 the Company had moved to be based in Rockhampton and the line-up of actors again changed, with only two continuing from the previous year: Michael Carman, Mark Daly, Susannah Fowle, Tanya Gristle, Wayne Jarrett, Lucian Mariucci, Nicola Scott, Lyn Shakespeare, Sharyn Steller (local Mackay radio announcer and actor), John Turnbull and David Wood made up the roster.

But even in their new location not everyone was pleased. The *Morning Bulletin's* Editorial felt "diddled": "The company which has revolutionised the theatre scene in CQ is backing out, offering only three programmes instead of four on its annual plate. Here we are, in May, with a promise of 'Guys and Dolls' in June. Rockhampton might hibernate [sic] in summer but June really doesn't seem good enough".[419]

It is probably as good a time as any to comment on the patina of nostalgia which overlies these two crucial years of New Moon's existence. They are heavily infected, if that is not too strong a term, with a bygone film culture. 'Gentlemen Prefer Blondes', 'Guys and Dolls', 'Key Largo' even 'Don's Party' had been most widely seen in a film version. 'BBT' was based in a 1960s film genre. 'On Our Selection' had been twice filmed: first in Raymond Longford's silent version of 1920, and again by Ken Hall in 1932. The revised George Whaley version which New Moon used was to be again filmed in 1995 with the unlikely casting of Joan Sutherland as Ma. All this does strike one as rather too much to be merely coincidental. It speaks of an aesthetic shaped by an almost fantastical world both far away from what was happening in the rest of the Australian theatre at the time (perhaps what Iles had earlier declared to be porno kitsch).

To take a selection only, by comparison, QTC's 1985 season featured: 'A Pair of Claws' (Michael Gurr*), 'The Family Room' (Ted Neilsen), 'Insignificance' (Terry Johnson), 'Salonika' (Louise Page), 'Pack of Lies' (Hugh Whitemore), 'Cheapside' (David Allen*), 'Three Sisters' (Chekhov), 'The Real Thing' (Tom Stoppard) and 'Macbeth' (Shakespeare); while MTC was playing inter al: 'The Sentimental Bloke '(Albert Arlen/C.J.Dennis*), 'The Celebrated' (Stephen Gard*), 'Season's Greetings' (Alan Ayckbourn), 'Fifteen Rounds with Gorgeous George' (Garrie Huntchinson*), 'Never in My Lifetime' (Shirley Gee), 'Victoria Bitter' (Michael Gurr*), 'Benefactors' (Michael Frayn), 'The Doll Trilogy: Kid Stakes/Other Times/Summer of the Seventeenth Doll' (Ray Lawler*), 'Too Young for Ghosts' (Janis Balodis*), 'Glengarry Glen Ross' (David Mamet), 'Cyrano de Bergerac' (Rostand), 'The Glass Menagerie' (Tennessee Williams), 'Reservoir by Night' (Barry Dickins*).[420] Of course, these companies had a much wider scope, longer seasons, were settled in their home base theatres that had loyal subscription audiences established over decades. Nevertheless, even this simple list offers a sense of the context in which New Moon was viewed nationally.

In the light of this, when that year's first production came along local critic, Judith Anderson was no more impressed. Writing that the Company lacked strong solo voices she complained: "there's a lot more work to be done".[421] Iles must by then have regretted being so rude to her two years before. Tom Lewis in the Gladstone *Observer* was a little more positive: "Another quality production" but he found aspects of the scene changes distracting [422] and SO'H in Mackay pronounced it: "good entertainment" but would not be moved to further praise.[423]

By the time it reached Townsville, Christine Salins was able to give it a more glowing report including for some "superb" acting, but agreed that the singing was not always up to it.[424] while Jan Lahney in the *Cairns Post* came to much the same conclusion.[425] Overall the response was that it was just ok and once more there is a sense that the media, and perhaps the public, were a little over the idea (as they perceived it) of old movies being turned into stage shows.

That being so, 'On our Selection' which followed was both a change of pace and perhaps rather closer to home. Memories of the silent movie were long past and George Whaley's version had given it a more modern feel without losing authenticity. More or less continuous musical accompaniment in Bakaitis's production added further to its appeal.

"Comedy, drama, great acting and intelligent stagecraft all combine to make this one of New Moon's best ever" Tom Lewis wrote in *Gladstone Observer* "piano player, Ralph Tyrell" came in for particular praise.[426] Judith Anderson was again more reserved but urged: "for nostalgia's sake, get to see 'On Our Selection' before it moves up the coast".[427] Given the subject matter, when it got there it was only appropriate that the *Daily Bulletin* should have selected one Ben Hall to review Steele Rudd's work and he proclaimed it: "digestible, light-hearted entertainment".[428]

Finally, in that foreshortened season came 'Trumpets and Raspberries' by radical, socialist, Italian playwright Dario Fo. Bakaitis had seen it only a year before in London[429] and it was a bare seven years after the abduction and brutal murder of Italian politician, Aldo Moro which it macabrely reflects. It was not by any means a "hit" which Judith Anderson makes clear: "New Moon's 'Trumpets and Raspberries' was greeted with more of the latter than the former by Rockhampton theatregoers who stayed away in droves from last night's Australian premiere performance". But she noted that at least: "the production was slick and fast. Michael Scott-Mitchell's cartoon style neo-roman set and his costumes in vivid primary colours bring the show visually alive, but it is the fantastic non-human presences on stage that add a dimension of sheer fantasy to the farce".[430] Jan Lahney in the *Cairns Post* regarded it mildly as: "an interesting choice with unusual humour – a spaghetti comedy with a little political meat on the side"[431] and Colin Campbell, found it: "a rowdy satire which uses ancient techniques of Italian farce and welds them to modern messages..." [432]

But wherever it went, nobody went and mostly the theatres were dismally vacant. Whatever the North wanted it was not political farce however uproarious or, at least, not from Italy. Perhaps by then Queensland had come to realise that it had enough of its own buffoonery not to need imports. This then was not a case of art reflecting life but rather that life had come to exceed art. And life did occasionally intrude. In the midst of this Mackay's deputy Mayor, Ald. Elaine Martin resigned noisily from the New Moon Board, citing concern over its: "lack of community involvement" and: "the financial situation". She had been a strong supporter of the Company but now described it as "the circus coming to town and then off again. They leave nothing behind."[433] It was not long after Paul Iles had seemingly come to the same conclusion and indeed left.

The Diane factor

By the fifth Season in 1986, New Moon was back based once more in Townsville from which it had first emerged. By now, with Iles gone and under new management, all semblance of maintaining an acting ensemble was gone. Plays were cast one by one and "names" were where it was at. There is a feeling of panic about the programming. 'Agnes of God' by American, John Pielmeier was to become something of a vehicle for Diane Cilento in three different productions with New Moon, QTC which also went to MTC as well as being presented in Sydney but with a variety of casts. Cornelia Frances and Kaarin Fairfax played the supporting roles for New Moon. Perhaps only Miss Cilento's local, if limited fame, explains the choice. If that were the motivation, it did not succeed. Certainly, it failed to lift the box office in the manner intended. So poor in fact were sales in Townsville that the 'star' gave a two finger salute to the small and, it is related, largely unappreciative audience.[434] Small numbers also were the cause of one cancelled performance. These were not actions calculated to win friends or sustain the few that remained to New Moon, but were a sign that it was running out of ideas.

Notwithstanding, Edwin Relf in the *Morning Bulletin* described 'Agnes of God' as: "Brilliant contemporary drama,"[435] In a letter to Mackay's *Daily Mercury*, Jack Sturgeon wrote: "I have been to every one of [New Moon's] productions and although I enjoyed many, most of the productions were not what I was looking for ... I got sick and tired of white faces – smoke – and flashing lights directed at the audience. Two weeks ago I saw 'Agnes of God' and tonight I saw a technical rehearsal of 'Return Engagement'. At last we have top class professional shows ... It is indeed a NEW Moon organisation". [436] Meanwhile, Colin Campbell, in the *Daily Bulletin* considered: "'Agnes of God' is the kind of play New Moon Theatre Company should have done a long time ago".[437]

None of that prevented Cilento making unflattering remarks to the *Cairns Post* about lack of public support[438] to which Say Choo Lim responded in a letter to the Editor stating that she found the tickets too expensive but also: "the program so far has not interested me". She had been a past supporter: "In fact, I found 'Beach Blanket Tempest' one of the most enjoyable and exciting live productions I have ever seen".[439] Clearly, you can't please all the people all the time.

But 'Agnes of God' influenced one local profoundly. For Campbell Young that occurred in an instant. Young operated a hairdressing salon in Mackay, a city that was Bakaitis's favourite on the New Moon touring circuit. "I fell in love with Mackay first off when we got up there. I couldn't get over this beautiful, battered old hall with louvres and a fan".[440] Campbell had a lifelong love of theatre and had at various times provided hairdressing services for the local Little theatre groups. So it was not surprising that when New Moon came along it drew on his talents for that purpose. He was excited by the Company's appearance on the scene and is not too much to say entranced by the quality and range of the productions it presented in his relatively sedate home town. However, the moment of revelation came in 1986 with the production of 'Agnes of God'. The Company had hired an expensive wig for Ms Cilento's role which the lady had sabotaged. Campbell was asked to see if he could repair it. "The local theatre groups had occasionally used bought hairpieces, but this was the genuine article, a beautifully made, bespoke theatrical wig. I thought to myself: I need to learn how to make these. That was the start of the rest of my career."[441]

A few years later Young sold up his business in North Queensland and headed off to London. He lurked around the theatre world for a while until somebody, knowing his growing passion for wigs, suggested he should work with the leading maker of the time, Peter Owen and learn the craft under that master in his Bristol-based studio. In time Young outgrew that relationship, but meanwhile he worked and continues to work with leading directors, costume designers and producers throughout Britain, across Europe, in the United States and, of course, in his native Australia.

Some 15 years ago he established his own business which continues that trajectory. Now, leading names of European theatre, opera, musical theatre as well as film fall naturally from his lips in discussing the many and extraordinary productions (including at one stage two 'Ring' cycles at the same time) in which he has been involved. "From amateur theatre in North Queensland to the great opera houses of Europe – it's been an immense journey and a wonderful life which all started from that encounter with New Moon!" he delightedly remarks today.[442]

But back in Queensland in 1986 there followed 'Return Engagement', again a vehicle for stars, with stage and television personality, Toni Lamond then arguably better known than her equally talented son, Tony Sheldon, later to be an international star of 'Priscilla' and much more. The production, originally entitled 'Madonna and Child', had been devised by Ron Creager with the two actors. Judith Anderson (perhaps with Iles having made good his escape) found: "The pleasure of watching two thoroughly professional troupers singing and hoofing their way through the popular musical comedy classics and of hearing that special blend of voices that only genetics and a lifetime of acquaintance can produce ... Thankfully, 'Return Engagement' suffers neither from the terminal cuteness nor the self-indulgence that its concept suggest – it's a thoroughly enjoyable evening's entertainment".[443]

Nevertheless, bookings were low that there too one performance was cancelled. Marketing Co-ordinator, Barbara Tiernan who had adopted some of Cilento's tendency to attack the public rather than trying to analyse the problem, stated: "we get more interest from Darwin than Rockhampton and it's becoming very tempting to take our shows there" she said.[444] Notwithstanding, Jan Jahney in the *Cairns Post* wrote: "Simply staged, the evening superseded a mere nightclub act, to become an emotional encounter with real people with real hurts and wants as each actor shows the polish with movement and style that has earned them acknowledgement in the fickle world of performing."[445] Kate Flamsteed noted what she called a: "shameful opening night turnout of fewer than 200 people who had the foresight to attend one of the slickest, most enjoyable performance the city had seen this year... 'Return Engagement' seemed to be written for North Queensland and self-respecting Townville theatregoers would be to look a gift horse in the mouth [to miss it]."[446] A Mrs J Allen of Lamberts Beach voiced a similar concern in Mackay: "What a pitiful response from a city that is crying out for a new cultural theatre. Where were all the people who for so "generously supported the theatre fund?"[447] The Brisbane *Courier-Mail* however, described it as a: "schmaltzy show about a schmaltzy show and creaks with embarrassing dialogue and 'just "a lot of entertaining twaddle".[448]

Reaching out

A small aside is offered at this point. Hot on the heels of 'Agnes of God' came a project in Rockhampton which could not have been a greater contrast. This was 'Crocodile Creek'. It was never a New Moon production per se though it had New Moon significance. Today, Bakaitis, perhaps over-modestly, declares that he had "little to do with it"[449] and of the production proper that is strictly speaking true, though the publicity does bear its name. But he and the Company did play an important role in its genesis during 1985 and into 1986. New

Moon had enabled the services of the designer located in Townsville as well as director, choreographer and stage manager. The project was ambitious by community standards involving at least a hundred Rockhampton participants and thereby was able to make a significant impact. Moreover, the idea could have pointed a way for New Moon to create wider, genuine engagement in the cities in which it played. It was also a noted local story. One may see it therefore as yet another missed opportunity.

Malcolm Calder, administrator of the Pilbeam Theatre and a New Moon Board member, had been offered a script by an unpublished, Rockhampton grandmother, Barbara Birchall. It was an historical piece set in 1867 on the Gavial Creek goldfields, part way to Mt Morgan and based on true events of racial conflict and riots. Calder described the plotline "R&J copybook star-crossed lovers, in this case: Irish-girl-meets-Chinese-boy-families-disagree-they-fight-some-die".[450] He felt it could have value as a large-scale piece of community theatre which might appeal to a wider audience if it could be enhanced with music. He submitted it to the new script advisory service which Bakaitis had established both as a way of involving New Moon and, in particular, a means of enabling New Moon to meet Australia Council requirements for improving its community outreach.

A composer, Felix Meagher was retained and worked with the playwright to create 'Crocodile Creek – the musical'. The Australia Council's Music Board and the Queensland Directorate of Cultural Activities came to the party with funding as did some local businesses. The New Moon ensemble gave the work a reading to obtain feedback and suggestions for development. The Company was also responsible for the provision and partial funding of choreographer, Garry Lester and designer William Marron from Townsville and located and negotiated recent NIDA graduate, and later to be eminent stage and film director, Baz Luhrmann to direct.

'Crocodile Creek' was given four performances at the Pilbeam Theatre on August 21-23, 1986 which interestingly are billed as a joint presentation of the Rockhampton Performing Arts Complex and the New Moon Theatre Company. The editorial in Rockhampton's *Morning Bulletin* proudly announced that: "the show would be good theatre anywhere",[451] while Edwin Relf in the Brisbane *Courier-Mail* wrote: "Rockhampton can be proud of its effort. It is an important achievement in a national context".[452] But that was not to be. Sadly, 'Crocodile Creek' never received a second production in Rockhampton and, although eminent Festival director, Antony Steel flew up from Brisbane to look at it for potential inclusion in his 1988 World Expo program, he demurred feeling, somewhat paradoxically, that a 'regional work' might be a bit of a strain for a metro audience.

Imagine that!

Then came 'Imagine', a saga all of its own which featured John Waters as John Lennon in a work devised by Rodney Fisher. The cast consisted of Waters, Graham Matters, Luz Yeomans, Bjarne Ohlin (all multi-skilled actors/musicians) and music director Stewart D'Arietta. If one were looking for the artistic "legacy" of New Moon and its ongoing benefit to the theatrical profession, one could with justice declare that, in part at least, this is it. John Lennon had been assassinated in New York City in 1980 but fascination with him lived and still lives on. Despite the post-Beatles careers of all four of the Liverpool lads and the varying success that these reached, that of Lennon took on a particular glow perhaps as much as anything for the increasingly political content of his work; the lure of his partnership with Yoko Ono; and his guru-like presence wherever he went.[453]

When the fatal gun was fired in Manhattan on, curiously, the Feast of the Immaculate Conception, December 8, 1980, Lennon ascended to a kind of secular sainthood. His boast that as a band the Beatles had been "more popular than Jesus"[454] came in a perverse way to be fulfilled. So it was not surprising that everyone wanted to claim a relic or create, as it were, a reliquary. Just as Roman Catholic saints had feast days with a ferial mass and processions of the image, so with Lennon it was to be shows about or around his life but, above all, his music and lyrics and what might, with some stretch of the term, be called his 'philosophy'. That, in a way, was the origin of 'Imagine' and in the context of New Moon it probably comes under the heading of "it seemed like a good idea at the time".

With 'Beach Blanket Tempest' New Moon had put its toe into the waters of creating a show that could tour beyond their home base, especially to major markets like Sydney and Melbourne. It would be a product that could pull in a commercial promoter with whom to share risk as they had done with the embryonic Gordon Frost organisation on 'BBT' and thereby generate fresh revenue. The aim was ultimately to reduce reliance on the ever-fluctuating grant income and perhaps even, *mirabile dictu*, build reserves for the Company against a rainy day since, as Auntie Mame famously observed, "it couldn't get much wetter" than it was by then in the North. What they needed was a cash cow. Iles had known that and shrewder heads around the Board table, like experienced businessman Bruce Shepherd, recognised that he was right and, given his flair and acumen, he was the probably the only one who could have pulled it off. But Iles was gone. 'BBT' had suggested a paradigm for this. There needed to be a follow-up act. It was a gamble, but probably one worth taking. However, time was running out.

In a way 'Imagine' was New Moon's last, best hope and the turning point in the Company's fortunes. If it succeeded, it could be blue skies or as much as they ever can be in such a volatile business. If it failed, it would be, as it turned out, a slow slide to oblivion. It was also a continuation of the switch from ensemble to 'personalities'. Not only Lennon's but that of John Waters. British-born Waters was an accomplished musician and was already a name in Australian entertainment. His first big break was in musicals, playing Claude in the Sydney production of 'Hair' in 1969, then Judas in 'Godspell' and Pontius Pilate in the Australian concert production of 'Jesus Christ Superstar'. He was in the original Australian production of the two hander 'They're Playing Our Song' with Jacki Weaver. So he was, as they say, a commodity. What he needed was a vehicle. In securing him,

New Moon had hit the nail on the head.

Now, there are various possible readings of what happened next and, indeed, what happened over subsequent years,[455] but this much is clear: since 1992 Waters has toured many times with his one-man show 'Looking Through a Glass Onion', co-written with friend and musician, Stewart D'Arrietta. That show is a tribute to John Lennon featuring numerous examples of Lennon's music, words and images. In addition to many Australian tours of this show, it has also played six months in the West End, London. In 2014, it played 120 performances at the Union Square Theatre in Manhattan.[456] Waters also has a double live album, 'John Waters Looking Through A Glass Onion' (2011). In none of the material associated with any of these is New Moon or any of the collaborators on "Imagine' other than D'Arrietta acknowledged. Their publicity material declares that in 1992, twelve years after Lennon's death, Waters and D'Arrietta first conceived and performed 'Lennon: Through a Glass Onion' on a small stage at the Tilbury Hotel in Sydney. That part of the story is beyond doubt. The show was an instant success. In the years that followed, Waters and D'Arrietta toured the show and played sold out engagements at venues including The Sydney Opera House.

At the time of the New Moon production, however, Colin Campbell in *The Daily Bulletin*' judged that 'Imagine – A story of John Lennon' "is the best thing to hit Townsville this year. ... I've never seen people dancing in the aisles before at the Civic Theatre ... the well judged paste-and-paper job by writer Rodney Fisher gave the impression that Lennon beat his angst by external whimsy and great songs ..." Director Helmut Bakaitis got a bravura performance from his band.[457] In the Rockhampton *Morning Bulletin* Judith Anderson declared it a "great piece of music history... Director Helmut Bakaitis has pared the action on stage to its absolute minimum. In less skilful hands than his and the cast's such immobility and sombreness would be a recipe for disaster, but the energy is sustained throughout and the result is first class entertainment".[458]

On the other hand a critic [name withheld] writing to the *Daily Mercury* found it all too loud and rather tedious: "what I saw was an average rock band (without drummer) with the ability to repeat lines". But the anonymous critic also claimed: "audience numbers and reaction to the company's latest touring product 'Imagine' which opened at Mackay's Theatre Royal last night proved New Moon is onto a winner."[459] Anne Brock writing in the *Courier-Mail* was also not swept away though she admitted there were: "standing ovations and an encore... a total success for the five actor-musicians ... Altogether the theatrical side is a bit disappointing but who cares? The main thing is the music, the dozens of Beatle and Lennon songs".[460]

Realistically, 1987 is the last truly recognisable touring season of New Moon according to the original formula. Still based in Townsville and confronting a series of misfortunes both personal and financial the Company struggled to keep afloat, to keep itself in front of the public, to keep an audience and to justify its continuing existence.

Denouement

Bakaitis had gone and his replacement, Ian Tasker had come and tragically gone having made only one real decision which was that, in an effort to buy time, they would bring in and present an external show. Now this was giving the game away even as a one-off, because it was exactly what the presenting theatres did and, with their increasingly active NARPACA network, were doing in concert. (Technically 'Return Engagement' was similar but that somehow seemed to pass muster). There was nothing 'Pleasure Tested' or original to see here. Nonetheless, something needed to be done urgently and that something was 'Intimate Exchange' by prolific British playwright Alan Ayckbourn. It was a direct buy-in of an existing two-hander from Sydney's long running Ensemble Theatre and billed by New Moon as an 'Alan' Ayckbourn 'Festival'. In fact, it was four works out of a much larger Ayckbourn menu from which it was intended some would be chosen at random on the night: Those that toured Queensland were: 'A Cricket Match', 'A

Garden Fete', 'One Man Protest' and 'Affairs in a Tent'.

The season, which played just Rockhampton, Mackay and Townsville in May that year did not sell, partly it was believed because of the difficulty of promoting the idea of a different play each night in a four night run in each city. Where there was a stable recurrent audience such as the Ensemble enjoyed in Sydney and where Ayckbourn was well known, that might be doable, but it proved daunting in the Queensland country towns. However, it had been bought at minimal risk. The loss was more than commensurate with that on one of their own productions and it had been necessary to keep faith with commitments to the region venues that were holding dates for the Company.

The cast was Gillian Axtell and Brian Young with the production directed by the Ensemble's producing director, Sandra Bates and designed by Tom Bannerman. Some measure of the deal may be seen from the fee of $3, 000 per week to the Ensemble plus 3% of gross box office; $1,000 per week to each actor plus living allowances, $760 to the stage manager and 10% royalties. While it cost little, it also left little trace behind. Tested today, even New Moon's then management were hard pressed to remember it.

Following that, Sydney-based actor and director Gary Down took over as guest director of the other two planned productions, both by Australian playwrights. This represented some attempt to return to the idea of an ensemble, albeit not continuous, by casting three of the same actors in both. The first of which was the Elvis Presley fantasy drama 'Are you Lonesome Tonight' by Pamela Van Amstel with David Brown, Graham Lancaster, Samantha Lovejoy, Andrew Windsor and Judith McGrath. It played Townsville, Cairns, Mackay, Gladstone, Rockhampton and Mt. Isa in August/ September.

Trevina Hall in the *Daily Bulletin* found it: "Funny if not over the top"[461] and Annette Bryan in *Cairns Post* saw it as an: "interesting production"[462] while WEM in the *Daily Mercury* approved of the:

"vivid performances". In the *Morning Bulletin* Judith Anderson offered: "Bouquets to New Moon for using Queensland talent for this production".[463] The *Observer* noting it was the first time the company had performed in Gladstone said: "New Moon Theatre Company gave Gladstone an entertaining Rock'n'Roll history lesson ... in a comic yet pathetic fashion".[464] The *Townsville Advertiser* declared it rather understatedly as: "well worth seeing."[465]

The last production of 1987 and, in effect, the last but one real touring season of New Moon was Michael Gow's hugely successful 'Away' with David Brown, Monica Maughan, Judith McGrath, Peter Cummins, Edwin Hodgeman, Liddy Clark, Samantha Lovejoy and Bevan Wilson. It played Townsville, Mackay, Rockhampton, Gladstone and Bundaberg from late October to late November. RLG in the *Daily Mercury* wrote that it: "Moved the audience to tears and laughter"[466] while Trevina Hall in the *Daily Bulletin* thrilled: "The Production was outstanding ... Once again, New Moon have come up with a production equal to the best in Australia".[467]

That year the youth branch, La Luna was also formally inaugurated with Jeremy Johnson, a recent NIDA graduate, running teenage classes. Jocelyn McKinnon. who had been the real initiator of the project in its earlier, less formal incarnation, continued to offer classes to the younger kids. It was by then charging participants a fee per term up-front and there was already a big waiting list. The Company provided marketing and administrative umbrella but no direct funding though scraps of support came to it indirectly.[468]

By the end of 1987, having nothing to do with La Luna, Johnson resigned minutes before he was pushed after some very complex disputes over the workshopping and potential production of his play 'Blotto'. Both Diane Cilento and the chair, Ald. Vallentine had a high opinion of it, a view that was not shared with the rest of the Board though that was not entirely as to the quality of the work. The Company had received a $6,000 grant from the Bicentennial Authority to run a playwrights' competition and subsequent workshop. Five plays had been designated by Ms Cilento as worthy of workshopping. But there was a view – supported by majority of the board – that the proper procedure had not been followed and that "Blotto" had been arbitrarily pushed to the fore by including it for consideration as a New Moon production in the Bicentennial year. Directors felt that that would be in conflict with Bicentennial contract and that after various debates the Company opted not to proceed and to sever all association with the author and his play. Those disputes had included his continued use of the Company taxi account after resigning, claiming expenses for work actually undertaken and paid in association with the opening of the Mackay Entertainment Centre, and so on.

Throughout 1988 and 1989 there are a series of false starts in attempts to revive mainstream touring while La Luna continued on its way and other venture such as Theatre Sports were undertaken. There were also newer contenders for the prize of being the North's professional theatre provider. These are related in the next chapter.

Last hurrah

The eighth and final touring season eventually occurred in 1990 – two years after its previous one. The much touted and often postponed "rebirth" was celebrated by John Lamb, Rod Wissler and the Townsville Mayor, Tony Mooney with balloons and promises of great things to come. His Worship's launch also had a touch of the valedictorian about it. "While celebrating the rebirth of New Moon we must not forget the achievements of the company in the 1980s"[469] Too true, one might say.

Finally they came around to what was in many ways the most obvious the play of all: 'The Summer of the 17th Doll' which had been one of the highlights of the Townville Summer Stock a decade and more earlier. As if to add to the symmetry, it was directed by Stephen Clark who had been a member of the original New Moon ensemble playing, we may recall, Ned Kelly in its very first production. The cast had impeccable credentials: Chris Bett was a veteran of the Queensland Theatre Company, Liddy Clark (incidentally, Stephen's sister and latterly a Minister in the Beattie Labor government) had appeared with New Moon in 'Don's Party', 'Beach Blanket Tempest' and 'Away'; Sue Dwyer was a North Queensland actor; Chas Green and Penelope Sheridan were both JCU drama graduates; Anthony Phelan was an experienced Queensland actor originally from Ayr; and Townsvillean, Kirsty Veron, who had we have noted among others things managed the Company during its challenging "down" years, completed the cast. Many considered it was the kind of line-up they should always have had, but that is easy to say with the benefit of hindsight.

As the Company's first tour was detailed at the beginning of this chapter, so it seems only appropriate the last should receive a similar dignity. Its schedule, also moved back to the early original time of year was: Mackay (which now had its new Entertainment Centre) – January 31 to February 3; Kelly Theatre in Ingham – February 6-7; Burdekin Theatre, Ayr – February 8-10; Cairns in the Civic Theatre which had replaced the older Civic Centre – February 14-17; Townsville Civic Theatre – February 21-24 and Pilbeam Theatre in Rockhampton – February 28-March 3, 1990. It is an extensive tour and might have set the future pattern. One other change worth noting is that with the passage of ten years, the published reviews had all shrunk in size. Just as in the capital cities, with the decline of advertising in print media the regional newspapers themselves had reduced, leaving less and less space for such fripperies as arts coverage. So while not unenthusiastic, the articles are terse in their praise.

Although hailing it as New Moon's powerful return, it is instructive that the (unattributed) review in the Townsville *Daily Bulletin* says: "with direction by Stephen Clark New Moon seems to be well on the way to re-establishing itself as *one of the top* North Queensland theatre companies." [My emphasis][470] So far had things changed. Kim Cathcart in the *Morning Bulletin* was content to note that the: "performance of the seven-member New Moon cast was a credit to the company.[471]

W.E.M wrote, thoughtfully, that while it is well to claim it as a "classic" Lawler's play may still need time to mature: "Mackay being a "sugar" (we usually drop the "cane") town, we are very much aware of changes in the industry and somehow the canecutter has not survived in heroic mould in the popular mind". Nonetheless "New Moon's production, directed by Stephen Clark, is a must for young people, trying to understand our past, and will give the older brigade food for thought." [472] Meanwhile "This is some of the best professional theatre seen at the Cairns Civic Centre in several years" noted the equally anonymous critic in the *Cairns Post*.[473]

The curious fascination with Dario Fo continued right to the end. New Moon's very last production 'Can't Pay, Won't Pay' directed by resident director, David Fenton came hard on the heels of its success with 'The Doll'. Kirsty Veron, Penelope Sheriden and Chas Green from that cast were joined by Andrew Buchanan, by then co-ordinator of La Luna and Theatre Sports, and Lewis Jones. It played just one week at the Townsville Civic Theatre before the money finally and forever ran out. The choice of play is perhaps less odd in the context of the year that had been planned, but was to be never staged. That had foreshadowed: David Williamson's 'Emerald City' in June, 'Zen and Now' a musical spoof on growing up in the '60s in July and John Romeril's 'The Floating World' in October. One asks: what if?

Borrowed robes

For all its claims to (artistic as against organisational) innovation, New Moon created little new work. It never told North Queensland stories as other regional theatre did of their domains, thus giving them a grounding in their communities. Nor did it find a playwright as HVTC did in John O'Donohue, Theatre South with Katherine Thompson or New England with Bob Herbert. There is no 'Essington Lewis, I am work' or 'Tonight We Anchor in Twofold Bay' in New Moon's history and that seems both an opportunity lost and a curious oversight.

To be fair to the Company's later incarnation, even the blueprint laid out from the earliest time by the steering committee, shaped one assumes by Lamb and perhaps Nelson, is in four rather unadventurous categories. One can accept these were indicative only, and to some degree selling points to public authorities and potential sponsors who had little or no background in the theatre arts. "Don't scare the horses" would have been a reasonable starting point. But nowhere is there any sense of exploring the immediate world around them (no more was there, for that matter, in the Queensland Theatre Company of the time). It was all still very much the old pilgrim Arts Council model that real art, professional art, comes from somewhere else. It is not something you can make yourself. In particular, vis-à-vis the bush, art came from the city. But a glance back at that initial selection of work from the first two seasons tells the tale and suggests from the outset what the problem might become: 'Ned Kelly', 'Macbeth', 'No Orchids for Miss Blandish', 'Tommy', 'Cabaret', 'A Midsummer Night's Dream', 'Life on Mars' and 'Royal Show'.

This is especially curious since Terrence O'Connell and, to a lesser extent, Peter Barclay had both had the advantage of setting up and running the RTC and so should have understood the value and importance of local engagement and embedding. The situation in Wagga Wagga was admittedly much less complex than the four-town New Moon model. But one has to ask: where then did loyalty lie? In HVTC and Theatre South it was easier to tell a Newcastle or a Wollongong story, but how to choose between Townsville and Rockhampton – two cities with wildly different settler histories, self-image and self-doubt. Each had, as Christina Stead might have observed: "an ocean of story", but oddly no one stepped forward to tell it. Or did they and were not taken up? In any event, it rather seems that everyone and the Company overall, was just too restless and itinerant and maybe just too busy with the day-to-day ever to give it a go. Perhaps it was too impetuous to do so.

Thus, it was not until 1984 that New Moon produced an original show. 'Beach Blanket Tempest'. It was reasonable that such a thing could take time. Otherwise Australian plays, for example those that had been featured, by Michael Gow, Pamela van Amsteel, Williamson and Louis Nowra were among the relative few produced across its history. We've seen that an abortive attempt to stage a new Dorothy Hewitt play ('Bush Tivoli') did not come off though it got to the point of being programmed and even advertised. The Company received Act 1 but clearly it was not ready. Like most early drafts it needed work and Hewitt's loose and baggy monsters often needed more than most. Accordingly, when the idea of Dennis Watkins's Californian adaptation of 'The Tempest' came along it seemed like a breakthrough.

Watkins and collaborators had earlier launched the tongue-in-cheek Theatre of Poverty of Intellect in Sydney. It was a rough and ready, often sardonic but still at times of oddly erudite and literary theatrical space. The idea that this might have been a palimpsest for rough-and-ready in your face tropical Queensland drama is an intriguing possibility and one we should not neglect. Yet again, one asks: what if?

On the other hand, Iles was notoriously a beach addict. Perhaps 'Beach Blanket Tempest' appealed to his love of skin, sun and surf. Yet his was a new chum's approach to that culture, not that of the Currency lads and lasses. Like the Hollywood beach blanket movie culture which the show reflected, his love was perhaps more of the skin than the surf. At all events, the production was intended to celebrate youth and the name alone punched its way into theatrical consciousness well beyond Queensland. Nonetheless, whatever its other virtues or defects, it was not a local story and made no pretence to be. However, before we rush to judgement, remember folks that those notorious purveyors of local "beachy" stories on the box which have gone on to conquer the world like 'Neighbours' and 'Home and Away' astonishingly first went to air respectively as late as 1985 and 1988. Too soon we forget how empty our popular coastal narratives were before their advent!

For all that, it is perhaps the only New Moon production widely remembered by theatregoers and the only one to tour extensively beyond the region, yet BBT grossed only $44,558 in the four base cities.

Some attributed this to the "Doplo effect" but in fact the receipts in Rockhampton were higher than for either 'Don's Party' or 'Key Largo'.

As well, shopping 'Beach Blanket Tempest' around to presenters interstate was also one of Iles's better endeavours making it in the process New Moon's most nationally visible product and probably the only one that those living outside of its immediate regions still recall. It toured widely in Queensland (though, as we've seen, never to Brisbane) and pushed across to Alice Springs and, as noted, then to the southern capitals. In Sydney it ended as an entirely commercial deal with a bunch of investors including company members and a last minute saviour in long-serving Mackay board member Bruce Shepherd with Gordon/Frost.

The last minute somewhat ramshackle arrangement was typical of the modus operandi of the Company and could have stood as a metaphor for what was both good and bad about its business dealings: on one hand bold, aggressive even, out there, entrepreneurial and outrageous; on the other, lacking in care, real underpinning and driven entirely by short-term considerations. In those respects, it was a runaway train, an accident waiting to happen. Iles was, in many ways, an old fashioned showman who genuinely believed in the philosophy of "razzledazzle'em". Had he played with his own money as Ashley Gordon and John Frost were doing, it would have been bravos all round. Today, Iles would probably have been producing burlesque in a spiegeltent, but in 1985 the times were not quite right. In Queensland the greater burlesque show was still to come: first in the State parliament and ultimately in its denouement through the Fitzgerald Royal Commission. Like the Mafia in Italy no theatre however brilliant could compete with that! By then, Australia was riveted by the greater political drama of the decline and fall of king Joh as it had not been since Whitlam's dismissal, and all competition faded into the background.

Yet burlesque was apparent on all sides. Let us remember, it was the era of the white shoe brigade; Alan Bond was syphoning cash from his corporations left and right while buying over-priced European art and creating an eponymous university on the Gold Coast; Christopher and Pixie Skase (who put Port Douglas on the map) were at the height of their notoriety, at once epitomes of business success, excess and overweening bad taste. In this context, New Moon it was not so much tropical as de trop. Add a faded movie star living a kind of Sunset Boulevard existence at Karnark (while operating her restaurant The Nautilus – a celebrity hotspot and something of a byword for high living and excess); a band of youthful thespians wild for the ride; a surfeit of chemical substance being ingested; and one had an almost perfect setting for life reflecting art.

This was seat of the pants, edge of the seat, sailing close to the wind, what you will. It was a grant here and, a deal there. Living dangerously was part of the thrill, one suspects, for Iles as least. The fact that the southern tour of 'BBT' made a modest "profit" helped the Company's overall fragile bottom line. But even Iles acknowledged that success in those cities could not disguise the fact that the work had largely failed in its home territories and was continuing to fail there. It was becoming clear that to whatever extent the audiences in the base cities had ever been tuned in originally to New Moon, they had now effectively turned off and dropped out.

Perhaps, it was because none of the key players in the Company was from the region or exhibited a commitment to living there year-round and being adopted into it, in any sense. In the off-season in a kind of ironic reversal of Barney and Roo, Iles went back to Adelaide to play with his kewpie dolls there. But New Moon was also too restless to sink roots in any one place. Witness the shifting of its base among Townsville, Cairns and Rockhampton – all perhaps for good reasons at some level – but never genuinely finding a place to be and thereby to connect or in turn allow a community to connect with it. Perhaps there was something in the gypsy caravan mode of life that appealed to Iles and that in turn infected the Company (mountebank, as Bakaitis observed). [474] Perhaps it was that being so young, single and largely without personal attachments they felt less need to settle or belong. Whatever may be the case, it became one of a number of fatal flaws in the mix. New Moon was never North Queensland. It was if anything Nimrod in North Queensland. (Bakaitis recalls that on first meeting Iles said: "think Glasgow Cits in the Tropics."[475] There was always a sense that the Company was trying to remake or reproduce something that was happening or had happened somewhere else.

Key Largo
Photo: Yon Ivanovic
Left to right: Steven Ford, Russell Kiefel, Denis Watkins.

Imagine
Left to right- Graham Matters, Bjarne Ohlin, John Waters, Luz Yeomans, Stewart D'Arrietta

Beach Blanket Tempest   Photo: Sheena Dunn
Left to right- Mark Daly and Liddy Clark

8

Why did it Fail?

> *Some people,*
> *no matter what you give them,*
> *still want the moon.*
> *The bread,*
> *the salt,*
> *white meat and dark,*
> *still hungry.*
> *The marriage bed*
> *and the cradle,*
> *still empty arms.*
> *You give them land,*
> *their own birth under their feet,*
> *still they take to the roads.*
> *And water: deep then the deepest well,*
> *and still it's not deep enough*
> *to drink the moon from.*
> *Denise Levertov – 'Adam's Complaint'*

What finally stopped it?

More than most other arts organisations in Australia one can think of there are "what ifs" swirling around New Moon's short history. As well, there are so many dangerous corners that might have been avoided. What if one of the original Brisbane candidates for Artistic Director had been appointed? Bryan Nason, in particular, was a seasoned regional Queensland touring veteran. The subsequent history of his hopelessly under-resourced but endlessly productive Shakespeare company, Grin & Tonic demonstrated he had the staying power. Another of the first round contenders, Rick Billinghurst, having led Brisbane's

La Boite for a while went on to success elsewhere. Then, what if John Milson's health had not forced him to pull out? He was a tough and hard working journeyman who might have been just what was needed in a regional start-up. Or what if Terrence O'Connell had stayed in 1983 and Paul Iles had left? He had a proven track record of founding and running a regional theatre company and a history of engagement with and development of local artists. His draft program for 1984 was startlingly original and risky in the right kind of way, perhaps more so than anything that was to follow. What if Ian Tasker had not died miserably before even starting the job? He was not a director but his entrepreneurial experience might have turned things around. What if Gary Down had wanted to stay and kick-start a new era of sense and sensibility? He was an actor/director with the common touch who had been everywhere and done everything. What if Rod Wissler had been in a position to take on the role and rescue the Company at the end? What if the youthful David Fenton brimming with ideas, had not had his time cut short by board conflict and confusion in the last days? What if they had been able to develop 'Beach Blanket Tempest' and/or keep and exploit 'Imagine' as cash cows that might have saved their bacon? [Mixed livestock metaphor intended].

There was always, and virtually built into the system, a lack of continuity and thus of "presence" giving rise to a lack of roots for the Company in the very places it aimed to serve. In the end, no one place (and above all none of the four cities to which its funding and accordingly its fate were bound) ever got the opportunity to identify with or love New Moon or its artists either individually or as a group. In particular, the distinctly secondary role that the two sets of Artistic Directors played in the critical five formative years meant that there was no one with whom the community could emotionally engage other than Paul Iles. However, the person who was the front man for the most critical period came across as alienating, flippant, disregarding and in the end rather unlovable. It was in fact far from the "pleasure tested" in or for the Tropics that had been promised. While Iles loved much and, anecdotally, many in the community, that love was not widely returned in any way that benefited or sustained the Company.

Compare its lack of local engagement with that of Dance North which, while it too serviced the region, was distinctly of Townsville and with those roots there has endured to this day. That company always had the advantage of being clearly based in one city while touring extensively in the neighbourhood and although it thereby lacked the much-touted benefit of multiple sources of local funding and institutional engagement, could invest itself in that city's life on many levels. Dance North also had a year-round presence with artists living and working there on a virtually permanent basis. Only very late in the day did New Moon really try to achieve that and then only when it had been effectively abandoned by its other base cities. With La Luna it achieved over time real depth of engagement and as a result of all its endeavours only La Luna survived. If evidence were needed, that surely is proof both of the failure and limited success of New Moon's basic model.

The Nimrod effect

Beyond doubt, Iles was good at making the deal. Probably none better in his day. But he wasn't always there for the delivery. For instance, he could put together a great accommodation sponsorship with charm and imagination but the sponsor never quite felt they got the quid pro quo and so more often than not walked away feeling they had been "gyped".[476] Execution was lacking and that was not helped by his part-time presence in the region. Not only did he, like the rest of the Company, retreat to their mostly Southern bases (and remember that to Capricornians that included Brisbane), but he was seen to move. It is hard enough to be accepted in such places after a 20 year presence, but to be viewed as a blow-in for just half the year, is and was fatal.

Such lack of follow-through eroded the very kind of loyalty in the business and general community that should have been vital in building constituency for a new company. What might have been goodwill turned to indifference in relatively short order, and even ill will in some cases, and the negative words spread like a stain around it.[477]

Iles had been shaped by Nimrod and one must remember that at those days Nimrod, although by then in decline, was still a stirring name in the Australian theatre. Despite the pioneering work in Australian theatre by Melbourne artists, it was Nimrod in the '70s that became the star turn, as it were.[478] Melbourne producers like APG and La Mama made their playwrights famous and many actors went on to solid careers, Sydney's Jane Street flourished for a while, but in Nimrod the triumvirate of directors Bell, Wherrett and Horler *were* the celebrities, especially Bell and Wherrett. In that context, Iles too was a star of a kind, attracting and dispensing propaganda and turning Nimrod from a hole in the wall (no Perth reference intended) to a theatre company translated from a stables to a sauce factory and taken seriously by all and sundry as the epitome of the new nationalist arts wave. (Note the way Nimrod is a frame of reference for HVTC as "Not the Nimrod of the north").

Interestingly, its successor Company B Belvoir would become all but synonymous with its Artistic Director, Neil Armfield though no one could be less in the "celebrity" mould that he. Iles, by contrast, was always the quintessential Englishman abroad of the kind that "went out in the midday sun". And though he had moved to Adelaide meanwhile, and the much more sedate State Theatre of South Australia, he trailed the clouds and arguably the mystique of Nimrod wherever he went, and above all as he travelled North. That had no doubt been much in the minds of John Lamb and his Townsville Council colleagues, just as it was to lay the foundations of the Company's eventual undoing.

Absence of local content

This is a tricky issue and goes back to what the New Moon founders wanted and envisaged in their original concept. Now, it does not follow that having laid down a plan it should have been slavishly adhered to nor did they, but as Terrence O'Connell has observed: "If they wanted a Queensland company they could easily have appointed a Queenslander. There were two qualified Queensland candidates.[479] As we know neither of them was appointed. A southerner, John Milson was (albeit with some Queensland connections) and after he withdrew the diarchy of O'Connell and Barclay came in, also from the Southern states. (Note that even the idea of collective artistic leadership could be traced to Nimrod, especially as Barclay had previously been a minor part of it.) So that connection cannot be regarded entirely as incidental. Again, one must be careful not to import ideas retrospectively which later flourished but which were not apparent at the time. The framers of New Moon sought locally produced, quality professional theatre made by ensemble company of the best talent that could be assembled. There is no sense in any of the available documentation or recollection of the surviving founders of wanting or needing it to be in any way chauvinistic in content.

"We actually auditioned in Brisbane twice and, I think, in Sydney. We did end up casting some Brisbane actors but, at that time, there was not the range of talent there that there is now. We were looking for actors who were strong singers and if they could play an instrument that was an added bonus. In fact, we had to have at least 50% of the company as instrumentalists to perform the musicals we chose. As things turned out, there were five or six Queensland-based actors who appeared with the company on and off over my two years there. It should be said that three other Brisbane-based performers were offered roles but declined as they did not want to, or could not, tour. It is true that, in the end, I had worked with many of the company before but only two of the permanent members were from RTC, others came from my work on Music Box Theatre Project in Sydney and Melbourne's Last Laugh."[480]

Whatever the blueprint or the mission, until too late there was little that came from or reflected the area, but more importantly and surprisingly there was little that reflected Australia, still less regional Australia. This was, after all, the age of what many have seen as a great Australian cultural re-awakening. This is also the decade when Mojo advertising's creative team were sweeping the nation with 'C'mon Aussie, C'mon', 'I feel like a Toohey's' and Paul Hogan was urging the world to 'put another shrimp on the barbie'. But all that had little counterpart in what was being offered by New Moon in such an intensely regional environment. La Mama and APG and Nimrod had been pumping out the "rough" Australian theatre of Hibberd, Romeril etc. Yet for the first five years of its existence pretty well all New Moon's actors and creative personnel came from elsewhere.

Now it is possible to argue, and as O'Connell suggests, that there wasn't the locally trained talent to sustain a company of the type envisaged. At the time this was probably true. Nor is it to suggest that among such skilled theatre professionals the idea of using as many locals as possible never occurred to them. That would be an absurd claim. But in the absence of such engagement, nothing replaced it. The Company was so constantly on the road that there was just little time or space for the kinds of activities such as workshops, outreach activities and the like which might have compensated for lack of local professional participation. They were a caravan passing through. Of course, they wanted the best and most multi-talented and multi-skilled artists they could find and without doubt, judging from both the public reports and the private observations, so did the paying public.

Like any audience they wanted to be wowed with brazen talent and bold choices and often they were. O'Connell recalls "even after all these years, I will still be approached by people who were in their teens then to tell me how much they loved the company".[481] Others in the business recall Riverina Trucking Company and New Moon as the two regional companies that had the greatest impact. Producer and Festival Director, David Malacari reflecting on O'Connell's role in both remembers them as the standouts.[482] Stephen Clark recalls years later meeting a woman at Mission Beach who still extolled her experience of seeing the Company's work.[483] One latter-day New Moon board member, Chris Cottrell who with his wife had transferred for work reasons to Townsville from Adelaide said of the New Moon productions: "We were subscribers to the SATC and these were as good as we had been seeing in Adelaide'.[484] That was high praise back in the day.

Remember too, that the broad brief was musical theatre. That was

O'Connell's background. "this was one of the reasons I was chosen for the job, that my work at the time was very music based and tended to attract a younger audience who were not necessarily regular theatregoers." [485] There is no evidence today that this was to be the dominant part of the original brief. But given the choice of Milson first who had a strong musical theatre background and wide experience of opera of the more *outré* kind and then O'Connell, this was clearly deliberate and continued throughout Iles's tenure to the end of Bakaitis's. So one can only assume it was Iles's particular spin on the broader remit. In saying all this, it is also important to note that stylistically the Company was clearly and unmistakably its own thing and in those first five years, even allowing for the very different styles and temperaments of the Artistic Directors there was a musical aesthetic which if not consistent then was at least continuous that ran through the whole.

When it comes to Australian or even local work, judging New Moon's shortcomings retrospectively is on surer ground. This is especially so as viewed within the context of what was and had been happening elsewhere in Australia at that time, including notably in many non-urban regions. Yet even here the choice of work which New Moon adopted, through successive artistic directorships, also seemed determined to emphasise the company's "otherness" from its immediate environment. In this respect, New Moon began promisingly with 'Ned Kelly'. Leaving all questions of the quality of the work itself aside, there could scarcely have been a more resonant topic or title than a piece of musical theatre about Australia's all but mythic colonial anti-hero.

Yet little followed of that ilk. Of the first eight plays presented in the initial two seasons, the only other Australian title was Louis Nowra's 'Royal Show'. While scarcely of the same rambunctious style or intent as 'Ned Kelly', the concept at least dealt with its quintessentially Australian experience of the annual agricultural fair and one to which if anything audiences in regional towns and cities could easily, indeed intimately, relate. But with such choices there was always the sneaking suspicion among the locals that they were being sent up. While audiences in these towns were not necessarily as experienced or as theatrically sophisticated as their urban peers, they had a developed nose for the phoney and the condescending. It may be that early in the piece some at least sniffed those traits. Whatever may be the case, between 'Ned Kelly' and 'Royal Show' the gap in content resonant with the locals was considerable. That is not merely to rewrite history. Bear in mind that we speak of a time when one might have thought that 'The Les Darcy Show', 'Flash Jim Vaux', 'Dimboola', 'A Toast to Melba' or even 'A Hard God' might have fared better than 'Cabaret' or 'Tommy', however well intended or executed. That is not to suggest that the post-Pram Factory world was the only possible one from which they might have derived.

There had also been an upsurge in the genuinely regional product made by local companies and reflective or their environments or history. At approximately the same time, the HVTC had produced the startling 'Essington Lewis: I am Work' and 'The Star Show'. Meanwhile Theatre South produced 'Tonight we Anchor in Twofold Bay' and 'Diving for Pearls' reflective of the meaning and savage decline of iron and coal cities in a post-industrial world. Moreover, it wasn't as though there was no local creative writing talent on which New Moon might have drawn. Where one might ask was 'Too Young for Ghosts' set in North Queensland by Janis Balodis who was raised in North Queensland and was a graduate of Townsville Teachers College just down the road? Ric Nelson, one of the original Summer Stock operatives in the same town was turning out plays, including, as has been seen, one on Northern pioneer identity, Christie Palmerston. For that matter even David Williamson's 'Travelling North' is set in the region and might well have made more sense that 'Don's Party' and been less offensive to the government (unless of course being offensive was the aim?) Even The Australian Opera had just produced 'Voss' based on explorer Ludwig Leichhardt, fatally mislaid in Queensland, and based on Patrick White's landmark novel. So it's not as though there was no consciousness of the region in wider artistic terms. One could imagine that Xavier Herbert's 'Capricornia' adapted for Belvoir Theatre by Louis Nowra in 1988 might not have been the least controversial choice for a theatre company in the Tropics, but then neither as it turned out was the bleak and Anglo-American 'No Orchids for Miss Blandish'.

However, it was not just a question of content but also arguably one of style. Reflecting on it all much later, Wissler observes: "too much of the programming probably, in those first three or four years felt like programming that should have been in Sydney and Melbourne."[486]

While it is easy to say what didn't happen and lament perhaps the opportunities missed, it wasn't as if New Moon was not pondering these matters or that the question of Australian or even Queensland content was being ignored. We've noted that Plans for 1984 as late as the grant application to the Australia Council outlined a short list of works which featured such ideas.[487] Sadly not one of them realised. All bear O'Connell's touch. So, we can if need be add these to our lists of "what ifs". What might have happened if any or all of that had succeeded? The fact is, however, that by year's end O'Connell was out and Bakaitis was in, bringing a very different style and intention to bear – one that brought a more international, even cerebral, vision to the Company

Thereafter, of the 10 productions under Helmut Bakaitis's artistic direction, four could reasonably be said to be Australian. None, however, is on a local theme or reflective in any way of the region. They are 'Beach Blanket Tempest' by Dennis Watkins very loosely after Shakespeare, Williamson's by then classic 'Don's Party'. George Whaley's adaptation of 'On our Selection' was at least set in Queensland albeit on the Darling Downs from which Steele Rudd hailed. (what is it about the persistence of Rudds in Queensland?) At a stretch, 'Return Engagement' was Australian by association rather than content, being a bio-show about a distinguished mother and son from an distinguished Australian theatrical dynasty. But none of this over six years could be called a commitment to telling or even developing North Queensland stories. Perhaps no one in the Company was around enough or connected enough to find them. When they were there the pressure of work and the pressure of life was such that there just wasn't time to stop and listen. All of that was compounded by the constant movement between cities, not just of the productions themselves which was inevitable in a touring company, but of the curious obsession with moving its base of operations.

A lack of roots

But New Moon sped through the four towns in succession and apart from mostly good memories in the audiences (as far as one can gather from anecdote and newspaper reviews) they left little imprint. Even when they were successively headquartered in Townsville, Cairns and Rockhampton there seems little evidence of deepening of engagement. At best, their sojourn was for six months of the year which was all the contracts provided for and all that the finance allowed and then like migratory birds they flew south. It is worth noting that even when the ensemble system was abandoned from 1985 paradoxically the fi/fo mode was exacerbated and the opportunities for engagement diminished even further.

Here's another paradox: the very structure of a full-time ensemble for an intensive six months constantly on the road to provide for maximum exposure in the region and to secure support especially from the city councils and the State government were the very factors that worked against putting down effective roots and growing genuine loyalty in the communities they sought to serve. That is not to say that some didn't try. Both O'Connell and Bakaitis wanted more local involvement and trialled internships and the like, but they were never around in one place long enough to make any of it stick. Only when La Luna came on the scene was there real engagement and then only really in Townsville.

Nonetheless, one must also acknowledge that these are concepts which were in their infancy at that time. Few talked of "community" in that sense let alone "outreach". Audiences were there or they weren't. That is not to underestimate the energetic role that the community theatre movement was playing at that time, but it was a specialised field far removed from the concerns of those who still aimed for the professional regional theatre company and both sides of that debate were keen to draw the line and mark the distinction.

The focus (some would say obsession) on marketing which today so dominates thinking in the arts often to the exclusion of other considerations, was barely apparent least of all in such regional centres. If anyone had asked why are you doing this; the answer would have come back (as justified by any number of pronouncements issued by New Moon and its peers at the time) to present quality theatre to the people of ... as outlined in the original prospectus and Sheila Keeffe's launching announcement right at the beginning. Today it would be "to engage with the community of ..." We should then always be wary of retrofitting our ideas of success or failure according to the mores prevailing in a later time to the actions of an earlier one.

An associated factor was New Moon's patent lack of engagement with local arts practitioners until late in its history. In defence again, one could argue quite plausibly there was simply a lack of time given the demands of their operating model. If so, was the model fit for purpose if the need was to sink roots somewhere, somehow? There is a certain charm and excitement perhaps even a frisson of risk when the circus rolls into town and no doubt a heightened expectancy which looked forward each year to its arrival. New Moon never quite captured that mood, or, lacking wild animals, its other eccentricities didn't quite measure up. As Kerry Saul observed: "we were just riding into town with a show in the hope that the local community would actually come and see it."[488]

It is noteworthy that in 1984 the two plays which succeeded were 'Don's Party' because it is an outstanding play written by Australia's most performed playwright relocated to Queensland and bizarrely enough 'Gentlemen Prefer Blondes' presumably because it was an ingenious production of an American script which furthermore featured six local supernumeraries from each city. It may not be entirely co-incidental to some of the adverse imagery that New Moon had acquired in certain critical circles that these were what were then known as "muscle men" or body builders, if you will – a phenomenon less apparent then than in today's rampant gym culture. Certainly, New Moon had learnt from some of its earlier mistakes in neglecting the locals but when it did so it was in ways that were not perhaps always as helpful as intended. One can almost imagine Iles urging the idea of hiring these extras while grinningly appreciating that the precise nature of it would scandalise some.

It is interesting that the analysis undertaken for and on the Company by Rodney Fisher in 1986 commented on these discrepancies. He was at that stage an Associate Director of New Moon. One of his central observations is telling: "The rationale behind artistic policy appears not to have been shared with the Board of Directors let alone disseminated through the press. Post performance discussion with audience members, pre-performance talks with students, open rehearsals, demonstrations of "how the company works": in fact the whole "getting to know you" structure seems to have been overlooked. The company has remained isolated".[489]

Now many might with reason argue that Fisher was not the least elitist director in the Australian theatre at that time, so that it is even more notable that he recognised these shortcomings in community relations and sensed the dislocation that they had caused. He was also a Queenslander by origin and perhaps had a better feel for the State and its sensitivities than many of those who had just flown in. But even those guests are neglected, he noted: "Moreover, the image making of the company has been at odds with the concept of a company belonging to its community. New Moon posters are astonishing for their anonymity. Only four of the fifteen play posters, as far as I can ascertain, have carried even the author's name. The names of cast members, designer, director etc have never been displayed. The results are self-evident. Actors who have spent six and, in many cases, twelve months of their lives in Northern and Central Queensland are as unknown in the region now as they were before they arrived".[490] One might add that Fisher was not a fan of Paul Iles, though it might equally be noted that Fisher has never been a fan of management in general, believing that it is put on earth to thwart directors. Nevertheless, his analysis of what had gone wrong with New Moon is shrewd and telling. More broadly, others considered that the design of marketing materials themselves, now curiously in the hands of one Scott Morrison, had seriously declined as well.

In an odd kind of way the Company was the obverse of Lawler's 'The Summer of the 17th Doll. New Moon is the untold part of what happens when Barney and Roo are up north cutting cane. Like them, the question arises where is their real life? Given that, one wonders (as Terrence O'Connell was later to ruminate): perhaps we should have started with 'The Doll'.[491]

Wear and tear

While the idea of a constantly touring, ensemble company was a visionary concept which would have been outstanding anywhere in the country at that time, in North and Central Queensland its organisation, maintenance and achievement was in those initial years often just sheer hard toil. The wear and tear of getting the Company up in short order and keeping it on the road was enormous. All those who were involved in that extraordinary combo who talk today remark on that but without complaint. The shows were large and some initially too heavy for touring; lessons had to be learned from that. They were making it as they went and literally making it up as well and while obviously neither the tiny crew nor the actors were spared: Bob Baines remarks: "We were really young and really fit – or we were at the end".[492]

In the face of all this, Barclay recalls that he wanted to adapt the touring model so that two plays in two blocks would alternate and thereby make it less demanding on the company and help make the seasons a little more accessible to the public in each of the towns. "I started to think we have got to re-conceive this. Maybe the idea is [that] we should get two shows up and then take them in repertoire. That would allow us to be in the town more than a week where we are running off our faces … that meant it would also have made savings on all of the travelling which was a significant part of our costs."[493] But he was gone from New Moon before anything like that could be properly considered still less implemented.

But it was not just the touring itself that was the problem. Some of the critical decisions made about how and what to do were killing: "the set for 'Ned Kelly' had three huge white scenes which were almost completely clad with Masonite and weighed a ton. They couldn't even fit all of it in the truck to take on tour and when they did get to the venues it was too big to put all of it out and this bunch of people had been carrying all of this stuff and it had become a big issue. So I took it on that I had to make a show that wasn't going to kill these people carrying all of this heavy, heavy stuff".[494] Stephen Clark remembers it as: "Two weeks on the road. Rehearse in the afternoons, do the show at night and rehearse the full days we weren't performing at night; then we'd go to the next town, set up. perform. Then get back to base camp with two weeks to put a polish on [the next show]. 3 days to get it into the theatre".[495]

The business model

One of the great paradoxes of New Moon is that, on the face of it, the great strength of the business model lay in its funding from three tiers of government and oversight across effectively five LGAs in a collaborative mode. However the Company's needing to satisfy the disparate demands of those Councils was arguably the seeds of its later weakness. Added to that was the fact not just of movement during touring, but also periodically moving the entire base. No city ever got to own them or just as they might have done so, they relocated. So gradually those cities lost interest. Not surprisingly, the Queensland Government hung in longest because its requirement for strong, widespread regional presence was most important to meet. Even when it clung on, one could never escape the feeling that the Australia Council always wanted to move on. That of, course, is as much a reflection of the agency's own flawed operating model in which a revolving door of board members and "peers" even to this day renders long term stable policy-making and execution well-nigh impossible. The LGAs themselves became progressively disgruntled mainly because they were treated so poorly. Though there, too, the nature of municipal government itself with (then) part-time elected officials overly sensitive and reactive to volatile constituent opinions especially on moral issues, played a large part – as the Doplo affair amply demonstrated.

Equally, the governance model, also based upon the municipal governmental collaboration, exhibited the seeds of its own destruction through discontinuous leadership for the Company and thus lack of corporate memory, as well as having directors scattered over four cities in the days before email and zoom or even mobile phones. The dominance of Local government appointees to the Board, which was part of the corporate structure, resulted in excessive turnover of directorships resulting from municipal elections, resignations from office for various reasons and changes of administration within Councils that rotated focus on its various suffragan entities. Continuity might have been provided by always (rather than occasionally) appointing the managers of the civic theatres to balance the elected officials. However, by ill-luck, two of the strongest contenders namely John Lamb and Ian Satchwell, both left for other jobs elsewhere and in one case at least the successor, David Gration at the Civic Theatre in Townsville seemed to show less interest than his predecessor or was maybe less confident of the New Moon project. In any event, continuity of oversight and concern was broken. There was also extraordinary turnover of chairpersons (eight in nine years not counting various times when someone acted in the role). One of them and one of the longer serving ones relatively speaking, Diane Cilento who, given her extensive acting career and profile, might have been expected to provide not only knowledgeable leadership but high visibility, proved temperamentally unsuited to the task and thereby incapable of offering the skills needed.

Paul's company

There is, too, the view that it was always his master's company. Even the media spoke of "Paul Iles's company". He was one item of continuity over the first five years of the Company's life even though he was only in the North for half the year. The Artistic Directors never saw themselves as seriously involved in other than in artistic planning. They had little contact with the Board or government agencies or sponsors, so they never became the face of the Company in any meaningful way. "It was always Paul's company. He played the administrative side very close to his chest".[496] That may well have been true of O'Connell who had much less "corporate experience", but the written record suggests that Bakaitis may be selling himself a little short in that matter. His regular reports to the Board suggest that, apart from financial matters, he earnestly sought to shape their thinking and made some valiant attempts to help lay members understand the creative side of the Company. Perhaps though everyone was just too scattered and too preoccupied to notice.

And to be frank, it is not clear from either of the two main artistic players that they would have wished to undertake a more executive role. Again, we have to put ourselves back in the times. Today we're accustomed to the idea that Artistic Directors are often CEOs of arts companies and, even where they are not, they are expected to engage in a range of promotional, fundraising and administrative activity much broader than the specifically artistic role. Of course, even then there were notable exceptions in the bigger companies such as John Sumner at MTC and Alan Edwards at QTC who combined both functions or there were the remnants of the old director/manager repertory model who were and did everything such as Hayes Gordon at the Ensemble and Irene Mitchell at St Martins. But they were rarities by then. Managers managed and Artistic Directors programmed and directed. In the case of New Moon, Iles was undoubtedly the driving force: setting the pace, making the pitches and cutting the corners. He maintained a voluminous correspondence with all and sundry, some of it wry, delicate and persuasive, some of it rabidly offensive, but all of it in the service of the Company's advancement as he saw it and the propagation of the grand theatrical vision for North Queensland.

All of the available evidence suggests that Iles was a white knuckle manager. That is as true of his time at Nimrod in Sydney and later at the State Theatre of SA as it was back in Britain in Blackpool and Edinburgh. Immense achievements stand out against major failings; extraordinary planning and foresight against sometimes disastrous spur-of-the-moment reactions. In many respects the history of New Moon from 1981 to 1985 during his tenure there reflects his temperament and manner which could veer wildly from cool-headed analysis and shrewd decision to extravagant outbursts and intemperate language. This is clear from his many Board reports internally, as well as from his correspondence with funding agencies, most notably the Theatre Board of the Australia

Council. His attitude to the Queensland Division of Cultural Activities seems to have been milder perhaps because they were more consistent in their support or because he was cluey enough to recognise that they were less likely to tolerate his verbal fireworks. Or maybe it appealed to his sardonic sense of humour to play (in reverse as it were) good cop/bad cop with the two contrasting funding agencies.

It is also likely that that pattern once set was hard to break. A degree of distrust among those whom we would today classify with the unlovely usage "stakeholders" continued to pursue the Company and its fortunes well after Iles's departure. Rodney Fisher's summary is very telling. Given his past close association with Bakaitis he was perhaps not the most detached observer and never one to hold his opinions back. Yet for all that, it is surprisingly stringent. In commenting on the Company's stated objectives, he wrote "here, it would seem we are dealing with false promises. From my research, it is clear that the idea of a theatre company providing assistance to local amateur groups and conducting workshops in various aspects of the performing arts was at the very heart of the foundation of the company. In its failure to provide these services the management of New Moon over the past four years is seen at its most cynical: promises of pending training and assistance schemes repeatedly unfulfilled".[497]

He observed that this was all the more remarkable seeing that Bakaitis was highly regarded and well-trained in the area of community theatre and youth training and Cilento was an expert in the Laban technique and her offers of workshops had not been taken up. Fisher, is of course, using the term community theatre in a sense which the then highly active community theatre movement in Australia would not have recognised. Nevertheless, his point stands. One must also acknowledge that while it was undoubtedly "Paul's company" neither of the first two Artistic Directors has suggested that he ever interfered in choice of plays or casting beyond the reasonable limits of any manager concerned for budgets and tourability. If anything, one is left with the impression that perhaps more restraint in that matter on his part might have helped the increasingly wobbly bottom line. But in none of his numerous and very detailed reports to the Board on financial progress is there ever a hint of blame to the artists or a suggestion that they had been prodigal. It always seemed that if there was a new and perhaps better way to do things, Paul was up for it. A good example here was Bakaitis's concept of a touring metal stage box to sit as a standard playing space in the variously scaled venues. It might have worked. In the end it didn't entirely realise its goal, but Iles supported it and in effect made it happen.

Above all Iles loved the theatre. There are various personal accounts of the almost visceral entrancement with the act of performance which, at least as long as he was in Australia, he never lost. No doubt that wish to share his pleasure in the experience with the theatrically under-served people of North Queensland was what kept him going through thick and thin in those very tough 5 years. That and, it must be acknowledged also, his equal attraction to the natural and human beauty of the place and their "pleasure tested" openness to him.

Yet the fact is that Iles was always too fond of cheap shots. Some of that arose from misreading the community, but some was just his natural instinct since it was as apparent in Sydney where no one cared and in Adelaide where it was too unimportant to notice and not just in the present but in the past. For instance, with the choice of Dario Fo's 'Trumpets and Raspberries'; anyone with half a knowledge of the North Queensland Italian Diaspora or a care to find out, could have told that it was most unlikely to be receptive to a Marxist message. Shots at Joh's government were foolhardy in the context, however well received in the wider world. And they were done from a position of weakness by fi/fo company with no stake in the region and no real knowledge of it or its inhabitants.

Lack of vision

The question also arises: did New Moon have a long term goal/vision other than that outlined in its first statement of intent.[498] That is harder to discern. The rapid turnover of artistic directors and therefore direction seems to suggest not. Its mission, if that is the right word, was always linked to the practical ends of servicing the four main centres specifically and central and northern Queensland generally with quality theatre product. There does not seem ever to have been a larger objective. Certainly, beyond quality, variety and entertainment there appeared to be no aesthetic stamp that any of the leadership wanted to place on the enterprise and equally there is nothing implicit in the choice of work which would lead even an acute observer to eke one out. Iles's remark about Glasgow Cits in the Tropics was not a plan but a whimsy. Now to be fair "quality, variety and entertainment" are not to be despised as theatrical aims. The obsessive urge to create plans in which the slavish pursuit of goals and strategies and KPIs that has of late reduced many a worthy arts organisation to a set of ciphers was still to come. Putting on good shows which attracted a paying audience was still regarded in the 1980s as a worthy pursuit. *Qui procul hinc...*

One of the essential flaws, perhaps the essential flaw, was that in devising the Company there was a great deal of attention paid to what it would do and not enough to what it would be. For sure, the business model was well argued and negotiated. But the founders plunged into it without ever giving it (literally) a road test. Of course, there was nothing new about theatrical touring. Actors had done that since the Middle Ages. The Arts Council movement in Australia with its far-flung network of branches was predicated on extensive country tours, especially in NSW and Queensland. But all were transplanted city productions rehearsed and premiered there and sent out to dazzle the bush. They were long ribbon tours playing night for night in dusty town halls and Schools of Arts.[499] "Arts Council tours are only fit for performing dogs and puppets', a character in Peter Kenna's play 'An Eager Hope' says. Kenna knew. He'd been on a few. But none of the touring shows were based in the bush itself. Almost none rehearsed the next show while playing the current one and certainly none did all that four times over in six months. That was brand new, perhaps dangerously new.

Moreover, the history of the permanently touring theatre company in Australia was not heartening. The Trust Players created in 1954 had been an attempt by the AETT to build a national theatre company to parallel similar efforts in opera and ballet and later marionettes. It was probably the only precedent for what New Moon intended and it had early come to grief.[500] Repertoire art forms like opera and ballet were different, but they rarely ventured beyond the city except with cut-down versions to piano accompaniment. But New Moon with an untried ensemble, no established audiences, an odd name, and a funding mix which would have been the envy of many a city-based company, launched itself on the road after just four weeks rehearsal. The wonder is not that it faded but that, in such a format, it lasted a year, let alone five!

Big money

To the extent that any memory of New Moon survives anywhere in Australian theatrical folklore it is that a) it was all a bit too racy for conservative, redneck Queensland b) it was all fi/fo and c) it lost money from day one and kept losing money. The first is a matter of opinion and the concept of "racy" will always be in the eye of the beholder. The second was and continued to be true right to the end as we have seen. But the third is a trickier proposition. It is fair to say that it is both correct and incorrect. Why and in what ways it was both successful and unsuccessful financially is an interesting and instructive tale.

First of all, let's take the two foundation years and a few key measurements. In year one – 1982, New Moon sold 15,740 seats over the four cities for $132,324 (or roughly $340,000 in today's terms) representing an average of $7.06 per ticket. In Year two, it sold 19,338 seats for $172,025 (an increase of 29% which is a remarkable achievement for any start-up business. That was an average of $8.89 per ticket. In each city the seats sold and cash receipts exceeded the previous year.

In the same period, Australia Council funding went up 18% while Queensland government funding went down by 45% and sponsorship rose by 237%!! (admittedly from a very low base). The State figure is somewhat misleading since in 1982 two years of funding had been rolled into one because the Company started a year later than had been planned and $79,000 was carried forward from 1981 to 1982 effectively doubling the grant income that year. As a consequence, its contribution appears to decline rather than remain steady in 1983. However, 1982 was the only year in which the Company recorded a surplus (of just $829) largely it might be argued because of that curious Queensland double subsidy. From then on it accumulated operating losses though in 1983 that shortfall was "covered" by funds retained from the previous year.

The chart in Chapter 6 offers a picture of the situation at the end of 1985 when Paul Iles departed and the state of play inherited by the untried new administrator, Ruth Bereson. One should note that it was the first year in which only three productions could be presented. The issue was not so much a failure of growth in income as a rising costs and a growing gap between the two.

Moving forward, as we have seen, 1987 is the last year in which it could be said New Moon enjoyed anything like a stable funding base. Even when carrying a deficit and dealing with the vagaries of death and disorder it was still a serious trading entity in receipt of considerable public subsidy (however hard fought at times), some private sponsorship and earning performance fees and box office receipts. The financial edifice was by then somewhat ramshackle but the key elements were all still in place. In the remaining three years those elements fell apart and, except for isolated moments, never really came together again.

In the eight years to 1988 the five core LGAs provided over $400,000 in direct funding plus extensive indirect support and value-in-kind. From time to time, this was supplemented by contributions from other LGAs (Mulgrave, Proserpine, Mirani, Sarina and Nebo) In 1982/3 the Company had secured sponsorship or donations from the private sector worth $59,600. That was an extraordinary achievement in those days. It would be still today. By 1987 it had effectively nothing from that source.

In 1982 the Theatre Board of the Australia Council gave $89,600. While Queensland contributed the same. By 1987 support from the Australia Council had evaporated. That from the State sat at $200,000. It is perhaps the most succinct measure of what had occurred to the Company's fortunes in that short time.

One can, of course, note that this was a period of considerable turmoil on many arts fronts. It was the height of the dispute between the "community" theatre and those perceived as "mainstream" companies and the associated debate – if that is not too mild a term – on the redistribution of public arts funding. It was a phoney war, but one which put considerable pressure on the Theatre Board as to what to fund. At the same time, demand for subsidy was spiralling out of control while a cautious Hawke government, anxious to distinguish itself on the one hand from the supposed prodigality of the Whitlam years and on the other from the parsimony of the Fraser era, was only mildly responsive to demands for an increased subvention to the arts. It would be easy to see New Moon, at least in part, as a victim of all this.

From the outset, however, as noted previously the Theatre Board, driven by then by the infamous Rotherwood Plan, had always been clear that funding to all regional companies, not just New Moon, was on a five year, annually reducing, sunset basis. One can, and many did, debate the wisdom of that formula and Iles regularly railed against it. Indeed he made some headway by persuading the Board to defer the annual reductions for two years or by securing project funding, and on one occasion a matching "incentive" grant, to make up the difference, at least in part. But that sunset provision was always a feature of the New Moon deal and a less reckless management than he might have negotiated the reality better.

It would be tedious to trace the financial ups and downs over the entire period but as 1984/85 is the turning point, let us look at it in a little detail. By late 1984 things were looking rough. The minutes of an extended Board meeting in Rockhampton report that box office had not grown that year at the same rate of the first two years of the Company's operation (by only 5% in 1984).[501] Accordingly, the estimates for 1985 were forecasting an alarming deficit of ($97,848). An option to reduce the main season to three productions would cut the projected deficit to ($10,374) assuming grants from all funding authorities remained at the levels offered (i.e. for a four-production season).

Added to that was an accumulated deficit at end of 1984 of ($15,606) which meant that the starting point for 1985 would be ($25,946). New Moon had by then survived three years of operation by annual "windfalls". It seemed, too, that the Company's attendance had plateaued at 320 paying per night or earned income of $241,230. This accounted for only 37% of receipts with $407,158 being grants, sponsorships and donations. The national average at that time for theatre was held to be around 55% earned income. So after much soul-searching by the Board, 3 productions it would be. Renegotiation with various funders had to be entered into. By delaying the season to the second half of the year they believed some ground could be made up. There would be more time to raise sponsorship and reset expectations. However, by mid-year 1985 it was apparent that the plan was slipping further still. On June 24 Iles reported in detail to the Board that there had been a serious decline in box office receipts (for 'Guys and Dolls') and an increase in costs which had a knock-on effect for the rest of the year.[502]

All sorts of mechanisms were tried to boost sales. One of the most telling was to do with price point. The Company had frequently debated the option of raising prices to bridge the deficit gap, but Iles rightly believed that increasing the number of paid bums on seats at whatever price was a greater priority. Accordingly, after the box office slump of 'Guy and Dolls', they took another tack: reduce prices. Now it might be argued that Steele Rudd had more natural appeal in Central Queensland than an aged Broadway musical about gangsters falling for a Salvation Army girl. At all events, of the four performances of 'On Our Selection' in the Pilbeam theatre the first two on Wednesday and Thursday were half price previews which did 316 and 379 sales respectively. Interestingly, sales for Friday and Saturday at full price soared to 420 and 514 respectively and all up the sales were 1,629 for the season as against 1077 for 'Guys and Dolls' or around 33 % higher than for the musical. Of course, the cash receipts were only $1,600 up, but over 500 members of the public either came for the first time or returned.

The experiment was continued with 'Trumpets and Raspberries' but like the Governor-General in 1975, nothing as it turned out, would save

Dario Fo. Overall, box office was down $28,139 on estimates with 'On Our Selection' perversely the greatest loss. An attempt to play Friday matinees in Townsville and Cairns failed to draw flies in either city. By October the budgeted deficit for 1985 had increased to ($60,360) as a result both of lower box office of $27,179 and higher expenditure of $22,796 with 'Trumpets and Raspberries' still to come. The end-of-year deficit was then estimated at ($76,000). To give a measure of this 'Guys and Dolls' took $63,924, heavily buoyed by Cairns. 'On our Selection' took $45,678 fairly evenly spread across all four cities. 'Trumpets and Raspberries' took $12,712 (!!) equally bad in Cairns Townsville and Mackay and catastrophic in Rockhampton. Total earned income was $122,323 for three productions as against $210,709 for four in 1984 which did not include 'Beach Blanket Tempest' attendances outside of New Moon's home turf. Meanwhile, the Queensland government had raised its grant for 1985/86 to $175,000, an increase of $17%. The accumulated deficit as at 31 December 1985 stood ($158,040) as compared with ($15,606) in 1984 and the net deficit was ($142,434) for the previous sixteen months' trading.[503]

On the positive side, it might be mentioned that the Company was the largest arts employer in Northern Australia at that time. In 1985 it employed 21 full-time theatre workers on fixed-term engagements. This was of course among the chief reasons why Dona Greaves was so determined to keep it afloat. Subsidies in 1985 represented about 58% of turnover; sponsorship a further 8% and box office and other earned income 34%. In 1984 it had sold 20,356 tickets in its own region (i.e. excluding sales of 'Beach Blanket Tempest' inter-state. In 1985 that fell to 12,000, reflecting three rather than four productions. By then, Local government had made a total investment of $352,487. Yet for all that the Company had no reserves and little hope of generating them.

Public opinion

Much of that decline had little or nothing to do with any of those factors of local engagement and content and mostly to do with its failure to deliver on the promises it made at its foundation. After so much time, it's hard to gauge how the work was received by audiences in terms of like, dislike or indifference. We have seen how newspaper reviews in the four cities give some clue and for the most part they were favourable to warm. As anywhere, opinions varied from show to show and place to place and as might be expected with any body of work. But there was never at any stage in any of its four markets sustained adverse criticism. The only exception is that one remarkable outburst by the Rockhampton Alderman in 1984 followed by an intense public skirmish. Such anecdotal commentary as it is possible to glean ranges from the extremely enthusiastic of the generally positive: "In that sense, apart from the reviews we never really knew what kind of an impact it was having."[504]

Occasionally, a letter to the editor took exception to some particular aspect of a production but probably no more than they might have in a capital city albeit more likely 20 years earlier. Even there, it has been suggested that some of this outrage might have been plants by Iles to stir up controversy and push sales.[505] If this is so, it seems rarely to have succeeded because the one true metric of New Moon's reception is that it never established a reliable recurrent audience and rarely met or exceeded its box office targets. That observable failure, more than any other factor, was responsible for eroding local government trust and ultimately support. Then, too, relations with those key LGAs was crucially linked to the use of their venues which were a critical component of the deals, both in cash and kind.

But it soon became clear that not all were equally suitable for the task. Despite John Lamb's drive in putting the whole package together, his own venue the Civic Theatre at 900+ seats was always likely to be too big for an emerging regional company even if it had done the most four square program. All but the most established state theatre companies in major cities would have struggled to fill a room of that size. Bear in mind that in the wildly successful Nimrod was playing in its 350 seat theatre in Sydney where indeed its successor Belvoir still does. At various times the managers of those venues were among their respective council's representatives on the New Moon board which must have added a further layer of complexity to the relationships. Similarly, with the private sector. While corporations rarely show their hand in these matters as clearly as governments, the fact that the Company was not reaching as many potential customers or opinion-makers as needed to justify the sponsorships was clearly a factor and that disappointment showed in their later correspondence about non-renewal or declining to join.

Unstable

Whichever way one looks at it, New Moon was never really financially stable. Although from day one it enjoyed the dual support of the Australia Council and the Queensland government in lock-step with a variable number of LGA grants and guarantees-against-loss together with a trickle of private sector contributions, the task they set themselves was always too wide and complex for the available resources. And yet paradoxically had it been narrower it is unlikely that it could have commanded the resources that were assembled to get it off the ground. Catch 22, as it were.

Iles had consistently argued that without a capital reserve the Company was always living on borrowed time: "We now regard the company as palpably underfunded." [506] In June 1988, Rob Adams came to a similar conclusion in his analysis 'New Moon – Future Directions': "The Company is unusual in that it is fully touring – serving four cities as if a resident professional theatre to each. 34 per cent of its costs are attributable to touring – over $200,000". Iles himself went on: "In our opinion, New Moon has been underfunded from the beginning".[507] The Australia Council's David Thompson agreed: "that the Company could not continue its present mode of operation on current funding levels".[508] His colleague, the Council's Finance Director Bob Taylor had reported a similar conclusion.[509]

All that was complicated by the fact that while the Queensland government's contribution continued to inch up, the Board's input – "core funding" we might call it today – gradually diminished. It was propped up from time to time with special "deals" or "initiatives" as they were more genteelly known. A Challenge Grant came to the rescue in 1984 which essentially matched grants for private sector fundraising. On another occasion, 'Beach Blanket Tempest' was toured to Mt Isa and Alice Springs with an Australia Council Touring and Access grant which many rebadged at the time as 'Touring to Excess' in that in promoted much travel but with little success. There were a number of interrelated financial problems. (A story circulated at the time that given the nature of the works selected for this purpose a post-modern dance company touring under the scheme to Alice Springs was so ill-received at its first performance that the locals queued next morning to hand back their comps before the second one.)

Yet, the simple fact is that almost from the outset, New Moon carried a series of rolling deficits which accumulated year-on-year until by the time Iles left and Bereson came in the Company was effectively $200,000 in the red (about $560,000 in today's terms). Bear in mind that when New Moon got its first grant in 1980, both the Australia Council and the Queensland Department were about 12 years old. There was no body of sophisticated monitoring to draw upon. A few harassed financial officers of the Federal agency tried to keep tabs on scores of fragile enterprises across the country overseen by governments at both Federal and state levels who were deeply suspicious of prodigality and who saw much of that as being redolent of socialist waste of public funds.[510] It is probable that trying to employ and sustain a "permanent" ensemble of 10 actors, not to say technical and production staff albeit for just six months a year, was unsustainable even in the medium term. Too much of the working capital was tied up in inflexible wage commitments. The scheme had been devised because the founders, and Iles in particular, believed that not only was it the best way to assure artistic quality since there was not an adequate pool (or some might have argued any pool) of local actors who could be relied upon in a venture such as they were embarked upon. There were also what they had calculated to be clear economies of scale in not having to bear the costs of casting and simultaneously rehearsing/performing each production with fresh talent in all probability flown in for the purpose from wherever that talent happened to be. All that was verifiable. Even the QTC in much more populous Brisbane suffered a similar drought as its long term Director, Alan Edwards was often heard to lament. But it was not the only solution. A mixed approach of a smaller ensembles with local apprentices might have lowered the financial load and at the same time deepened local engagement. It is of course easy to be wise after the event. Whatever the answer to that might have been, the financial lock-in was huge in the context and until 1986 that burden remained in place.

Certainly too, there is some occasional evidence of lack of control on expenses but not to any great degree and no more than might have occurred from time to time in other comparably sized companies, bearing in mind the cost of constant travel and freight and the need to supply accommodation. The real problem was that New Moon never really realised its full income potential and insufficient steps were taken to respond to that until too late. It meant that despite the impressive level of private sector support (in the context of the scale of the Company and the times) New Moon was always excessively reliant on public funding and never seemed to develop a coherent plan for how it would transition out of that pattern. Accordingly, a huge amount of administrative time was expended, and in reality needed to be expended, on securing and retaining that support and on occasions entering into rather public dispute over it. If and when that support began to erode, as it was always bound to do at Federal level, and began quite early to do among the local government authorities, the only recourse was the State government. Despite much goodwill, that was always going to be finite and hotly contested by more Southern interests, if one may put it so delicately.

While in minor ways other LGAs came on board from time to time, New Moon never really broke out of its primary reliance on the four main centres. It is arguable if servicing more towns in pursuit of more local government funds would necessarily have benefited the bottom line, but it might have shared the risk making the Company less vulnerable to just one or two of the major cities pulling the plug, as eventually Cairns and Rockhampton did. That greater breadth might also have strengthened its political arm vis-à-vis other tiers of government and increased the geographic spread of its audiences and thereby their lobbying clout. Longer tours might also have enabled the Company to produce fewer shows embedded in seasons with longer runs. One could go on in this speculative vein. Eventually, all these cost-push factors came down to unattractive and, to the minds of the public authorities, unacceptably blood-stained balance sheets.

As well, only 'Beach Blanket Tempest' broke out of the Queensland touring mould. If anyone might have made a more extensive circuit function it would have been Iles, but that product while fine was far from exceptional. The attempt to reproduce the reach made sense but with 'Imagine' it came a gutzer on issues of royalties and ownership which were predictable and indeed were predicted by a young general manager who was ignored and out-gunned.[511] Iles, for all his hubris, would not have fallen for that. But then he would not have allowed the product to be repackaged into the lead actor's meal-ticket and then lost to the Company. Its final attempt at salvation slipped away. Another wotif?

When some of us were still at school it was customary to enumerate important "facts": Three reasons for the Norman conquest, the five causes of the fall of Rome; the seven outcomes of the 100 years' war. That is not to mention the 10 Commandments, 8 Beatitudes, and however many gifts there were of the Holy Spirit. These were faithfully litanised in class and repeated in end-of-year exams. Marks were given out of 10. Later the world (or educationists at least) recognised that life is rarely so ordered. Pace Bertrand Russell, human history is too messy to be reduced to numbers. The probable causes of New Moon's failure listed above are just that: speculation, possibilities, maybes. The reality is that everyone involved was so busy trying to make it happen that the whys and wherefores like strategy were lost in the heat of battle and while there was time to count the casualties and bury the dead, it was over too soon for deeper reflection.

So are we left with a choice of bad luck or bad management or somewhere in between? Was it too early or too late? Too hot or too cold? What can be said with certainty is that it never, even for a moment, reached that

Goldilocks position of just right. Perhaps above all, if there is an answer that is the answer: that there was never a point of respite. It was always helter skelter.

Return Engagement
Tony Sheldon and Toni Lamond

9

What can we Learn?

Romans came across the Channel

All wrapped up in tin and flannel:

Half a pint of woad per man'll

Dress us more than these

National Anthem of the Ancient Britons

Art by decree

There are many ways of looking at learning. Soon after an event one might see a myriad of mistakes that could have been avoided, chances that were missed, actions that might have been performed better. Then, there is the medium view when the process is still live and is not yet too late to evaluate, amend and move forward. Further off still, when the specifics have been forgotten or are no longer of real account, general lessons emerge from the mist that may guide the present or the future. To conclude this rambling tale of wonder and woe, here are a few which might be of use if only because too often we seem historically "doomed to repeat", as Santana almost said, our small excesses and large errors.

New Moon was a prime example of the risk, seen many times and in many places, of creating arts ventures by government decree, that is to say when, for whatever political or administrative aim, a decision is taken that this or that cultural activity will or should occur in a certain place and under certain conditions. Now, It is true that no one actually stood on the Town Hall steps and proclaimed New Moon into existence like the issuing of a Papal Bull, but it came close. It matters little whether the idea being promulgated may in itself be good or desirable, the essential problem is that it is invariably top-down and even where the choice may have involved some response to demand or assessment of need, as it did in the case of New Moon, it may still be essentially flawed.

There are, of course, degrees of this behaviour. One would not argue on those grounds that the Hermitage is a bad thing or that the Prado should not exist. Many of the best of their kind were in origin personal whims or passions of absolute monarchs rather than state enterprises. (Would the UK government have finally created the National Theatre in the 1960s were it not for the eminence of Laurence Olivier?) But the closer it comes to the human level – in this case a small, roving theatre company – the more problematic becomes foundation by fiat rather than from creative practice.

Accordingly, if one compares, let us say the Murray River Performing Group and Theatre South (the two longest surviving Australian regional theatres) with New Moon, the differences in origin are stark. Although impoverished and often endangered, both those Southern companies were driven from the outset by artistic and social vision and by personal rather than institutional energy. For good or ill and through many changes of pace and policy, they lived in and survived through the swirl of local cultural circumstance. Both, it is true, had just one base rather than four although they each exercised some regional responsibility. Both had some institutional backing and government financing at various times and borderline Albury-Wodonga could always play Victoria and New South Wales off against each other. But the real distinction is that they (like Q Theatre and the Riverina Trucking Company) started with artists wanting to do something fresh in a particular time and place. Certainly, there was an opportunity that presented itself in these cases, but above all there was a genuine artistic mission framed and followed by artists, even if implemented in fits and starts.

New Moon was, beyond doubt, an impressive and visionary plan by officialdom of the day. It secured a remarkable spectrum of "backers" from both the public and private sectors, it put together a "cartel" of interests which was unprecedented then and may not soon be seen again. It had money in the bank before the doors opened, comparatively more than any of its regional peers. But artists came late in the piece and were somehow always an appendage to the big picture. The audience, in order of consideration, came later still. It was, in short, imposed on the communities; it was set up to serve rather than growing from them.

That approach, which also privileges the organisational over the aesthetic, was part and parcel of the times. In some ways it still is. Bureaucracies are forever coming up with grand schemes which tend to leave artists in their wake. Plans are hatched and schemes devised and somehow those who create are required to fit in. Biennials and sesquicentenaries are the happy hunting ground of such thinking. In the recent past, a determination to enshrine the arts in legislated fortresses was a case in point. They included turning state theatre companies into statutory corporations as a prime example. In the early 1970s this became a feature of the "it-seemed-like-a-good idea-at-the-time" syndrome from which so much arts planning in Australia has suffered. In fact, for a while in South Australia at least, it seemed as though everything in the arts would be a statutory body. It is also a reflection of the Australian geist, where compared with other countries in the Anglosphere, that government has long played a leading if not dominant role even to the point of contradiction, in all aspects of economic and social life. Is it sparseness of population? Scarcity of private capital? Dependency born of convict foundation? Over a century of long-distance decisions from the Colonial Office in London? Take your pick. Yet how often have we heard business interests, usually the first to decry red tape and regulation, demand the government to "take action" and intervene when it suits them. How quickly rampant capitalists turned to the welfare state when Covid-19 hit their bottom line.

So, not content with urging governments to create funding and advisory agencies in the 1960s and '70s, the arts were also prepared to let those agencies shape activity and create infrastructure and thereby make critical choices among a range of content: which dance, whose music, what plays, how many of what in any one territory, and so on. They still do, uncritically, and as though there was no other way to manage affairs. Witness the scurry to defend the Australia Council whenever it is deemed to be threatened by marauding cabinet ministers, as though it were a sacred cow at all costs in need of preservation by its adherents. It is sad, really, in a business that loudly and proudly proclaims itself to be innovative and independent, that it should be so supine in these matters.

Part of the problem is that too often funding has become a prerequisite for making art and so a cult of dependency has developed. On the other side, government has got onto the drug of grant-giving and finds it hard to get off so, that it has become central to thinking rather than thinking itself.

Paul Iles may have been wilful and sometimes wrong-headed, but in a braver world than today's he was prepared to stand and be counted; to argue, albeit on occasions with intemperate language, that the federal government's agency was on the wrong track; and that, for instance, sunset funding in regional Australia was frankly bullshit and demeaning because it assumed that its withdrawal would leave not – as it proved – a black hole but an opportunity for others who step into the gap. Who those others might be was never explained and what evidence there might possibly have been for that was never disclosed. Nowadays, grant dependents patiently wait for that same body to evolve another set of platitudinous "strategic goals" so that they can faithfully reproduce them in their funding applications rather in the way school children used once to chant the times tables back to their teacher.

That is not to say that every government initiative anywhere has been ipso facto bad. That would be an absurd claim. We can decry the so called edifice mentality that has spawned a colossal arts and cultural building program across the country (and many countries) over the last

50 years, while acknowledging that it has transformed the attendance habits of generations and made access possible to many who had little or none. Festivals by government imprimatur may rightly be considered anything from questionable to a plague. They are now spread generously across the land often linked to the dubious aim of "cultural tourism", but notably two contrasting cases will suffice to show they can have opposing results. The Sydney Festival was in the late 1970s without question a government-corporate stitch-up, but it turned an inert January into a joyous summer feast. Melbournians, by contrast, have never embraced their equivalent event no less dreamed up in a Minister's office, but have continued to prefer perhaps the greater and more heartfelt spectacle of the Spring Racing Carnival and end-of-season Aussie Rules tournament. Thus MIFA (now rebranded as 'Rising') wanders around the calendar seeking comfort.

Notwithstanding, it was also that very edifice mentality that build the regional arts centres in Queensland (as elsewhere) which, as we have seen, spurred the John Lambs of that parish to search for suitable content and ultimately decide to create a resident theatre company to provide it. So far so good. But all too soon it was clear that a mismatch between the sheer physical and logistic demands of those venues (usually around 700 seats) and the best averages of 300 attendances per performance was killing the experience while piling up the Company's costs. The local governments and their venue managers had an imperative to fill those halls which naturally pushed them towards the popular and commercially successful as their stock-in-trade. The Company (and indeed other high-end providers such as the Arts Council, QTC and the like) had other imperatives driven by genre development, presentation of quality work and the artistic benchmarks demanded by their conditions of grant, especially from the Australia Council. There was a disequilibrium from the start, though occasionally New Moon's more populist efforts e.g. the works built around Bowie and Lennon were able to bridge the gap. Bakaitis very early put his finger on the problem: the municipal architecture was wrong for the art but those who controlled the purse strings, owned the architecture and demanded its use.

New Moon was not the first theatre company in the world to confront this dysfunction, nor sadly will it be the last. Many have lamented it at some point in their history. However, for New Moon it occurred in an infancy the Company never escaped and which made it arguably the more fragile in the face of it. Among the many lessons New Moon offered, but which seem still not to have been learnt, is to avoid shoehorning performing companies into spaces unfit for purpose for some vainglorious political end. Allied to that is the worldwide trend of converting post-industrial sites (factories, power stations, old wharves and railway workshops), into arts "precincts" often at greater cost than erecting a new, purpose-built home, whether in the belief deep down that anything will do for the arts, or "artists like old things" or just plain indifference dressed up as concern to preserve built heritage.[512]

So perhaps another lesson might be to steer clear of "government initiatives" in the arts. They mostly have little to do with art but much to do with civic pride and [whispered] votes.

A further moral may be gleaned from the biblical adage that one cannot serve God and mammon. Let us allow for a moment that in this instance God may be equated with Art (and in doing so the author makes no special claims of divinity for any artist). On the mammon side, New Moon had simply too many masters. The glory of the model was in bringing many cashed up players into the game, but that was good only so long as they agreed with the rules. Iles was a master at pitching one against another and for a while he kept most satisfied. However, once they lost confidence in him and through him the project, that web quickly unravelled and the mirror cracked from side to side…

That might be summed up as a lesson which goes something like: the more to whom one is beholden, the harder it is to please anyone.

Change-making

Yet for all that, New Moon did change lives and mostly it would seem for the better. Some actors went through a baptism of fire and came out more adept, aware and resilient than they went in though others came away bruised by the encounter. No one knows or has ever known what makes art of any genre act on its spectators or, in doing so, whether its effect may be judged good or bad. Nor indeed can we know if any two people observing the same work of art at the same time have the same experience. What we can say is that in the relatively fallow ground of North and Central Queensland at that time audiences from school kids to grandparents had theatrical experiences that they would not otherwise have had and anecdotally that had impact then and in some cases still.

A small cadre of local theatre aficionados, students, technicians and managers were turned to significant careers in the performing arts or related disciplines. Judging from contemporary accounts, for a few short years the theatre-going public of the region was shocked and awed and entertained and hopefully had their eyes and minds opened by what New Moon offered. Some time ago, the late British director, Jonathan Miller said of the theatre that the greatest claim he would make for it was that the audience might go away having thought differently about something than they did before.[513] There is some evidence New Moon achieved that in some small way and we can never underestimate what the ripple effect of that might have been; somewhere perhaps there is "some mute inglorious Milton" who was changed forever. Throughout this tale we have tried to indicate a few.

Legacy

Legacy is a complex thing to assess in any enterprise. Some institutions leave material benefits that are easily measurable, even quantifiable: hospitals can record the number of patients, procedures, recoveries; schools the number of pupils, scholarships, successful alumni; transport the number of vehicles, journeys, passengers. Of course, the impact of the arts may be measured by the number of admission, tickets sold or even by surveys of audience satisfaction. But few in the business would be satisfied by statistical analysis alone and indeed many rebel against the current trend of over-reliance on those factors.[514]

But, as we have seen, no one would dare to claim lavish numbers for New Moon. Its success in that area was marginal at best and then only spasmodically. With the partial exception of La Luna, New Moon left little tangible legacy such as a body of revival theatrical work, a successor company or companies, a school of performance style or dramatic theory such as one might make a case for Nimrod with Belvoir. But how in any of these is one to measure satisfaction, still less delight, among those who attended? The many definitions that have been evolved over time may well be useful in the broadest sense, but it tells is little of impact on the individual or their intimate story.

There are, as we have seen and will see a cohort of people's lives and careers that were in some way materially touched and changed by their encounter with the New Moon Company in a variety of ways. Some were a gradual experience of seeing its work over a period of time. In some cases it was the sheer gratification of knowing that professional theatre production and presentation was actively in their midst. For others still, it was the impact of a single night in the theatre at a performance the like of which they had never seen before or even quite imagined. Perhaps an actor should have the last word on this: "Every now and again (and I hear this from other actors who I meet from time to time), someone asks me 'weren't you in New Moon? That was great'. All these years later".[515]

La Luna

Throughout this chronicle there have been many references to La Luna at crucial moments in the overall tale. This is the moment to tell a more coherent story of this remarkable enterprise and arguably the survivor from the wreckage of New Moon. The name itself was coined by the

Company's publicist, Sheena Dunn who also designed its original logo of a man in a spacesuit with the moon reflected in the visor of his helmet. While there had been some scattered youth activities before this time, one version of the history is that the program itself began in 1987 with the arrival of Jeremy Johnson from Sydney to build on work which had already begun by Jocelyn McKinnon in response to community requests for some activity of this kind.

There is, however, a parallel view which holds more accurately perhaps that the initiative which led to La Luna was begun in April 1986 as the proposed youth arm of New Moon and held its first workshops then. McKinnon comments: "New Moon at this time had a perceived need to be more involved in the community partly to meet funding requirements and because feedback suggested that the 'southern' leadership of the company had steered New Moon away from their initial path". [516] McKinnon was asked to conduct a program from April to December that year to ascertain whether the perceived community need would justify a permanent program and to gauge how much interest and support there was actually for a youth theatre particularly for less privileged participants.

It began with workshops for children aged 6 to 12 years while a large number of inquiries from teenagers then led to the establishment of an additional group aged between 13 and 16. As well as workshops, there was also a program of group-devised and in-house productions. Throughout all this, parental involvement and support was integral in the early stages, For instance, parents made costumes and props, assisted backstage, attended workshops, served on the support committee, ran fundraisers for the group and publicised it. The aim was to provide a service for low income families, though some children from comparatively affluent backgrounds also attended. One of the early organisers remembers the first batch of students included the then young daughter of Prof Henry and Senator Margaret Reynolds.

Either way, one could argue that La Luna, as it was to become, was engendered in an almost off-hand manner. We have seen that there were a variety of stop-go initiatives over time: a workshop here, schools audience of mainstream shows there and various talks and encouragements to young people as early as 1985. Bakaitis noted some of the constraints he had faced in that respect: "After Paul left I decided that I needed more time just to go visiting schools and drama groups; coming to rehearsals and helping them and so making connections which Paul had never done."[517] Nonetheless, there is some evidence in the records that it was also the result of a growing belief in the importance of the Company's undertaking work of this kind. In fact, there had been abundance of talk about it over time but little in practical terms happening until late in the day. Arguably too, it seems to have been more likely a response to pressure from funding agencies not only at State and federal levels but also from the city councils that were seeking value for money.

At all events, La Luna rented a shopfront opposite the New Moon offices in Sturt Street, Townsville which was in turn next to the abandoned Kings Theatre. It began with few if any resources but with volunteers lending a hand to get the business up and running. So it lurched uncertainly into life beginning with just four classes a week. Until recently, La Luna was the longest running youth arts company in Queensland and one of the country's most successful. Based in the splendid Riverway cultural centre it catered in a variety of classes across the performing arts in theatre dance music and circus to between 300 and 400 children and young people annually.

It is for others to trace La Luna's distinguished track record after the effective demise of New Moon. That is a different story. It suffices to say that its endurance and ongoing success for just over 30 years is in stark contrast to the fractured progress of its parent company. That can be attributed readily to a commitment maintained to this day to community engagement and outreach – the very things with which New Moon failed to grapple in any other dimension of its work but which, especially given the outstanding skills of one of its artistic directors, Helmut Bakaitis, one would have thought it could so easily have encompassed. Nevertheless, La Luna did happen and it did continue and we have seen how at crucial moments it was the only element in the New Moon endeavour that provided continuity, attracted funding support, offered public appeal and in the end when all else failed went on its own way.

Going bush

In the English-speaking world at least, there has long been an obsession in culturespeak with what might loosely be termed devolution. It is either a great leap forward or a dead end depending on one's preferences and experience, but it is almost never painless. The history of the arts including theatre in Australia – a land of many isolated population centres – is littered with the mantra of decentralisation usually dressed up as regional "initiatives" aiming to give power and choice to where it was deemed to belong i.e. at the local level. That has a long history. In the late 19th century the Schools of Arts/Mechanics Institutes were a first valiant attempt to bring a certain kind of cultural enrichment to the nation. That movement was not confined to the bush but flourished equally in capital city CBDs and suburbs as well as in country towns. Yet it brought everything from libraries, music recitals, social dancing, amateur theatrics and even billiard rooms to previously deprived communities. The Adult Education movement did something similar and, if that seems remote from the performing arts, it is worth recalling that it was that scheme in the 1950s which made possible touring in Victoria by the infant Union Theatre Repertory Company which in turn gave birth to the august Melbourne Theatre Company.

Post World War II the Schools of Arts faded or were subsumed into local government. Meanwhile, the Arts Council movement, forged by redoubtable women like Theosophist contralto, Dorothy Helmrich in New South Wales and in Queensland, Viennese-born art critic, Gertrude Langer, rose to take its place. Run rather like the Colonial Office, from their bases in capital cities with a quasi-religious mission to take civilisation to the backwoods, those circuits lived and died by the strength and fervour of branch committees spread across the length and breadth of the land rather as the Raj had depended on district Patrol Officers. They billeted artists, booked and crewed the halls, put up posters, sold tickets from their kitchen tables, dragooned their friends and neighbours into attending, baked the lamingtons for the after-show receptions and waved the touring companies on their way to the next town. They were the local doctors, teachers, small business proprietors and vicars' wives. They were the salt of the earth and a more committed, caring, bossy and irritating body of human beings it would have been hard to find anywhere. Theatre, dance and music of all kinds toured the regions: staying in country pubs where one got little sleep until the last noisy imbiber had left the downstairs bar; living allowances unknown; the roads bad with many a bus and truck lodged in a flooded creek or a giant pothole. And before the days of internet, Skype or even reliable public phones it was far from home and often very lonely.

Then, as we have also seen, arose the idea of the resident regional theatre company which came and went with just a few surviving even to this day in one form or another.[518] The occasional youth theatre in the regions has also struggled on. At more or less the same time, other establishments like the impressive chain of regional galleries have proven more enduring. Sometimes linked to these and sometimes not, came the equally impressive explosion from the late-1970s onward of the regional arts centres which eventually coalesced into statewide and even nationwide networks. Many if not all of these have contributed to bringing or producing live professional theatre outside the main urban centres of population. More recently some of the performing arts centres have been stimulated by various government funding initiatives [e.g. the Local Producers' Scheme] to make their own work and even tour it beyond their base. But with the best will, it has been spasmodic and one would be hard-pressed to argue that, viewed nationally, there is a coherent picture of regional theatre that is consistently resourced or even coherently regarded. Almost none it seems, even in the immediate Queensland region, remembers let alone reflects on the rise and fall of New Moon.

Pace the ABC's 'Landline', mainstream media have long forgotten the Bush. The regional media have all but vanished to be replaced in country towns by the news bulletin equivalent of the ATM in place of banks. So, too, chains of commodified motels, nationally operated fast food and retail outlets dominate in place of locally owned and run shops although here and there marginal cafes and craft shops somehow survive.

All those trends were apparent or emerging during the New Moon decade though, sad to say, few discussed them or took them into account in their planning or prognosticating. So perhaps the one big thing that we ought to have learned was that the New Moon model was probably always swimming against the tide of history. It was relying on a mode of delivery that the rest of world was fast abandoning namely that a local theatre producing and retailing enterprise could thrive when all other locally based enterprises were being made redundant by the march of the giant called Franchise.

The matrix

The one outstanding characteristic of the Company, clear from its very beginning, was the originality of its funding model. Original, that is, in its application to non-metropolitan Australia. It has been observed many times before that the three tiers of Australian government have been both a strength and a weakness in our political and administrative history. Even allowing for the grotesque difference in scale of the six states (Tasmania and Western Australia at the extremes of that) the Federation has at least resisted the urge to further subdivide, avoiding the risk of the absurd 50 US states or even Canada's 10 provinces and 3 territories. On the other hand, we have proliferated local government to an extravagant extent and, interestingly, only Queensland has managed to reduce that to a working model of more consolidated regional authorities in two mighty reforming sweeps in 1925 and 2008. But despite many tries, attempts to bring federal, state and local government into a consultative still less collaborative alignment have largely failed. The Murray-Darling basin is perhaps the most spectacular and tragic example of this failure in recent times. In this, the arts have fared no better than, say, housing or roads, but have inherited a multiplicity of funding fiefdoms all striving "to work out their salvation with diligence", to quote the Buddha. To this day, one could count on the fingers of one foot the number of successful three way ventures in the arts which involved even one LGA with other tiers of government beyond project funding.

So it is all the more remarkable that this strange Tropical endeavour to bring together not one but initially five (and later more) councils with the state of Queensland and the Australia Council could have prospered, if only for a time. To be fair, there was one great precedent, mostly forgotten except by a few chronicling drudges like the present writer, which did indeed find a formula for such a linkage. The Australian Elizabethan Theatre Trust established in 1954 brought together the Federal government, the six states and the councils of the capital cities in a joint funding deal to support a collection of elite performing arts activities (theatre, opera and ballet) with a then unique tax-deductible status for private donations. It took a royalist Prime Minister in Robert Menzies and a royal visit by EIIR to knit all this together (an odd collocation of a politician and a monarch neither of whom could have cared less about the arts.) Ain't history strange? But it sort of worked and lasted for thirty years and the curiosity is that few have since thought it remarkable and a fewer still have tried to make it happen again.[519]

Bold venture

So on the positive side, one can argue that the founders of New Moon embarked on an astonishingly bold venture. If in many ways it proved fractious to run, it demonstrated that it could be achieved and in a highly contested political space. The framers of the scheme saw the benefit of those regions coming together and created a formula in which they could do so and exploited the common need each had to supply content to their theatres and thereby for their constituencies. While no one would claim that they are lineal descendants of that, in later times both Queensland and NSW have trialled and to some extent maintain regional arts development groupings in which a number of contiguous LGAs and the State co-fund community arts activity. It is far from ideal and often unstable, but somehow the memory lurks that it is possible.

On the negative side, the New Moon founders neglected or never came to grips with the forces that pulled them apart. Above all, curiously, they seemed not to care that each of the towns which composed the four legs of their composite stool were wildly different. If one needed evidence of that on an intellectual level one has only to read back through the reviews quoted in Chapter 7. But more significantly, whatever their apparent differences there was the recognition that it was vital not to treat those heavily guarded castles all alike. Queensland was never "Sydney or the bush". It was more – and in many ways still is – Anglo Saxon Britain: many small kingdoms in search of an enemy.

Despite the tensions that always existed between "head office" and the branches, the Arts Council model which is the only working template for regional arts co-operation of scale we have ever had, allowed and even encouraged local "buy-in" to choice of product and the sale of product. It was imperfect and conflict was not unknown, but it provided space for the critical dimension of community involvement. New Moon never offered that outlet. In all fairness, it probably never could have. So it sought to impose a model made in Townsville and no doubt entirely plausible in Townsville, on the rest of the regions neglecting local opinion and interests. One did not have to go to the extremes of Ald. Dopplo to conclude that Rockhampton was a different world to that of Cairns. Nor was it necessary to conduct a poll of suitable plays in each city to form a program. But some attempt at grassroots engagement that went beyond moving the base of operation every couple of years and have having local councillors on its board would have/could have reshaped its destiny.

The lesson surely is to remember that the second half of the oft-quoted phrase "vox populi" is "vox dei" or in other words: note where the real power lies.

Reinventing the wheel

But what all this highlights is that we do keep repeating the same formula for producing theatre. When the New Moon Company got together in North Queensland it unhesitatingly shaped itself into a pyramid that would have been instantly recognisable in Hobart, Spokane or Wolverhampton. Its program may or may not have been daring, foolish or run of the mill; its artists may have been extraordinary and hard-working; its public image smart or obscure depending on the show; its management variously ambitious, wayward or gamely hanging on. But despite the time and the place and the *tabula rasa* that was offered, none of it tried in the slightest degree to rethink or reinvent the idea of a conventional theatre company that might have been more flexible or more adaptable to the strange new circumstances in which it found it – possibly as a partnership, as a co-operative or even as a dictatorship (one might that thought that if ever a time and place was ripe for the Intendant system it was Queensland in the 1980s!) So it plodded on with an administrator (by whatever name), an artistic director (or two), a group of contracted artists and artisans working to order and a board of directors from hither and yon who almost never saw enough of anything close up to form a collective view and were left to be wise or otherwise after the event. So the question arises in this as in many similar contexts: can one be steady as you go on top and (as Paul Iles often claimed) revolutionary underneath? Is it fair to ask if New Moon should have chosen to be radically different in form as well as function?

We have only to look around to see how little we have learned anywhere of that lesson. Arts companies in what some are pleased to call the not-for-profit sector still overwhelmingly exhibit the same tired structure with a few changes of nomenclature to make them seem modern. Now those who were once managers have become executive producers with little genuine acquiring of new executant skills; "cultural leadership" programs abound but none seem to lead to new ways of thinking or leading; and compliance, like the Old Man of the Sea, increasingly clings to the back of everyone who tries to make change.

Perhaps we may take heart at the more recent explosion of independent theatre production where feisty or just younger artists decline to apply for government grants; crowd-fund or self-fund their work; and share the results good or ill among the participants. In Australia's case it's a pity that this mostly occurs in inner city spaces. It's regrettable too that with so many dark nights more regional arts centre don't open their doors to the recent graduates of the all too numerous theatre studies courses to encourage them to make theatre in their locale. But for all the Jindyworobak mythology white Australia is still scared of the Bush and what it implies and has been since 1788.

Are you Lonesome Tonight? Photo: Townsville 'Bulletin'
Gary Down and Richard Roberts with set model.

The Summer of the Seventeenth Doll
Left to right: Chris Bett, Anthony Phelan.

Bibliography

Adams, Rob. *New Moon – Future Directions*. Arts Action, Sydney, 1988.

Australian Biography. 'Diane Cilento', National film and Sound Archives, 2002.

Australian Political Chronicle: July–December 1987, *Australian Journal of Politics and History*. 34 (2): 239–240. June, 1988.

Cadogan, Patrick. *The Revolutionary Artist: John Lennon's Radical Years*. CreateSpace Independent Publishing Platform, 2008.

Cilento, Diane. *My Nine Lives*. Penguin, 2007.

Condon, Matthew. *Three Crooked Kings*. UQP, 2013.

Crosby, Sam. *The Trust Deficit*. Melbourne University Press, 2016.

Davis, Des. 'Opportunity Lost: NSW Regional Theatre Companies –1976-2003'. Wollongong University Theses Collection, 2007.

Dickie, Phil. *The Road to Fitzgerald*. UQP, 1988.

Evans, Raymond & Ferrier, Carole (ed). *Radical Brisbane – an unruly history*. The Vulgar Press, 2004.

Evans, Raymond. *A History of Queensland*. Cambridge University Press, 2007.

Fielding, Trisha. *Queen city of the North: a history of Townsville*. Kirwan, 2016.

Fotheringham, Richard (ed). *Community Theatre In Australia*. Currency Press, Sydney, 1987.

Freudenberg, Graham. *A Certain Grandeur: Gough Whitlam's Life in Politics*. Penguin, 2009.

Glover, Stuart. 'Revisiting the Cultural Policy Moment: Queensland Cultural Policy from Goss to Bligh', *Queensland Review*, 18, Brisbane, 2011.

Hedge, Douglas. *The Company We Keep: Queensland Theatre Company, 1969-1979*. QTC, 1980.

Hooper, Guy. 'Renaissance in the Regions – the Hothouse Theatre Artistic Directorate'. *Proceedings of the 2008 conference of the Australasian Association for Drama, Theatre and Performance Studies*.

Huy, Liz, McDonald, Lorna & Myers, David (ed). *Sin, Sweat and Sorrow: the Making of Capricornian Queensland 1840s-1940s*. UQP, 1993.

Macdonnell, Justin. *Arts Minister: government policy and the arts*. Currency Press, Sydney, 1992.

Macdonnell, Justin. *Fifty Years in the Bush: the Arts Council Movement in New South Wales.* Currency Press, 1997.

Macdonnell, Justin. 'Cultural Precincts: Art or commodity', *Platform Papers* No 44. Currency House, 2015.

Lunn, Hugh. *Joh: The Life and Political Adventures of Sir Johannes Bjelke-Petersen.* University of Queensland Press, 1987.

McKinnon, Jocelyn: 'Towards a Social Aesthetic of Community Theatre in the Australian Political Economy – A Regional Perspective'. James Cook University Thesis, 1996.

Meyrick, Julian. *See How it Runs: Nimrod and the New Wave,* Sydney: Currency Press, 2002.

Meyrick, Julian. *Australian Theatre after the New Wave – Policy, Subsidy and the Alternative Artist,* Brill Rodopi, 2017.

Meyrick, Julian, Phiddian Robert & Barnett, Tully. *What Matters? Taking Value in Australian Culture.* Monash University Publishing, 2018

Parsons, Philip (Ed). *Currency Companion to Australian Theatre.* Currency Press, 1995.

Richards, Michael. 'Arts Facilitation and Creative Community Culture: a study of Queensland Arts Council'. Queensland University of Technology PhD thesis, 2005.

Robinson, Shirleene 'Homophobia as party politics: the construction of the 'homosexual deviant' in Joh Bjelke-Peterson's Queensland'. *Journal Queensland Review,* 2010.

Rogers. Meredith. *The Mill: Experiments in Theatre and Community.* Australian Scholarly Publishing, 2017.

Rowse, Tim. *Arguing the Arts: The Funding of the Arts in Australia.* Penguin/Random House, 1985.

Schmoyer LoMonaco, Martha. *Summer Stock: An American Theatrical Phenomenon.* Palgrave Macmillan, 2004

Spearritt, Peter. 'Rum Corps to white-shoe brigade'. *Griffith Review* 2, 2003.

Ward, Peter. *A singular act: twenty five years of the State Theatre Company of South Australia.* Wakefield Press, 1992.

Whitton, Evan. *The Hillbilly Dictator: Australia's Police State.* ABC Enterprises, 1989.

Endnotes

Chapter 1

1. https://www.facebook.com/LaLunaYouthArts/ February 8, 2020
2. John Lamb, letter to Rob Adams, February 14, 1979 and to Kevin Siddell, September 28, 1979, JCU arch
3. New Moon, Steering Committee, *History and Resume of the Project* meeting agenda, JCU arch
4. Steering Committee Minutes, May 7 and 8, 1980: JCU arch
5. New Moon, Board Minutes: JCU arch
6. John Lamb, *Prospectus Central and Northern Queensland Theatre Company Ltd*, JCU arch
7. Ibid
8. Ibid
9. Terrence O'Connell, letter to the author, November 13, 2017
10. New Moon, Board Minutes: JCU arch

Chapter 2

11. New Moon, Grant application to Theatre Board – Appendix "C", February 14, 1979: JCU arch
12. Mike Reynolds, Interview with the author, Sydney, May 20, 2018: JCU arch
13. Ibid
14. Kevin Radbourne, Interview with the author, Maleny, July 25, 2017: JCU arch
15. Arthur Frame, Interview with the author, Brisbane, July 24, 2018: JCU arch and see also Justin Macdonnell, *50 years in the Bush* 1996, Currency Press, passim]
16. John Lamb, paper delivered at the Drama Seminar, Foundation for Australian Literary Studies (Townsville), May 19-20, 1979: JCU arch
17. Ric Nelson, Interview with the author, Adelaide, July 13, 2018: JCU arch
18. Macdonnell, op. cit.
19. Nelson, op. cit.
20. Grant application, op. cit.
21. Macdonnell, op. cit.
22. Grant application op. cit.
23. Nelson, op. cit.
24. Ibid
25. Rod Wissler, Interview with the author, Brisbane, July 28, 2017: JCU arch
26. Ibid
27. Ray Dickson, interview with the author, Townsville, June 20, 2018: JCU arch
28. cf: Townsville 'Daily Bulletin', April 24, 2008
29. Wissler, op. cit.
30. New Moon Board Minutes, March 7, 1981:, JCU arch
31. Elizabeth Perkins, *New Moon* 'Currency Companion to Australian Theatre', Philip Parsons ed. 1995, Currency with Cambridge p399
32. John Lamb, letter to Paul Iles, January 1, 1981: JCU arch
33. John Lamb, Memorandum to Board, July, 31, 1980: JCU arch
34. 'Daily Bulletin, August 16, 1978

35 Peter Barclay, Interview with the author, Sydney, January 21, 2018: JCU arch
36 Ibid
37 Margaret Bornhorst, Interview with the author, Brisbane, December 12, 2018: JCU arch
38 Reynolds, op. cit.
39 Nelson, op. cit.
40 Margaret and Henry Reynolds, Interview with the author, Hobart, June 1, 2018: JCU arch
41 Brian Sweeney, letter to John Lamb, August 13, 1980: JCU arch
42 Townsville 'Daily Bulletin', May 19, 1981
43 Macdonnell, Justin: 'Arts Minister: government policy and the arts' Currency Press, Sydney 1992 p207
44 Robert Ellicott, letter to Brian Sweeney, September 11, 1979: JCU arch
45 'Townsville Advertiser', July 10, 1980
46 Robert Love, Interview with the author, Sydney May 28, 2018: JCU arch
47 Aku Kadogo, Interview with the author, Sydney, June 14, 2017: JCU arch
48 Cheryl Stock, Interview with the author, Sydney, June 27, 2018: JCU arch
49 Margaret and Henry Reynolds op.cit
50 Ibid
51 Reynolds, op. cit.
52 *Sin, Sweat and Sorrow: the Making of Capricornian Queensland 1840s-1940s*, Ed LizHuy, Lorna McDonald , David Myers, UQP 1993
53 Helmut Bakaitis, Interview with the author, Blue Mountains, August 2, 2017: JCU arch
54 Ray Dickson, op. cit.

Chapter 3

55 Graham Freudenberg, *A Certain Grandeur: Gough Whitlam's Life in Politics*, Penguin, 2009
56 Bob Baines, Interview with the author, Sydney, April 6, 2018: JCU arch
57 Malcolm Calder, Interview with the author, Auckland, March 12, 2017: JCU arch
58 Michael FitzGerald, Interview with the author, Melbourne, March 20, 2017: JCU arch
59 Wissler, op. cit.
60 Frame, op. cit.
61 John Lamb, letter to Kevin Siddell, September 28, 1979: JCU arch
62 Alan Edwards, *Drama Touring in Queensland*, August 1981: JCU arch
63 Frame, op cit
64 Lamb to Siddell op cit
65 New Moon, Board Minutes, November 18, 1983: JCU arch
66 Love, op. cit.
67 David Fenton, Interview with the author, Sydney, July 11, 2017: JCU arch
68 Stephen Clark, Interview with the author, Brisbane July 25, 2017: JCU arch
69 Kerry Saul Interview with the author, Sydney, August 23, 2017: JCU arch
70 Stock op. cit.
71 Richard Fotheringham, Ed: *Community Theatre In Australia*, Currency Press, Sydney 1987
72 James McCaughey, interview with the author, Melbourne, March 2, 2017: JCU arch
73 Brian Debnam, *Notes on Harvest Theatre*, letter to author, January 9, 2017
74 FitzGerald, op. cit.

75 Des Davis, *Opportunity Lost: NSW Regional Theatre Companies -1976-2003*, Wollongong University Theses Collection, 2007
76 Meredith Rogers, *The Mill: Experiments in Theatre and Community*, Melbourne, Australian Scholarly Publishing, 2017
77 Jocelyn McKinnon, *Towards a Social Aesthetic of Community Theatre in the Australian Political Economy - A Regional Perspective*, Department of English James Cook University, 1996
78 Julian Meyrick, 'Australian Theatre after the New Wave - Policy, Subsidy and the Alternative Artist', Brill Rodopi, 2017
79 Davis op. cit. quoting Tony Trench interview
80 conversation with the author
81 cf: Guy Hooper, *Renaissance in the Regions -the Hothouse Theatre Artistic Directorate*, proceedings of the 2008 conference of the Australasian Association for Drama, Theatre and Performance Studies
82 Davis op. cit.
83 'Courier-Mail', April 23, 2016

Chapter 4

84 Debnam op. cit.
85 Bornhorst, op cit.
86 https://narpaca.com.au/?p=2231
87 John Lamb, letter to John Milson, July 15, 1980: JCU arch
88 September 14, 1980
89 John Milson, letter to John Lamb, August 1, 1980: JCU arch
90 Barclay, op. cit.
91 Terrence O'Connell, letter to author, September 19, 2017
92 Anthony Babicci, Interview with the author, Sydney November 28, 2017: JCU arch
93 Barclay, op. cit.
94 Ibid
95 Bakaitis, op. cit.
96 'Steven Gale. 'The Stage'; May 16, 2011
97 Babicci, op. cit.
98 Paul Iles, letter to Julian Meyrick July 16, 1996
99 New Moon, Board Minutes: JCU arch
100 New Moon Board Minutes: JCU arch
101 http://www.mackayecc.com.au/__data/assets/pdf_file/0003/149214/Mackay_Regional_Theatre_-_Building_Fund_Programme_1985.pdf
102 Bakaitis, op. cit.
103 New Moon, Board Minutes, November 18, 1983: JCU arch
104 Bornhorst, op. cit.
105 Clark, op. cit.
106 Bornhorst, op. cit.
107 Ibid
108 Clark. op. cit.
109 Ibid
110 Kerry Saul, Interview with the author, Sydney, August 23, 2017: JCU arch

111 Ibid
112 Ibid
113 Ibid
114 Ibid
115 Ibid
116 cf Brisbane 'Courier-Mail', November 27, 1953, as a sample of her rabid views
117 Diane Cilento, *My Nine Lives*, Penguin 2007
118 Bakaitis, op. cit.
119 Bakaitis, op. cit.
120 Ruth Bereson, Interview with the author, Brisbane, December 2, 2017: JCU arch
121 Ibid
122 Ibid
123 Ibid
124 Ibid
125 Ibid
126 Ibid
127 Ibid
128 Ibid
129 Kirsty Veron, Interview with the author, Brisbane, July 26, 2017: JCU arch
130 Ibid
131 Ibid
132 Robert Spencer, Interview with the author, Cairns, May 16, 2019: JCU arch
133 Ibid
134 Ibid
135 Ibid
136 Ibid
137 Ibid

Chapter 5
138 New Moon Board Minutes: April 29, 1983 JCU arch
139 New Moon, Board Minutes: JCU arch
140 New Moon, Board Minutes: December 15, 1980: JCU arch
141 John Lamb, letter to Paul Iles, January 7, 1981: JCU arch
142 Paul Iles, letter to Russell Hinze: September 24, 1980: JCU arch
143 John Lamb, Memorandum to Steering Committee, August 8, 1980: JCU arch
144 Steering Committee Minutes, March 7, 1981: JCU arch
145 John Lamb, Memorandum to Steering Committee, March 31 1981: JCU arch
146 Hilary Furlong, letter to Paul Iles: April 2 1981: JCU arch
147 Vicky Harper, letter to Paul Iles, May 28 1981: JCU arch
148 Paul Iles, letter to John Lamb, May 29, 1981: JCU arch
149 O'Connell, op. cit.
150 Baines, op. cit.
151 Saul, op cit.
152 Babicci, op. cit.
153 O'Connell op. cit.

154 Paul Iles, Report to New Moon Board: March 11, 1983: JCU arch
155 Ibid
156 Love, op. cit.
157 Barclay op. cit.
158 Paul Iles, letter to Michael FitzGerald, October 4, 1982: JCU arch
159 Paul Iles, letter to Michael FitzGerald, Oct 7, 1982: JCU arch
160 Ibid
161 Lucy Wagner, 'Sydney Morning Herald' , October 15, 1982
162 Paul Iles, letter to Michael FitzGerald, October 7, 1982: JCU arch
163 Australia Council Press Release, September 30, 1982 from Elizabeth Butcher: JCU arch
164 Paul Iles, letter to Alan Edwards, July 10, 1982: JCU arch
165 Wagner op. cit.
166 Michael FitzGerald, letter to Paul Iles, October 21, 1982: JCU arch
167 Paul Iles, letter to Carmel Daveson, 20 October, 1982: JCU arch
168 Bruce Shepherd, letter to Michael FitzGerald, JCU arch
169 Iles to Daveson op. cit.
170 Bob Katter, letter, to Peter McKechnie, November 23 1983: JCU arch
171 Michael FitzGerald, letter to Paul Iles, October 21 1982: JCU arch
172 Michael FitzGerald ,letter to Paul Iles, November 23, 1982: JCU arch
173 Pat Galvin, letter to Paul Iles, December 13, 1982, JCU arch
174 Paul Iles, Report to New Moon Board, March 11, 1982: JCU arch
175 Ibid
176 Bakaitis, op. cit.
177 New Moon, Board Minutes, JCU arch
178 Allan Callaghan, letter to Paul Iles, March 29, 1983: JCU arch
179 Diane Cilento, letter to Hon J Bjelke-Petersen, April 11, 1983: JCU arch
180 Report of General Manger to New Moon Directors: JCU arch
181 Macdonnell, 'Arts Minister' pp273-4]
182 Bruce Shepherd ,letter to Michael Fitzgerald, April 29, 1983: JCU arch
183 Ibid
184 Ibid
168 Ibid
185 Ibid
186 New Moon, Board Minutes, October 5, 1983: JCU arch
187 O'Connell, op. cit.
188 Hugh Lunn, *Joh: The Life and Political Adventures of Sir Johannes Bjelke-Petersen* (2nd ed.). Brisbane: University of Queensland Press 1987 pp. 351-76
189 New Moon, Board Minutes, November 23, 1983: JCU arch
190 Paul Iles, letter to Michael FizGerald, October 18, 1983: JCU arch
191 Michael FitzGerald, letter to Paul Iles, October 27, 1983: JCU arch
192 Paul Iles, letter to Town clerks: June 1, 1984: JCU arch
193 Macdonnell, 'Arts! Minister' pp340 & ffg
194 New Moon Board Minutes, November 18, 1983: JCU arch
195 Ibid
196 Bakaitis, op. cit.

197 New Moon, Board Minutes, November 18, 1983: JCU arch
198 Bakaitis op. cit.
199 Paul Iles, letter to Rea Francis, March 19, 1984: JCU arch
200 Evan Whitton, *The Hillbilly Dictator: Australia's Police State*, ABC Enterprises, Sydney 1989 esp pp 91–92
201 media release: 'Rocking the Tropics: New Moon moves to CQ': May 18, 1984: JCU arch
202 'Morning Bulletin' February 18, 1984
203 Malcolm Calder, letter to author, November 17, 2017
204 Progress Statement No 2 for the Four Months ending 31 December 1984: January 3, 1985L JCU arch
205 Ibid
206 Bakaitis, op. cit.
207 Ibid
208 Ibid
209 Paul Iles, 'Future Options' August 14, 1985: JCU arch
210 Bob Taylor, interview with the author, Sydney, July 17, 2017: JCU arch
211 Matthew Condon, *Three Crooked Kings*, Brisbane: UQP 2013, p330
212 Board Report, op. cit.
213 New Moon, Board Minutes, August 14, 1985: JCU arch
214 Ibid
215 Bakaitis, op. cit.
216 New Moon, Board Minutes, August 14, 1985: JCU arch
217 Ibid
218 Bakaitis, op. cit.
219 cf. S. Robinson, *Homophobia as party politics: the construction of the 'homosexual deviant' in Joh Bjelke-Peterson's Queensland*. 'Queensland Review' 17, 2010: pp29–46
220 as reported in the 'Sydney Morning Herald', Aug 15, 2018
221 New Moon, Board Minutes, October 10, 1985: JCU arch
222 Bakaitis, op. cit.
223 R. Fisher: *A status report on the Central and Northern Queensland Theatre Company*: JCU arch
224 Bakaitis, op. cit.
225 'Morning Post' Rockhampton August 21, 1985
226 Obituary: 'The Herald Scotland' May 5, 2011
227 Bereson, op cit
228 Ibid
229 New Moon, Position description Administrator November 1985: JCU arch
230 Report of secretary to Board of Directors Meeting, November, 8-9, 1984: JCU arch
231 New Moon, Board Minutes: December 4, 1985: JCU arch
232 New Moon, Board Minutes July 6, 1986: JCU arch
233 Bakaitis, op. cit.
234 Administrative and Artistic, Report op. cit. JCU arch
235 Dona Greaves, letter to Val Valentine, May 29, 1986: JCU arch
236 Malcolm Calder, letter to Val Vallentine, May 21, 1986: JCU arch
237 McKinnon, op.cit. pp175-196
238 Fisher op. cit.

239 New Moon, Board Minutes, December 5, 1986: JCU arch
240 New Moon, Board Minutes: JCU arch
241 Calder, letter op. cit.
242 New Moon, Board Minutes: December 4-5, 1986: JCU arch
243 New Moon, Board Minutes, May 30. 1987: JCU arch
244 Ibid
245 Spencer, op. cit.
246 New Moon, Board Minutes, October 31, 1987: JCU arch
247 Minutes of Round Table meeting, July 8, 1987: JCU arch
248 *Australian Political Chronicle: July–December 1987* 'Australian Journal of Politics and History'. 34 (2): 239–240. June 1988
249 New Moon, Board Minutes 31 Oct, 1987: JCU arch
250 Gary Down Interview with the author, Maldon, June 2, 2018: JCU arch
251 Bereson, op. cit.
252 Veron, op. cit.
253 New Moon, Annual Report, December 31, 1987 p 7: JCU arch
254 New Moon, Annual Report, December 31, 1988 p6: JCU arch
255 Ray Dickson, Chairman's Report, July 29, 1989: JCU arch
256 Rob Adams, *New Moon- Future Options*, Arts Action: June 14, 1988: JCU arch
257 Wissler, op. cit.
258 Dickson, op. cit.
259 New Moon, Board Minutes, October 27, 1989: JCU arch
260 Wissler, op. cit.
261 Ibid
262 John Lamb, Memorandum to Directors, October 6, 1989: JCU arch
263 Premier's Department, Media Release, January 12, 1990: JCU arch
264 New Moon, Board Minutes, March 25, 1990: JCU arch
265 as reported in the 'Daily Bulletin' March 30, 1990
266 op cit March 31, 1990
267 Radbourne, op. cit.
268 New Moon, Board Minutes, March 3, 1990: JCU arch
269 Wissler, op. cit.
270 Fenton op. cit.
271 Ibid
272 Ibid
273 Ibid
274 Ibid
275 Frame, op. cit.
276 New Moon, contract with Belvoir Theatre, July 17, 1990: JCU arch
277 David Fenton, letter to Tim Wilson July 3, 1990: JCU arch
278 New Moon Open Forum 'Synopsis of Meeting': May 26, 1990: JCU arch
279 O'Connell op. cit.
280 'New Moon 1991 and Beyond', [Board Minutes, JCU arch] October 16, 1990: JCU arch
281 New Moon, Board Minutes, November 6, 1990: JCU arch
282 New Moon, Board Minutes, November 19, 1990: JCU arch

283 cf- Stuart Glover, *Revisiting the Cultural Policy Moment: Queensland Cultural Policy from Goss to Bligh*, 'Queensland Review', 18, 2011 pp 190-206

Chapter 6
284 Clark, op. cit.
285 Barclay, op. cit.
286 Clark, op. cit.
287 Ibid
288 Ibid
289 New Moon, Board Minutes, March 19-20, 1982: JCU arch
290 Bakaitis, op. cit.
291 January 28, 1982
292 'Cairns Week' January 31, 1982
293 February 4, 1982
294 Clark, op. cit.
295 February 5, 1982
296 February 19, 1982
297 'Daily Mercury ' February 13, 1982
298 'Morning Bulletin', February 18,1982
299 'Morning Bulletin', February 20, 1982
300 'Morning Bulletin,' February 24, 1982
301 'Daily Bulletin' March 18, 1982
302 March 26, 1982
303 April 7, 1982
304 'Morning Bulletin', April 1, 1982
305 Gladstone 'Observer' April 3, 1982
306 'Morning Bulletin ', April 3, 1982
307 April 19, 1982
308 Number 2, June 1982
309 Babicci, op. cit.
310 April 22, 1982
311 'Cairns Post', April 23, 1982
312 'Post', April 29, 1982
313 Cairns 'Post' April 26, 1982
314 April 24, 1982
315 Ibid
316 G Welch, letter to the Mayor of Cairns, May 25, 1982: JCU arch
317 April 28, 1982
318 'Post', April 29, 1982
319 April 30, 1982
320 'Morning Bulletin' May 15, 1982
321 G. Jorgensen, letter to Ian Satchwell, May 19, 1982 JCU arch
322 Bornhorst, op. cit.
323 May 25,1982
324 'Morning Bulletin' May 19, 1982

325 Clark, op. cit.
326 New Moon, Board Minutes, March 19, 1982 and see also Barclay, op. cit.
327 Babicci, op. cit.
328 Cairns 'Post' June 5, 1982
329 'Daily Bulletin ' June 11, 1982
330 Clark, op. cit.
331 'Daily Bulletin', June 15, 1982
332 'Morning Bulletin' June 21, 1982
333 June 22, 1982
334 June 23, 1982
335 'Post' June 23, 1982
336 'Post', June 24, 1982
337 Ibid
338 June 26, 1982
339 June 19, 1982
340 'Daily Mercury', June 26, 1982
341 June 17, 1982
342 Cairns "Post" June 29, 1982
343 'Morning Bulletin', June 24, 1982
344 Meyrick, op cit p83
345 July 14, 1982
346 Baines, op. cit.
347 Ibid
348 Ibid
349 Ibid
350 Ibid
351 Ibid
352 March 9-12, 1983
353 March 24, 1983
354 April 3, 1983
355 April 7, 1983
356 April 4, 1983
357 Cairns 'Post ', April 24, 1983
358 April 20-25, 1983
359 'Daily Bulletin' April 21, 1983
360 Christine Dyer letter to editor 'Daily Bulletin', April 27, 1983: JCU arch
361 letter to Editor, 'Daily Bulletin' May 3, 1983: JCU arch
362 'Daily Bulletin', June 3, 1983
363 'Morning Bulletin', June 16, 1983
364 June 17, 1983
365 Cairns 'Post' June 22, 1983
366 Jan 12, 1985
367 Lucinda Shaw, letter to author, June 6, 2019
368 Ibid
369 Ibid
370 July 28, 1983

371 Cairns 'Post', July 7, 1982
372 July 13-16, 1983
373 Malcolm Calder, interview op.cit.
374 Helmut Bakaitis, letter to Richard Cottrell, January 18, 1984: JCU arch
375 Ibid
376 Ibid
377 'Morning Bulletin', Feb 26, 1984
378 March 2, 1984
379 letter to Cottrell op. cit.
380 Clark, op. cit.
381 letter to Cottrell op. cit.
382 Cairns 'Post' March 22, 1984
383 March 29. 1984
384 April 6, 1984
385 Cairns 'Post' May 3, 1984
386 May 10, 1984
387 Mackay 'Daily Mercury', May 18, 1984
388 'Morning Bulletin', May 24, 1984
389 'Daily Bulletin', June 21, 1984
390 'Post' June 14, 1984
391 'Daily Mercury' June 28, 1984
392 July 5, 1984
393 'Morning Bulletin', July 6, 1984
394 Ibid
395 Ibid
396 July 14-15, 1984
397 'Morning Bulletin', July 17, 1984
398 'Morning Bulletin' May 21, 1984
399 Ibid
400 Ibid
401 Ibid
402 Ibid
403 undated notes: JCU arch
404 July 26, 1984
405 'Daily Bulletin' August 2, 1984
406 Aug 17, 1984
407 'Morning Bulletin', August 8, 1984
408 October 29, 1984
409 October 29, 1984
410 September 21, 1984
411 November 9, 1984
412 'The Sun-Herald', October 28, 1984
413 'The Canberra Times', September 26, 1984
414 Karen Jacobsen, letter to the author, February 2, 2020
415 September 9, 1984
416 November 5, 1984
417 October 3, 1984
418 'Daily Bulletin' August 4, 1984
419 May 5, 1985
420 source: Austage, Australian playwrights indicated by *

421 Morning Bulletin, June 13, 1985
422 June 14, 1985
423 June 20. 1985
424 'Daily Bulletin', June 27, 1985
425 July 5, 1985
426 August 2, 1985
427 'Morning Bulletin' August 3, 1985
428 August 22, 1985
429 Bakaitis, op cit
430 'Morning Bulletin' September 21, 1985
431 October 4, 1985
432 'Daily Bulletin' October 10, 1985
433 'Daily Mercury', November 1,1985
434 Bereson, op. cit
435 July 24, 1986
436 August 14, 1986
437 August 7, 1986
438 August 8, 1986
439 August 13, 1986
440 Bakaitis, op. cit.
441 Campbell Young, interview with the author, Brisbane, October 22, 2020: JCU arch
442 Ibid
443 'Morning Bulletin', August 7, 1986
444 'Daily Mercury, August 12, 1986
445 August 28, 1986
446 'Daily Bulletin' August 21, 1986
447 'Daily Mercury', August 16, 1986
448 August 8, 1986
449 Bakaitis, op. cit.
450 Calder letter to author op. cit
451 August 23, 1986
452 August 23, 1986
453 cf. Patrick Cadogan, *The Revolutionary Artist: John Lennon's Radical Years*, CreateSpace Independent Publishing Platform, 2008
454 John Lennon, quoted in the 'London Evening Standard' March 4, 1966
455 Bereson, op. cit.
456 https://theharbouragency.com/artist/looking-glass-onion-john-waters/ ref
457 November 2, 1986
458 November 13, 1986
459 November 8, 1986
460 November 7, 1986
461 August 27, 1987
462 September 2, 1987
463 September 19, 1987
464 September 18, 1987
465 August 27, 1987
466 November 5, 1987
467 October 29, 1987
468 cf. McKinnon op. cit. esp. pp147-195

469 'Daily Bulletin', January 23, 1990
470 February 22, 1990
471 March 2, 1990
472 'Daily Mercury" February 1, 1990
473 February 15, 1990
474 letter to Cottrell op cit.
475 Bakaitis, op. cit.

Chapter 7

476 Calder, op. cit.
477 cf David Thompson and Fred Thompson comments, New Moon Board Minutes August 14, 1985 JCU arch
478 cf Meyrick 'See How it Runs' op. cit.
479 O'Connell letter op. cit.
480 Ibid
481 Ibid
482 David Malacari Interview with the author, Sydney January 9, 2017
483 Clark, op. cit.
484 Chris Cottrell , Interview with the author, Brisbane, July 27, 2017
485 O'Connell, letter op. cit.
486 Wissler, op. cit.
487 Paul Iles, letter to Michael FitzGerald, op. cit.
488 Saul, op. cit.
489 Fisher, 'Status Report' op. cit.
490 Ibid
491 O'Connell, op. cit.
492 Baines, op. cit.
493 Barclay, op. cit.
494 Babicci, op. cit.
495 Clark, op. cit.
496 Bakaitis, op. cit.
497 Fisher, 'Status Report' op. cit.
498 e.g. in the 'History and Resume of the Project' op. cit.
499 Macdonnell, 'Fifty Years in the Bush' op. cit.
500 'Currency Companion to Australian Theatre', Philip Parsons Ed, 1995 pp 615-6
501 New Moon, Board Minutes November 8/9, 1984 JCU Arch
502 New Moon, Board Minutes: JCU arch]
503 As reported at AGM, March 1986
504 Clark, op. cit.
505 Calder, op. cit.
506 Paul Iles, letter to Michael FitzGerald and Kevin Siddell, June 1, 1984] and again in his 'Options Paper', 1985 op. cit.
507 'Future Options' p3. 1988: JCU arch
508 New Moon Board Minutes, August 14, 1985: JCU arch
509 Taylor, op. cit.
510 Taylor, op. cit. and supporting document
511 Bereson, op. cit.
512 cf Justin Macdonnell, *Cultural Precincts: Art or commodity*, 'Platform Papers' No 44. Currency House 2016

513 BBC 'Hard Talk', March 25, 2013
514 Meyrick, Phiddian & Barnett op cit.
515 Baines, op. cit.
516 McKinnon op. cit
517 Bakaitis, op.cit.
518 Hothouse: https://hothousetheatre.com.au; Jute Theatre Comapnyhttp://jute.com.au/etc
519 'Currency Companion', op. cit.

Index of Key persons and references

'A Midsummer Night's Dream' 105, 114, 117, 189-90, 223

Adams, Rob 153-5, 163, 255

'Agnes of God' 77, 141, 144, 209-12

'Are you Lonesome Tonight?' 150, 218

Australia Council for the Arts 23, 28, 40, 47, 49, 51, 83, 106, 113, 120, 122-4, 127, 130, 139-40, 143, 147-8, 150, 152, 157, 203, 206, 213, 237, 242, 249, 254-5, 262-3, 272,

    Theatre Board 10, 26, 30-1, 41, 48, 53, 104-5, 107-9, 113, 115, 120, 153, 245, 250

'Away' 89, 150, 219, 221

Babicci, Anthony 59, 66, 69, 76, 101, 117, 171, 178-9, 182. 185

Baines, Bob 39, 101, 171, 176, 186-90, 241

Bakaitis, Helmut 6, 35, 51, 54, 76, 80, 81-3, 116, 121-4, 128-9, 132-9, 141, 146, 148, 152, 175, 193-8, 208, 210, 213, 216-7, 227, 235, 237-8, 243, 245-6, 263, 268

Barclay, Peter 11-12, 14, 26, 28, 52, 54, 64-6, 70, 97, 99-100, 104, 171-2, 174, 179-80, 182, 187, 223, 233, 241

'Beach Blanket Tempest' 89, 97, 126-8. 130. 195-6, 202-5, 215, 221, 223-6. 230, 237, 252-3, 255, 257

Bereson, Ruth 45, 82-5, 88, 95, 136-9, 141, 146, 149, 152, 161, 249

Bjelke-Petersen, Johannes 37, 39, 44, 96, 112, 117-8, 121, 123, 125, 132-4, 139-40, 149-151

Bornhorst, Margaret 28, 62, 72-4, 171, 176, 181, 186

'Cabaret' 98, 114-7, 128, 188-9, 191, 223, 236

Cairns City Council 10, 70,

Cairns Civic Centre 62, 172, 180, 221

Calder, Malcolm 40, 80, 82, 102, 124, 140, 193, 213

Cilento, Diane 44, 77-80, 82, 87-8, 91, 102, 110-2, 131, 137, 141, 144, 146, 209-11, 219-20, 243, 245

Clark, Stephen 45, 73-4, 156, 162, 165, 171-4, 176, 182, 186, 192, 196, 220-2, 234, 242

Cottrell, Chris 90, 234

'Crocodile Creek' 212-4

Debnam, Brian 59,

Dickson, Ray 36, 85, 87, 89, 91, 151-3

Division of Cultural Affairs (Qld) 10, 26, 31, 41, 62, 83, 113, 130, 139-40, 143-4, 152-3, 155, 158-60, 166, 213, 245, 249-50, 252, 255

'Don's Party' 23, 124-5, 132, 195-6, 198-9, 201-2, 206, 221, 225, 236-7, 239.

Doplo, Teresa 125, 199-201, 273

Down, Gary 54, 150-1, 218, 230

Edwards, Alan 41, 42, 107, 178, 256

Fenton, David 45, 54, 156, 161-4, 166-7, 222, 230

Fisher, Rodney 81, 82, 135, 142, 144-5,

175, 197, 214, 216, 240, 245

FitzGerald, Michael 40, 47, 105-8, 114, 120

'Gentlemen Prefer Blondes' 195-7, 206, 239

Gratian, David 243

Greaves, Dona 83, 136-7, 140, 153, 160, 166, 252

'Guys and Dolls' 98, 128, 130, 145, 206, 251-2

Iles, Paul
6, 14, 19, 26-8, 35, 45, 59, 64, 66, 68-9, 70, 75, 77, 79, 80, 94, 97-100, 103-110-15, 117, 120-3, 125-9, 130-6,138, 140,145, 152, 175-6, 179-80, 183, 193, 195, 197, 200-1, 205, 207, 215, 224-6, 230-2, 240,243-4,246, 249-51, 253-4, 256, 262, 274

'Imagine' 144, 146, 195, 214-7, 236

'Intimate Exchanges' 146, 217

James Cook University 8, 23, 32-33, 45, 84-5, 90, 94,

Keeffe, Sheila 10-11, 25, 28-9, 31, 32-3, 35, 62, 70-1, 91, 99, 239

'Key Largo' 116, 195-7, 206, 225

La Luna 6, 95, 131, 141, 150, 153, 157, 162, 219-20, 222, 231, 238, 266-9,

Lamb, John
10-11, 18-24, 26-8, 31, 36, 41, 62-3, 65, 70, 87, 89-91, 95, 109, 152, 155-6, 160, 165,220, 223, 232, 243, 254, 263

Lamond, Toni 144, 211

'Life on Mars' 114, 117, 187, 190, 193, 223

Love, Robert 45, 104,

Luhrmann, Baz 213

'Macbeth' 100-1, 172, 177-8, 182, 184, 223

Mackay City Council 10, 29, 70, 87,

McKinnon, Jocelyn 48, 141, 219, 267

Milson, John 63-4, 97-8, 230, 233, 235

'Ned Kelly' 3, 100-1,175-6, 182, 184, 188, 223, 235-6, 241

Nelson, Ric 22-5, 29, 62, 157, 223

'No Orchids for Miss Blandish' 88, 101, 179-83, 195, 223

O'Connell, Terrence 6, 11-12, 14, 26, 51-2, 54, 64-6, 70, 77, 79, 97, 99-100, 104, 111-2, 114, 117-21, 165, 171-2, 175-6, 177, 182, 187, 190, 193-5, 206-8, 223, 230, 232-5, 237-8, 241, 243

'On Our Selection' 128, 195, 206-8, 252

Perkins, Elizabeth 87, 89-90, 156, 160, 167

Pilbeam Theatre Rockhampton   10, 29, 35, 40, 101, 123-4, 172, 181, 200, 213, 221, 252

Pioneer Shire 10, 29, 87, 91, 147, 184

Radbourne, Kevin 19, 83, 130, 132-3, 137, 160

'Return Engagement' 144, 210-12,217, 237

Reynolds, Mike 17, 33-4, 79, 206

Reynolds, Henry 33, 84, 85, 89-90, 198, 267

Reynolds, Margaret 30, 33, 77, 267

Rockhampton City Council 10, 35, 79, 123-4

'Royal Show' 13, 114, 117, 128, 193-4, 223,

235-6

Saul, Kerry 74-6, 101, 171, 175, 239

Sheldon, Tony 144, 211

Shepherd, Bruce 11, 70-2, 77, 79-80, 91, 108, 111, 114, 132, 184, 215, 225

Siddell, Kevin 41, 62, 109, 120

Spencer, Robert 82, 85, 87-90, 150

Stock, Cheryl 46

Tasker, Ian 96, 148-9, 217, 230

Taylor, Bob 130, 255

'The Summer of the Seventeenth Doll' 22, 89, 157-8. 165, 173, 220-2, 240

Theatre Royal Mackay 40, 88, 116, 172, 195

'Tommy' 100-1, 182-5, 223m 236

Townsville City Council 8, 21, 24, 33, 85, 89, 91, 116

Townsville Civic Theatre 17-19, 29, 31, 41, 62, 172, 181, 221, 254

'Trumpets and Raspberries' 128, 132, 135, 195, 208-9, 246, 252

Veron, Kirsty 85, 90, 152, 221

Voos, Jean-Pierre 154-6, 161, 165

Waters, John 145, 214-6

'We Can't Pay, We Won't Pay' 90, 159-60, 162, 166, 222

Wissler, Rod 24-5, 41, 62, 64, 86, 90, 154-6, 160-1, 164-5, 220, 230, 237

www.ingramcontent.com/pod-product-compliance
Ingram Content Group UK Ltd.
Pitfield, Milton Keynes, MK11 3LW, UK
UKHW021327180426
11947UKWH00017B/1495